"*Mesmerizing—that is the only word for the effect Tony* and eyes for detail bring you into the moment of any st· who wants to understand American policing must read Tony Bouza's testament.*"

PROFESSOR LAWRENCE SHERMAN, DIRECTOR, INSTITUTE OF CRIMINOLOGY, CAMBRIDGE UNIVERSITY, ENGLAND

"*There is no one I know who loves American policing more passionately and more critically than Chief Anthony Bouza.*"

CHIEF DEAN ESSERMAN, NEW HAVEN POLICE DEPARTMENT, NEW HAVEN, CT

"*In his latest book, Tony Bouza describes his experiences as an expert witness in a wide variety of cases involving police-citizen interactions. Should be required reading for every law enforcement officer, criminal attorney, criminal justice student and anyone else involved with or interested in law enforcement. His "case study" approach provides a "behind the scenes" look at both the highlights and lowlights of police work. The cases are more riveting and compelling than any fiction – and serve as a reflection of the best and worst aspects of the U.S.'s criminal justice system.*"

PROFESSOR MICHAEL KLAUSNER, ASSOCIATE PROFESSOR OF SOCIOLOGY & ORGANIZATIONAL BEHAVIOR, UNIVERSITY OF PITTSBURGH

"*A police chief for Minneapolis - a strong professional - and outsider - was what I thought was needed in Minneapolis in 1980 when I became mayor. I liked his resume and when I met him I thought "Wow. This guy is something." A committee of thoughtful citizens liked what New Yorker Tony Bouza wrote in his application and he got the job. After nine years of making both good decisions and news, he retired and continued his writing and began service to litigants involving police.*

This newest book is consistent with the values he brought to the Chief's job in Minneapolis. He recites 59 cases in which the rights and wrongs of citizens and police are outlined in cases where he was asked to play a role. He remains committed to the fundamental principles of fair play and is not hesitant to identify departures by police or citizens from that standard.

Always articulate, Bouza conveys each story with clarity as he identifies the breaches that led to disputes. For both the professional and the lay person, this book will be an enlightening read."

MAYOR DON FRASER, MINNEAPOLIS MN (RET.)

"Tony Bouza is a cop's cop and a master story teller. His wit and insight will draw the reader into the world 'behind the badge'."

"Bouza's career as an officer of the law is distinguished and exemplary, first in New York, where he rose from the starting ranks of the NYPD to the highest positions, and then in Minneapolis where he had two terms of service at the highest rank as Police Chief. He is a man of courage, both physical and intellectual. One of the unusual things about him is that he has always been reflective about his service, and has written more than a dozen books. All of them are swift-paced and highly instructive on the various facets of the law he encountered in his work. This newest one is no exception.

Expert Witness is essential reading for anyone concerned about the damage done to justice by the abuses of the law that its police officers have inflicted on the people they are sworn to protect – and the role that expert testimony has played in the attempt to shift the balance more favorably to the just claims of the those harmed by the police."

"This book is an invaluable tool for citizens to better understand the limitations in power their police face. Attorneys litigating claims against the police will also want to read and refer to it to recognize just where is the invisible "line" between a police officer and a citizen when it comes to the lawful use of force.

Bouza has the advantage of a depth of experience, combined with a keen intellect, that has me, as one of the readers of his many books, unable to put one down once begun. He does not take fools kindly and often finds himself on the wrong side - politically, socially, or sometimes even as weighed by the current morality of issues. And he just "Don't care." He's a tough man to argue with as he thinks through his opinions carefully and weighs his words with rare attention to detail."

"I have known Tony Bouza both as Chief of Police in my city, Minneapolis, and as an expert witness in a civil rights case that I handled for the family of a Native American man who died in police custody. Tony is tough on bad guys, be they criminals or be they the occasional rotten apple in a police department, but he is always fair."

"*This is an important read for all levels of law enforcement. Allegations of misconduct range from clear cut to complicated with many unknowns. Tony gives the best advice to police leaders: patterns of behavior indicating abuse* **cannot** *be ignored. He gives the best advice to expert witnesses: tell the truth.*"

ALLEN GARBER, AGENT, FBI (RET.), CHIEF OF POLICE, CHAMPLIN, MN PD (RET.), UNITED STATES MARSHAL (RET.)

"*If the reader is open to thinking about police work in an important new way, this book is the ticket. It will challenge the reader to think deeply, philosophically, and practically.*"

JOE SELVAGGIO, PRESIDENT AND FOUNDER OF MICROGRANTS, WWW.MICROGRANTS.NET

"*Tony Bouza is that rarity who never deviates from an internal moral compass calibrated to a sense of honesty, justice and equality for all. Despite attaining high status as a law enforcement officer in New York and Minneapolis, he has never wavered in his belief that it's the cop walking the beat who matters most in maintaining law and order in a manner effective and equitable to all segments of society, rich or poor, black or white, young or old. In his book, Expert Witness, he tells it like it is in the enforcement of the law – freely admitting the deficiencies of people and procedures in all too many instances. It's what we call an eye-opener!*"

HAROLD BURSON, BURSON-MARSTELLER, WWW.BURSON-MARSTELLER.COM, NEW YORK CITY

"*In a style that is true Tony Bouza—forthright and fair—Expert Witness is illuminating! Packed with such alive stories and solid interpretation, Bouza helps us all understand the complexity of the "quality of justice." A must read for all!*"

MARILYN MASON, PH.D., CONSULTING PSYCHOLOGIST, AUTHOR OF FORTHCOMING BOOK, BECOMING A GENUINE LEADER

EXPERT WITNESS

Breaking the Policemen's Blue Code of Silence

BY TONY BOUZA

EXPERT WITNESS: Breaking the Policemen's Blue Code of Silence

ISBN # 978-0-9888672-1-5

PUBLISHER

A Bigger Play
Brookline, Massachusetts
www.abiggerplay.com
anne@annebraudy.com

COVER DESIGN by Ana Grigoriu at www.anagrigoriu.de

Unattributed quotations are by Tony Bouza.

This book is intended to provide information about the subject matter covered. It is sold with the understanding that the publisher and author are not engaged in providing legal or other professional services. If expert assistance is required, the services of the appropriate professional should be sought.

First Edition 2013

http://expertwitnessthebook.com/

TABLE OF CONTENTS

Prologue 13

Part I My Cases 15

    Case 1: A Victim's Sense of Guilt 17

    Case 2: The Constitution in the Porn Parlor 19

    Case 3: A Justice Intervenes 21

    Case 4: Women in Policing 23

    Case 5: Kafka Would've Loved It 26

    Case 6: Police Chases 28

    Case 7: Driving While Black 30

    Case 8: Rodney King 32

    Case 9: Post–Rodney King Roundups and Sweeps 35

    Case 10: The Press 37

    Case 11: "I'm Already Dead" 40

    Case 12: Lynchings 43

    Case 13: The Sword of Litigation Has Two Edges 48

    Case 14: Rugged Individualism 51

    Case 15: Life Is a Sperm Lottery 54

    Case 16: Doin' Time 56

    Case 17: Drunken Indian Stereotypes 59

    Case 18: Cowboys and Indians 62

    Case 19: Being an Asshole Is Not a Crime 64

    Case 20: Indirect Responsibility 67

    Case 21: The Central Park Jogger 69

    Case 22: No Good Deed Goes Unpunished 77

    Case 23: Extracting Defeat from the Jaws of Victory 79

    Case 24: Preventable Tragedies 81

Case 25: Even Schmucks Have Rights 83

Case 26: Psychos 85

Case 27: Those Whom the Gods Would Destroy They First Make Mad 87

Case 28: A Maverick's Ordeal 92

Case 29: The Constitution Has Few Real Defenders—or Even Believers 94

Case 30: The Imperial Presidency 98

Case 31: Attica Prison 101

Case 32: Sports Riots 103

Case 33: War Protesters 106

Case 34: Poisoning the Wells of Justice 109

Case 35: A Victim Perennial 112

Case 36: Killer Tots 116

Case 37: Tortured Confessions 121

Case 38: Small Town Teens 129

Case 39: Sex, Power, and Official Myopia 131

Case 40: Rites of Spring 134

Case 41: Random Shots in the Ghetto 139

Case 42: Constitutional Rights vs. Hamstringing the Cops 141

Case 43: Life among the Underclass 144

Case 44: No Justice, No Peace 146

Case 45: Hiring Practices 148

Case 46: Another Failed Attitude Test 150

Case 47: Blown Cover 152

Case 48: Swabs, Sprays, and Videotapes 154

Case 49: Why Do Blacks Respond Differently Than Whites with Cops? 159

Case 50: Profiling and Its Dangers 161

Case 51: Royalty in the Ranks 163

Case 52: By Starting Well, Ending Badly 168

Case 53: Tree Huggers 173

Part II: Cases Declined, but Worth Noting 185

Case 54: Minor Victories 187

Case 55: The Right to Kill 189

Case 56: Gray Areas 191

Case 57: Mall Rats 193

Case 58: Avoidable Problems 195

Case 59: Innocently Wreaking Havoc 198

Why Hire an Expert Witness? 201

Gunslingers 201

Fixing What's Broken 203

The Role of Expert Witness 203

If the Case Goes to Trial 206

The Ever-Popular Good Faith Defense 206

The Expert's Most Important Contribution 207

Epilogue 209

My Most Important Work 209

About The Author 213

Books By Tony Bouza 215

As for me, the question is what to put on the gravestone:

My loves were family, America, and policing.
I hope I served them as well as I could, and should.
Amen.

PROLOGUE

I am an unapologetic supporter of the use of police violence, even lethal force, but it has to be guided by the law, the standards of reasonableness, and the U.S. Constitution.

Even after the LAPD had been pressured to abandon the chokehold, I permitted and encouraged its use, which is the policy even today. I have presided over clubbings, shootings, gassings, and other assaults by the police. I see violence as a key weapon in the police arsenal and trained cops in the full range of possibilities available to us.

My only caveat is that the use of force has to be legally justified, measured, and appropriate, and that the weapons have to be in conformance with the law.

While the Constitution does not lack for champions, it has few defenders in arenas where unpopular causes breathe life and meaning into its words. Great constitutional questions are usually embodied in the defense of derelicts, molesters, psychos, murderers, and other pariahs that society finds easy to loathe. Accepting that their rights represent the advance guard of our rights is what is so hard for most of us to grasp.

A client – frequently a black man – alleges the police falsely arrested and physically abused him. How to evaluate the merits of the case? How to distinguish between probable cause, necessary legal force and their opposites?

A cop shows up in court in uniform and modestly asserts, to an already persuaded white juror, that he is the only thing between that juror and rapine and slaughter. How do you combat that?

Navigating the maze of "testilying", the Blue Code of Silence, cover-ups, evasions and other mendacities is difficult. Penetrating the hermetically sealed culture of the police world is both daunting and beyond the reach of outsiders.

This book identifies the forces that shaped my outlook as an expert witness. It describes scores of cases—most of which were settled out of court—to which these forces were applied, and it attempts to draw lessons from the experience. I brought more than three decades of police experience to the table as expert witness.

For anyone with a personal or professional interest in the criminal justice system, maybe you all can learn a little something from my small triumphs and major defeats.

I don't think I could teach anyone to be a better cop, detective, or first-line supervisor. I do think, however, that I can pass along lessons I've learned about a mostly hidden Atlantis in our midst. My hope is that the fifty-nine cases cited here demonstrate that the American justice system can be navigated successfully, but only if you grasp its complex realities and only when we hold its practitioners to account. Only then will the system work more effectively. Only then will the quality of justice improve.

I've gradually come to see expert witnessing as a pretty effective way of altering police behavior on the street for the better. That reform occurs through the impetus of fear—the terror that lawsuits inspire—not only doesn't faze me, it actually confirms my view that this is the most effective route to reform.

Maybe cops reading these cases will learn that guys like me examined police actions first to determine whether they were performed in good faith. I always supported errors of judgment if I believed the cop was really trying to help and if the results were not too tragic to overlook.

Maybe lawyers can compare their cases against mine and deduce their chances of success.

Even citizens who had been wronged by cops might weigh their prospects against the dramas described here.

And for the general reader, I hope to enlighten and entertain, both with a better understanding of the justice system and the bizarre actions of other humans mostly acting badly.

The central fact is that I am an immigrant, grateful to a great country and particularly thankful for having had the chance to serve in a police world I love. As an expert witness, I've tried to better that world.

PART I
MY CASES

CASE 1: A VICTIM'S SENSE OF GUILT

Positions of authority—doctors, teachers, cops, even priests—enable the libidinous to exploit the opportunities their leverage affords. Victimizations are frequently followed by attempts to get the victim to accept responsibility for an outrage. These are among the factors that turn many sex crimes into convolutions manufactured by the guilty to escape the consequences of their depredations. A Wisconsin case proved a model of the genre.

An ex-boyfriend pounds on the door of a twenty-nine-year-old single mother of three at 2:30 a.m. in mid-August 1998. She had previously secured an order of protection to shield herself from his assaults. She now called the police. Three uniformed cops respond, but by the time they get to the house, the abusive lothario has disappeared.

While two cops search the area, the third enters the house to interview the woman. One of the searchers, clearly suspecting something, goes in and announces that they all should leave. They do, and the incident appears over. A few minutes later, however, the third cop knocks on the door and tells the woman he has a few more questions. She is wary but complies. The cop enters and quickly gets down to business: does she want to see his show? He quickly removes his erect penis from his pants, masturbates, and attempts to force it into her mouth. He lifts her sweatshirt and ejaculates on her face, sweatshirt, and breasts. Trapped in a chair, she is unable to resist or escape. Her three small children are sleeping down the hall.

The woman lodged a complaint and the cop was criminally prosecuted. The semen served as damning DNA evidence. Recognizing how hard it is to prosecute cops, the district attorney accepted—wisely, in my view—a plea of guilty to a misdemeanor. This may strike the unknowing reader as exceedingly lenient, I know, but allowing you to understand such complexities is one of the key reasons for my writing this book.

Had this case simply proceeded as described above I'd have commended the supervisors for their prompt and effective action, and then declined to participate. But the federal suit that followed—the officer was charged with another sexual assault, a mirror image of this one—appealed to me because of the chief's and the city's complicity. The officer in question was a ticking bomb when they hired him, and they knew it. I thought the chief's adoption of this horror show an absolute outrage and relished the thought of taking him on.

The state of Wisconsin wisely requires a thorough background check of a police applicant and the chief certified the cop's suitability. The background is a doozy. The cop was a personal friend who had worked on the chief's house and who came with heavy baggage. The chief acknowledged that he knew the cop was "misbehaving," as if he were a mischievous but relatively innocent child. But the cop was hired at the chief's insistence despite the explicit misgivings of the village council. In fact, the cop's current actions were remarkably prefigured in prior incidents that attested to his unsuitability for the position.

The estranged mother of his children charged that the cop had been forced to resign a previous police post over stalking a young woman. She alleged physical, psychological, and sexual abuse during her relationship with the cop. The mother had alerted the chief, who ignored her warnings.

The cop was fired from a high school security job for inappropriate behavior with students. Photos of girls in bathing suits were found in his car. The cop even made suspicious inquiries about a female high schooler that a staffer suspected constituted stalking. The chief was notified and ignored the issue. The cop is pulled off a job as a driver because he is considered too unstable.

The cop's ex-girlfriend even goes to see the chief, four months before this crime, to describe the cop's actions. He promises help if she won't snitch to the village council. The cop's behavior against his ex-girlfriend escalates and she files for an order of protection in the adjoining state. The order, ironically, forbids him to carry a firearm. The chief accompanies the cop to court as he retaliates by seeking an order of protection from her.

Amazingly, the cop was also charged, in May 1998, with exposing his penis to a fifteen-year-old girl who'd been visiting his family. He put his penis in her mouth and ejaculated in front of her. Her mother wasn't notified until months after the incident. The case was combined with the original assault of the twenty-nine-year-old woman.

My lawyer troubled me with accounts of her reaction. She felt partially responsible. She had, after all, given the cop $20 so he could buy cigarettes and pop before the sexual assault. Had she unwittingly encouraged him? She had a DUI on her driving record and feared a stint on the stand. Her devastation included unresolved feelings of guilt.

I urged the lawyer to steel her client's resolve and work to erase any sense of complicity or cooperation with this criminal sexual assault. Sadly, he failed, and the woman settled for about $20,000. I thought it a very unhappy outcome notwithstanding the "victory" of the city's having to cough it up and our dotting the record with the chief's shameful behavior.

The twenty-nine-year-old victim had suffered severe and documented psychological problems following the incident. The fifteen-year-old's prognosis can only be imagined.

CASE 2: THE CONSTITUTION IN THE PORN PARLOR

As a young cop on the NYPD, I saw us as the good guys and marveled at how much evil there was in the world. We seemed to swim only among scumbags. Dispensing street justice seemed right and felt good.

It was my experience with the NYPD's intelligence unit that gradually instilled in me an appreciation for the U.S. Constitution as a sure guide to police actions. Even as I advocated infiltrations of subversive organizations—trolling for muggers with decoys, staking out places where hold-ups were expected, setting up shops to fence burglars' proceeds—I began to see the value of adhering to the limits the Constitution imposed. Even as I ran aggressive police operations in three agencies, focusing mercilessly on productivity (more arrests, more summonses, faster responses to emergencies), I adhered to constitutional restraints, which tolerate aggressive police tactics but resolve the issue of limits.

As I plunged into expert witnessing, I encountered street people, hustlers, militant groups, unrepentant lefties, thugs, and other "undesirables" who had been wronged. These unlikely heroes proved the bodies into which I could beat the life of constitutional vigor. My evolution may not have been complete, but it sure had come a ways. And so it was with a bitter inner taste that I accepted the case that I nicknamed the "Breasts and Bottoms" suit, which came with the city's very own heir to William Kunstler.

A guy in Minneapolis ran a shop that sold what might be called legal pornography and rented stalls in which guys would watch coin-operated videos and whack off. The reek of semen was stomach-turning. Kleenex was strategically positioned to capture discharges. Some stalls were equipped with "glory holes" into which one client would insert his penis while the guy on the other side gave him a blow job.

A handful of uniformed cops entered to inspect the premises, hoping to catch some literal jerk-off in flagrante delicto. The owner, a streetwise entrepreneur, not only objected vociferously to the intrusions into stalls, but he failed the "attitude test" by grabbing a video camera and filming the cops as they made their rounds. In the close quarters of the booths one of the cops banged against the camera. Claiming he'd been struck, the cop grabbed the owner. His fellow officers joined in, and they roughly marched him out, where they "took him to the ground" (a police euphemism) and handcuffed him. In the process they banged his head against the surface and twisted his arm behind his back so violently he later required medical attention. They charged him with the usual plethora of events signifying official displeasure: resisting arrest, assault on an officer, disorderly conduct. Nothing relating to the activities that provoked the inspection.

The owner fought the criminal charges and won. Not surprising, since all the players in the criminal justice system know how to spot the extralegal punishments that signify more a failure of attitude than a breach of law. Now the owner was suing for false arrest, brutality, and more. I loved the case, especially after reviewing the material, all of which confirmed my suspicions.

The outcome of the criminal charges was critical to me for two reasons. First, I wanted a client who had been examined by the system and cleared, whether this meant acquittal or failure to prosecute. Second, I needed to be assured that my client was a fighter.

The legal dance began. The city surprised me by offering what I thought was a generous settlement (about $250,000). I was shocked when the lawyer said his client had summarily rejected it.

My job was to work with and for the lawyer once I decided to take a case. I usually met clients, if at all, in court during the trial. Now I did something I'd never done: I asked the lawyer if I could meet with the client before a trial was scheduled. He eagerly agreed and they came to my home.

I told the client that I would be happy to testify to the points he already knew I'd make. But trials are uncertain affairs, I said. Jurors, especially white ones, mostly love cops. Their testimony will not look much like the client's memory of events. His robust appearance belied his assertion of permanent injuries to his neck, shoulder, and head. In short, it was losable, and I counseled nudging the city upward a bit and settling for whatever their final offer came to be.

His response took me by surprise. He'd only come to see me because he admired me, but he wouldn't consent to the deal even if a machine gun were held to his head. He'd fight.

We fought.

The cops described a scenario at some odds with reality. The jurors, whose body language seemed to say they were onto me as a hired gun, willing to soil my reputation in this meretricious business, didn't eagerly lean forward for my testimony.

We lost.

But the case had been a great example of false arrest and malicious prosecution.

CASE 3: A JUSTICE INTERVENES

I was frequently asked about the culture shocks I experienced when my family and I moved from New York to Minnesota in early 1980. The Midwest and the East Coast were, I had to admit, undeniably different. Everything started about ninety minutes earlier than in New York and ended accordingly. The landscape was sprinkled with Rufuses, Basils, and Elmers, names I thought appeared only in comics.

I finally figured out that the response people most wanted to hear about culture shock was that life in the Midwest was better. I told the truth: I liked the people, I loved the space, and I found walking into movies, theaters, restaurants, and concerts a pointed contrast to the hassles of New York, where I'd spent forty-two years and which had worn me out.

But cultural differences within the justice system? There weren't any. Cops were cops the country over, and I couldn't tell you where I was if you blindfolded me. The complaints were all the same: "This job sucks" (but nobody quit). "The chief is a psycho" (this they fervently believed). "We're going to hell in a hand basket" (difficult to measure). And the one absolutely uniformly held view: "Morale has never been lower." How that indictment could span thirty-six years and three police agencies never came clear to me.

So it didn't surprise me when a black federal judge I'd never met called me one morning early in the new millennium to ask for my help in exposing the well-entrenched cop behavior known as the blue code of silence.

"Chief"—an honorific everyone in government insists on observing, although I begged for "Tony"—and the judge continued, "I'm in the middle of a civil trial involving a woman who was swept up in a police raid, abused, and released. She is suing the police. We're just mid-trial"—it was Wednesday and the trial had started Monday—"and when several cops testified this was a textbook example of how a search warrant should be served, and then added that none of them had ever heard of a blue code of silence, I just lost it. I've recessed the trial and called to ask if you'd serve as a neutral expert on the case."

I was flattered by his unprecedented offer. This was the first time I was hired as a neutral expert and the first time my fee would be shared by the plaintiff and defendants. Within the hour I received a stack of documents that I tore through, taking notes, in about sixty minutes. My Catholic schooling, army experience, and career as a police officer had taught me two things: arrive early and work fast.

The facts of the case were straightforward. The Minneapolis cops had made a buy of drugs from the occupant of an apartment building and secured a search warrant to make the arrest and seize the drug stash. All perfectly kosher. But when the police arrived to storm the apartment, they grabbed a black woman who was passing by on the sidewalk in a way that must have aroused their suspicions. They twisted her arm behind her back, force-marched her up the stairs, subjected her to a humiliating search, and, finding nothing, let her go after about an hour. Unlike the overwhelming majority of blacks who fatalistically accept such treatment, this feisty citizen sucked it up and sued the police.

I met with the lawyers that afternoon in my Minneapolis living room. The plaintiff had hired an unimpressive black lawyer. The city's defender, a white male, paled as I described what my testimony would be.

There was a blue code of silence in police departments throughout America. It basically held that you support your cop siblings no matter what and keep quiet about what really goes on within the ranks. Corralling a black woman on the sidewalk who had no connection to the suspects, when the search warrant was to be executed on a building's second floor, hardly constituted a model of its type.

The lawyers left and I went back to studying the materials.

The next morning the judge called, thanked me for my services, and said the woman had received a quarter million dollars from the city. When the plaintiff's lawyer came to pick up materials he'd left with me, I asked why it had been left to the judge to intervene to secure justice. It was the lawyer's duty to get an expert in a case that clearly cried out for one. If he didn't, who was going to contradict the cop's assertions? White jurors, contrary to commonly held wisdom in police ranks, loved cops and believed their testimony. The lawyer offered a lame excuse that I interpreted to mean he wasn't going to risk the expense on such a chancy case.

This was a great example of the quixotic appeal of expert witnessing for me. It was precisely for such cases that I adopted the policy of not making my affordability the issue. Poor street people like this particular plaintiff needed access to testimony like mine, which is why I usually didn't send a bill until a case concluded successfully. In the end I was thrilled with the thought of a poor black lady walking off with a bag of gold and a judge ascending as the unexpected hero.

That the case involved the Minneapolis Police Department and an officer I'd tried to fire over drug use also caused me no problems.

CASE 4: WOMEN IN POLICING

By the 1970s I was the only high-ranking official in the United States willing to fight for the entry of women on police forces. It would be romantic to describe my evolving into a feminist as the pursuit of a winding, torturous path leading to an epiphany, but it wouldn't accord with the facts.

I was raised by a strong woman, but my mother believed so firmly in a man's world that she automatically turned to me, when I was fifteen and she a widow in her early forties, for consultations on serious family matters. I married Erica, an equally feisty woman, but I slipped so naturally into the role of pater familias in 1957 that I never gave a glancing thought to the fact that she worked outside the home and inside as well. She cooked, cleaned, and shopped. Until, that is, she dramatically started losing weight only months into our marriage. Frantic, I took her to doctors and was appalled to hear her list for them all that she did to maintain our home and my absence from the process. I resolved to change and I did, permanently helping around the house, though I never did learn to cook.

In 1953, the year I entered policing, there were two models of females in the New York Police Department, and everywhere else, for that matter. The familiar one was of compliant policewomen (we didn't adopt the androgynous "police officer" until years later, and the union stubbornly calls itself the Patrolman's Benevolent Association to this day) who had made their roosts with administrative sinecures that could be remunerative, but could be given or withheld by males. The second model, represented by a minority of two as far as I knew, fought, scratched, kicked, and litigated for the right to take promotional exams they'd been barred from. They were not popular and I saw them as uppity bitches.

Gradually, however, I came to secretly admire them. My regard grew when I worked closely with one of them, literally in the same room, just the two of us, for many months. I emerged from that room a convert. I was convinced that women would promote negotiating, mediational, conflict-resolution skills altogether lacking in a world that saw problems as opportunities for physical domination.

By 1975 I published a lengthy article in the prestigious FBI Bulletin titled "Women in Policing: An Idea Whose Time Has Come." I addressed a "Women in Policing" conference in St. Paul, Minnesota, in 1978. There was still a lot of resistance in the ranks, but the NYPD was hiring women in greater numbers. At the time, I was commander of the Bronx and had scores of women on patrol in the toughest sections of the borough. I regularly forbade them the cushy, safe, clerical, inside jobs they'd been cosseted with in prior years. I did allow them—in explicit and dangerous defiance of a conservative police commissioner's orders—to wear trousers instead of the miniskirt that had the hardened denizens of the South Bronx whooping and whistling every time these officers emerged from their patrol cars.

Without intending it, I'd become a sort of hero to the idea of women in policing. I was the only expert witness who regularly testified throughout the country that women could function as cops. Civil liberties lawyers asked me to attest to the proposition that there was no bona fide occupational qualification, physical or intellectual, that precluded women from serving interchangeably with men in the ranks. In other words, were men and women equally capable of serving as police officers? Issues such as physical strength, agility, height, and such were introduced and it was my job to mow them down. And so I did.

I experienced some pain when I had to testify against Bill Connelie, a brilliant guy whom I'd studied with for lieutenant and who had gone on to head the New York State Police. He refused to hire women because they weren't tall enough to fire over the roofs of automobiles. We won, as we'd won every other case, half a dozen in all.

The toughest nut was the Los Angeles Police Department, whose chief, Ed Davis, famously said, "When the Rams [then the resident NFL franchise] hire women as linebackers, I'll hire them as cops." My response? "The reed that doesn't bend to the prevailing wind gets broken." And break them we did. The LAPD got saddled with a consent decree that compelled them to hire Hispanics, blacks, and women, in defined and generous quotas, well into the twenty-first century.

Armed with the decrees, women marched into the ranks, my sister's daughter among them. Women now occupy the full spectrum of ranks and offices in the police world and the issue has been replaced by other controversies. In fact, many major cities now have female chiefs.

That's not to say I'm the patron saint of female officers. Take, for instance, the case of two cops I suspended for what Admiral Elmo Zumwalt referred to as "friggin' in the riggin'"—his reply to the question of what concerned him most about women in the navy. I was not excessively troubled by such liaisons if conducted discreetly, but it was altogether different when they spilled into working lives, as happened one evening during my stint as Minneapolis chief of police.

A bunch of cops had gone to a bar after their tour and drunk themselves into near oblivion. At least one was female, who wound up in a car with a male cop. She was single, he was not. They drove to the parking lot and fumbled their way to making out, only he was too tanked to get it up, despite her receptivity, and relieved his frustrations by pissing in the lot. There were angry verbal exchanges with what we'd euphemistically describe as irate neighbors.

I had Internal Affairs investigate, then ordered a departmental hearing in which the two cops were found guilty of "conduct unbecoming a police officer." I suspended him for twenty days without pay and her for three. She appealed to me and I explained my sense that she was complicit and needed to be punished for unseemly behavior. I added that she was foolish to think she could go drinking with the fellows and escape unscathed. She'd "never be one of the boys." She then sued me and other supervisors for sex discrimination.

On the stand I was put through the usual preliminaries relating to my background and the events in question. After a few verbal sorties her lawyer paused pregnantly and shouted, "Did you tell the plaintiff she'd never be one of the boys?"

Yes, I replied.

"What did you mean by that?"

I had carefully crafted an answer, knowing the question would come.

"I know male police officers are indefatigably libidinous sexual predators who would seize any opportunity to exploit females."

He had not expected my response. He had confused women's rights with their being identical with men. They weren't. Women and men were different. They had equal rights, but they weren't identical specimens. Her suit against me was dismissed.

A second female officer sued me in 1986. It all began on my fifty-eighth birthday. I was in the lobby of the Opryland Hotel in Nashville, attending a convention of the International Association of Police Chiefs. One of my deputy chiefs whispered to me, "I just heard a cop's been shot in the chest in Minneapolis." My heart sank.

Then came the best birthday present I've ever received. "He was wearing a bulletproof vest and suffered only a deep bruise." And the suspect had been captured.

I ordered an immediate investigation, knowing incidents frequently concealed unexpected complexities. One quickly surfaced, one I'd never encountered in thirty-three years of policing: the cop's partner had run off.

The shot officer was adamant that she'd deserted him, a claim that was supported by the evidence and witnesses. A hearing was held on the shocking charge of cowardice and she was found guilty. I fired her. She sued me for wrongful termination, and I testified against her in 1989. The firing was upheld.

Both suits validated, for me, the freedom my championing their cause had helped grant women in the ranks. They owed me nothing. I fought for their inclusion as a way of preserving my own constitutional rights, just as I had fought for the inclusion of minorities, mostly black males, in the NYPD and helped to insert "without regard to sexual preference" in the MPD's hiring policy in the early 1980s. We may or may not have been the first police department to openly welcome gays (they were, I knew, already there), but we were certainly the only department I knew of that openly welcomed them at that time.

Vainglorious claims? I hope not. In each case, it was simply the right thing.

CASE 5: KAFKA WOULD'VE LOVED IT

A guy is sitting behind the wheel of an idling car, outside a just closed bar. It is the late 1990s, and another frigid night in St. Paul. As curious cops pull up, a female's head pops up on the passenger side. They recognize her, she them, and the cops nod and drive off.

When she shows up at roll call the next day—where attendance is taken and instructions given—a few smirks and snickers announce the beginnings of trouble. During the "tour" (the work day) squad radios click on and off, a sure sign of restlessness. A slurping sound emerges. Laughter erupts in echo. Derisive comments. "Hey, Kate (not her name), how about me?"

Angry and disturbed, but not yet afraid, she confronts the cops who saw her in the car, separately. One lamely acknowledges making some reference to the troops but meant no harm. The other embraces a more traditional police approach and stonewalls her.

OK, she'll tough it out, laugh it off, shrug her way through it. It will pass.

Only it won't. Snickers, smiles, laughter haunt her. Others part suddenly or stop talking at her approach. She begins confronting her colleagues without really knowing what real harassment is and what's imaginary.

Tensions grow. She complains to supervisors who, accustomed to the libidinous macho culture that never saw women much beyond the warrens of desire, resent her approaches and respond in ways she finds unsatisfactory. Her anger feeds on itself. The radio comments escalate. Any references in the roll call that can be seen as double entendre, however innocent the context, now produce bursts of titters. Sensitive issues, like backup on calls where she might need help, exacerbate. She is derided as a bitch.

In the way of these things, her ordered world begins to fall apart. Her work suffers. Her evaluations deteriorate. She is seen as a troublemaker and is transferred to another precinct. She reacts with increasing fury, which produces late night calls at home, followed by hang-ups or laughter or silence. Items are delivered she hadn't ordered, such as subscriptions to magazines she hadn't requested. Funeral businesses respond to "her inquiries" about their services. Leaving the force is not an option. As a single mother, where is she going to find a job that places her in the lower rungs of the middle class? Her job means survival, pure and simple.

Late one night she is pulled over on suspicion of driving under the influence. She refuses to take a breathalyzer and is arrested. She is suspended but gets a lawyer experienced in these cases, fights the charges, wins, and gets reinstated.

That the cops were lying in wait for her was inescapable to me. A couple of quick, inconvenient transfers follow, mostly predicated on evaluations that depict her as a malcontent. In truth she is disintegrating to the point of fulfilling her critics' prophecies.

She happens to run into the chief at a Christmas party and seizes the chance to buttonhole him. After an excited recitation that gets her thinking how quickly we can lose our grip on the world around us, he airily advises her to "go through channels." This innocently bureaucratic rejoinder serves as the hammer blow that brings her to her knees.

Beleaguered and desperate, she approaches a lawyer without really knowing where this might lead. She is driven not by thought but by anger. The lawyer calls me, referred by another attorney who'd worked with me, and asks if I'll take the case, a classic example of sexual harassment. I agree.

I review the material—police reports, arrest documents, court depositions, performance evaluations—and testify on video, since I'd be away during the trial. I am critical of the abusive internal culture and the indifference of the chief, mostly centering the blame for the continuing abuse on his inaction.

I was surprised the case went to trial, but we won. The female officer received a judgment of $90,000. Not much, but it was vindication, and her fellow cops all were put on notice. Either their behavior would be corrected or it would result in another public embarrassment. Although we never met, she generously and surprisingly credited me in a newspaper account with championing her cause. I had, midway through the process, written to her to buck her up.

So I was shocked when her lawyer said to be prepared for a reprise. It came when the city appealed the verdict. Her attorney explained that an appeal had the effect of sealing the record. There was a governor's race. Norm Coleman, the city's mayor, was running and William Finney, the police chief, hoped to slip into the mayor's chair in the next election. My video might prove a devastating commentary on his competence, so the city appealed and kept the file under wraps. Predictably, they lost. The verdict stood.

The female officer picked up her life and the chief, a really nice guy I've always liked (which is not a professional assessment of his competence), waited for the next chance to run. It came after he left office in 2004, but he, surprisingly, chose to pass.

I came to see the case as a feminist issue in the end. The officer, however, is black. But so, for that matter, is the chief.

CASE 6: POLICE CHASES

Police chases are hugely controversial. Sometimes they end tragically—with the death of a child, for example—and sometimes they're sparked by minor infractions. Know-nothings choose to abolish them altogether except in the most violent and egregious circumstances.

I supported the notion of police chases and issued written orders, both in New York and Minneapolis, that they would be controlled by a supervisor, that strict radio discipline was to be maintained, that there would be no caravanning (the Keystone Cops vision of a line of squads in frantic pursuit) or cowboying (feats of derring-do by testosterone-charged cops), and that the police had to know why they were chasing, even though this could change in the climax of capture. The importance of this latter subtlety was made clear by a Minnesota case.

The drama began in the 1990s in a Minneapolis suburb, in an apartment with a domestic argument, the prelude to a horde of police messes. The guy involved was notorious in the area and the target of previous police calls. He pulled the woman out of the apartment and into his car for the inevitable, and inevitably futile, "talk." There was a twelve-pack of beer in the car.

The guy had no license and wasn't supposed to have keys to the car, but he did. He drove the woman to a nearby parking lot for apartments. A resident must have called the cops because a squad was dispatched to investigate a suspicious vehicle. As the cop approached he recognized the guy. A small tussle ensued but the suspect tore off. The officer radioed the pursuit and the chase was on. It never exceeded 80 mph, which sounds like cold comfort, except they were mostly on a freeway.

Other squads joined in, including a supervisor, whose car was struck by the guy. A bit of wild and erratic driving followed and a blown tire brought the event to a climax. Six officers from three police agencies in six vehicles took part in the chase that wound up on the side of the highway. Now they approached the vehicle, guns drawn.

What did they have? This is the question every cop must have the answer to before he or she acts. At worst, in this case, they had an unlicensed driver who later turned out to be drunk.

The driver refused to get out and had to be pried from the car and wrestled down. He was struck three to five times on the head with a flashlight. Curiously, one of the officers had tried to stay this assault, futilely, with the admonition, "Tony, don't."

On the passenger side, the female—also allegedly drunk—was unable to open the car door and climbed into the back seat, shouting she had shoulder problems and mustn't be cuffed. She stumbled out of the car and was helped by one officer. Two officers started to struggle with her. A male officer brought her left arm back hard and heard a bang. He wandered off, sheepishly, knowing he'd done major damage.

The driver's head was bleeding and the lady complained of her left arm. Both were taken to the hospital. The driver had stitches to the head, a dislocated right arm, and a broken left elbow. His blood alcohol level was .07—under the then limit of .10 to constitute a crime. His hostage (because basically that's what she was) suffered the additional injury of a broken left arm and dislocated left shoulder, plus contusions and abrasions.

In the end the driver was charged only with fleeing a police officer in a motor vehicle. The lady was not charged.

The complaints of brutality ignited an investigation in which the officers characterized their actions as forgettable caresses. One was punished for using excessive force and the lady's arm-breaker speedily retired.

The lady sued the police. Her lawyer called me and, after reviewing the facts, I took the case. It was a mixed bag. The original contact was a response to a call to investigate and was appropriate, as was the officer's subsequent contact with the suspect and, given that the officer recognized the guy and suspected a crime, even the chase. But two officers (the flashlight wielder and the one who broke the lady's arm) behaved appallingly while the others were far more professional. One of the miscreant cops even brazenly asserted that, sure, he'd lie in a case like this, but was grateful he didn't have to because all of the actions in this case were justified.

My report didn't so much blister the two wrongdoers as it simply recited the facts. They were damning enough, as the internal police investigation verified.

The city settled with the lady rather than risk a trial. Adherence to the most rudimentary principles of policing would've spared the taxpayers the cost of this settlement, whose amount I did not know. I don't think the guy sued, and I know I wouldn't have taken his case. A drunken bully who essentially kidnapped his friend. A true asshole.

If I had any advice to offer responding, or chasing, officers, it would be this: Know what you're responding to and act in such a way as to convince a neutral observer, like me, that you were trying to be helpful.

It ain't brain surgery.

CASE 7: DRIVING WHILE BLACK

A forty-two-year-old electrical engineer on a field assignment was driving his ten-year-old Mercedes-Benz on a Minnesota highway on his way to Texas. A little after 3:00 p.m. a state trooper vehicle had driven parallel to the engineer's car. The engineer looked over and made fleeting eye contact with the trooper.

Was this an act of unforgivable defiance? You might think so when the additional fact of the engineer's blackness gets factored in.

The engineer saw an oil light blink a problem, so he pulled off the highway at the next exit and into the first gas station. He went to another service station across the street because the first had no oil. He noticed the state trooper's squad in a vacant lot and saw it return to the highway. The engineer bought oil and resumed his trip.

Back on the highway, he soon noticed the trooper behind him. This continued for four or five miles, at times coming perilously close. The engineer felt he was being provoked into a violation and took extra care.

The trooper flashed his lights and pulled the engineer over. He asked for his license and stated he'd checked the plate and it came back "salvage vehicle." The classification turned out to be a computer error. The trooper gave the engineer an administrative warning for going one to two miles over the speed limit and making an illegal lane change. The warning has no legal effect and is merely advisory.

The trooper discovered that the engineer's driving privileges had been suspended for failing to pay traffic fines. The engineer came up with receipts proving he'd paid the fines. The trooper had the man sit in the back of the squad car and called to verify this information. Another trooper responded and they asked permission to search the Mercedes. The engineer refused. The second trooper nevertheless rummaged through the engineer's belongings. Both troopers later reported they'd smelled marijuana.

The troopers had the Mercedes towed to an impound lot and searched the vehicle for three hours. A sniffer dog found nothing. They emptied the car and had the dog sniff everything. Still nothing. Finally a cane with a blade inside was found, wedged under a tire on the car floor. The first trooper then handcuffed the engineer and announced he was under arrest for possessing "a concealed weapon." The law prohibits a knife with a blade over four inches within reach in a vehicle. This sword was not anywhere within the driver's reach.

The engineer was booked on the weapons charge. The troopers further alleged they'd found marijuana, but Trooper #1 claimed he had thrown it away. The engineer was lodged in jail, bailed out by his brother about five hours after the arrest or about ten hours after the start of his ordeal. He was forced to stay in town an extra week to recover his car and to straighten out his driving records.

Neither trooper prepared a police report on the incident, but the original officer did prepare one, a week after being served with the lawsuit that led to my hiring. The state police require a police report on a bookable offense. The city attorney, possibly smelling a failed "attitude test," dismissed all charges before the engineer's first appearance.

Any white person reading this narrative would blanch incredulous over the account. It is, however, a classic example of racial profiling by America's police on the dawn of the twenty-first century. Shades of a northern version of Emmett Till, the black teen whose brutal murder in 1955 helped spark the Civil Rights movement when the men tried for his death were acquitted.

I was happy to take this case, but the state settled with the engineer before my deposition or testimony was taken. In a delicious legal reversal of roles, the defendants—the state troopers and their superior—had a report from me. (Usually I'm the one to receive their reports.) It was blistering in its simple recitation of the facts listed here, without embellishment. They'd have to imagine what a courtroom confrontation would look like.

I never did learn how much the settlement was, but I was satisfied that I'd helped strike a blow at racism. There was little doubt in my mind that the engineer's stare at the officer was perceived as an impermissible act of defiance that had to be put down. Not a single black male in America would have trouble understanding this transaction and its aftermath.

The miracle was that the cops had been called to account.

CASE 8: RODNEY KING

I had long thought the Los Angeles Police Department a kind of Marine model of policing in America: tough but disciplined and free of corruption. Its leaders, only three between 1953 and 1993, played a clever game of keeping the LAPD "out of politics," thereby enabling them to exercise untrammeled political dictatorial control. No irony was intended when one police chief treated LA's long-suffering, long-serving mayor as the police lieutenant he'd once been.

It was in this setting that the Rodney King case flowered.

On March 3, 1990, the police engaged in a fifteen-mile chase for speeding, ending with King, a twenty-seven-year-old black male, being surrounded and stopped. When he emerged from his car, four white officers clubbed and kicked him while scores of officers looked on and made no move to interfere. It was, in the words of such knowledgeable observers as police executives and a high-powered commission charged with examining the episode, business as usual.

The extraordinary thing about the event was that a thirty-two-year-old in the plumbing-supply business recorded the assault on an extended videotape. The incident garnered international celebrity on the order of Zapruder's film of Kennedy's assassination decades earlier. The plumber's video offered dramatic visual images of a shocking reality that America had been only too happy to overlook for eons.

So, when an attorney's bird dog called me in January 1992 to explore the possibility of my serving as an expert on the case, I was both flattered and eager. My impression of the lawyer was not my usual sympathetic one reserved for devoted libertarians in it for the cause, and for the occasional payoff that enabled them to continue their quixotic pursuits. This guy was a sharpie. I broke with my practice and asked for a retainer, which was promptly sent.

I eagerly set to work on the case, feeling I understood it perfectly. The blue code of silence would be a cornerstone of the defense. I expected all of the officers involved to stonewall any administrative inquiry—one that was sure to be conducted by notably unenthusiastic members of the LAPD.

Criminal prosecutions by assistant district attorneys who worked daily with these cops wouldn't get far. They would be presenting the case to jurors eager to believe the cops. Testifying would be a tough sell, as it turned out. The acquittals of the officers on April 29, 1992 resulted in lootings, burnings, assaults, and devastating street violence, including dozens of deaths, all on the evening news.

The avid lawyer had another case, also involving a white cop's brutalization of a black street person, which I accepted at this time. As I set to work on the second case, the first fell apart: even cannier and more aggressive lawyers convinced King to fire his lawyer (my employer) and hire them, which King promptly did, not ever realizing he was also firing me since he wasn't even aware of my existence. And this ended my direct connection to the Rodney King case. It was a blow, but I kept the retainer—the only tangible proof of my connection to the case.

The second case involved a black street wino who'd been clubbed by an officer assigned to "clean up the area," always a nebulous charge. "Just get rid of these unsightly creatures" was society's Thomas á Becket approach to perennial street conditions it found unattractive. The methods for accomplishing this goal were not a major concern. Had he resisted the vaporized allure of street life, our homeless client could, very likely, have made a score with his case. Pity.

And so this case vanished too, into the evanescent mists of the urban landscape of these unanchored humans.

There's a personal postscript to the Rodney King case, one of those highlights of my life's film that gathered no notice, except for those that might employ it to my detriment. They did.

After serving as Minnesota's gambling commissioner for two years, I became president of the Center to Prevent Handgun Violence in Washington, D.C. Having already served on the center's board, I understood the problems and moved swiftly to attack them.

A couple of weeks into this task, I appeared on the "Today Show" in connection with the Rodney King case and the riot that had exploded following the cops' acquittals. In response to Bryant Gumbel's scripted questions, I said that the only aberration of the King case was that the assault had been videotaped and that most black males in America (perhaps including Gumbel) could identify easily with King.

Hadn't the advent of black police chiefs and mayors tempered police behavior on the street? I answered, "Colin Powell [then the Armed Forces' chief of staff] may think he's black, but he's doing the bidding of the white power structure." I went on to suggest President Bush (the elder) ought to part his curtains if he wanted to see homeless people camping out on Lafayette Park across the street.

Fairly inflammatory, but no different from stuff I'd been mouthing, and I thought little of it. No one commented on it, including Gumbel, who seemed to be listening more to his producer through his earplug than to me. No one, that is, with one notable exception. I was taken aback when the chair of the board of the Center for Handgun Violence called to demand an eleven o'clock meeting the next morning and instructed me not to talk to the press. What was this about? The "Today Show" had nothing to do with guns.

The guy, a nice person with impeccable Republican credentials who'd tragically lost his son to serial killers in California (such tragedies swelled the ranks and coffers of anti-gun groups), asked for my immediate resignation, and ultimately I resigned, settling for six months' pay and an exchange of polite letters.

As I thought back on my tortured and futile peregrinations in the King case, I was glad to have been fired from the Center for Handgun Control, because, knowing myself, I'd surely credit myself with the victory King inevitably secured—in the form of millions—in a case anyone could've, should've, would've won. My swollen ego didn't need such strokes. It was only the credible threat that I'd fight: sue the center and force a board vote (I was a member) and denounce them through the "Today Show," which I was sure would salivate at the thought of my being fired over comments on their broadcast that caused these guys to buckle.

You don't always have to sue, but it does help to convince them you will, if pressed.

CASE 9: POST–RODNEY KING ROUNDUPS AND SWEEPS

Given a choice between being rich or famous, anyone who has experienced either knows rich is better.

Public figures are celebrities, visible and accessible. The pressures on them cannot be imagined by those who have not experienced the fishbowl existence. Council members, the news media, the public, every type of association, and even everyday citizens think nothing of importuning officials wherever they encounter them. I remember a governor's wife complaining bitterly about people "standing over us, spitting into our food" on the rare occasions they ventured out to eat.

This is the story of two San Francisco officials, one a police chief who was a gifted, liberal intellectual with impeccable credentials (he once went to jail rather than evict elderly tenants from a Chinatown hotel) and the other a mayor who was a vastly experienced former police chief with decades in law enforcement. Under the inexorable pressure of public events, they buckled. When the shit hits the fan at that level, it splatters all over officialdom, and messily.

The videotaped assault on Rodney King (*Case 8: Rodney King*), by officers of the Los Angeles Police Department in March 1991 simmered in anticipation that the system would respond to such egregious abuse. Predictably, however, at least to insiders, a sympathetic jury, a reluctant prosecutor, and outrageous police testimony led to an acquittal in state court. It was not until the no-nonsense federal inquiry, undoubtedly spurred by the pressure of riots, that convictions were obtained and cops punished. By then the pot had boiled over. Outraged blacks rioted in Watts and sporadically elsewhere.

On April 30, 1992, the day following the verdict, San Francisco experienced disorders in the form of overturned and vandalized cars, looting, fires, and other crimes. Seven hundred arrests followed, one hundred of which were prosecuted. Frank Jordan, the city's mayor, imposed a state of emergency, instituting a 9:00 p.m. to 6:00 a.m. curfew. On May 1 the police made another 465 arrests, at five different locations throughout San Francisco, for failing to disperse. There had been a demonstration scheduled for 7:00 p.m. on May 1 and many of those arrested were attending it. Phalanxes of extra police corralled the crowds all over the area.

Richard Hongisto, the city's police chief, had ordered the arrests on May 1. Mayor Jordan was present, directing these actions. There were no disorders or violence connected to these arrests. All of the police actions in question took place well before the 9:00 p.m.

curfew went into effect. However, the record did reflect a testosterone high in the SFPD. The police later attempted to justify their actions by complaining of the hurling of such epithets as "pig" and prominent references to one bottle breaking harmlessly. Near hysterical reports of missiles, Molotov cocktails, and weapons crackled over the police radio.

Those arrested were herded onto a pier and transported to the Alameda County jail in Santa Rita. They were held for the better part of a weekend, with the last prisoner cited and released about thirty-six hours after the arrests took place. Not one of the 465 was prosecuted. The police were not able to attach one instance of even minor criminal wrongdoings to a single one of the arrests.

Usually elected to office, prosecutors are invariably more sensitive to questions of law and politics than the appointed players in the criminal justice system. What would they charge the 465 with—mopery, perhaps? Failing to mosey? It was a measure of the validity of these arrests that the same prosecutor who'd chosen to charge and try 105 of those accused of looting and property damage on April 30 declined to present any of the May 1 cases to the court.

This had been an indiscriminate sweep and roundup of innocent citizens, a classic example of false arrests on a massive scale, performed by seasoned, knowledgeable police commanders any reasonable person would've guessed simply had to know better. And so, when Dennis Cunningham, one of those legal advocates who regularly embrace such causes, called me to take on the case, I accepted.

There was no doubt that San Francisco and its officials were alarmed by the disorders of April 30, which infected their thinking thereafter. The board of supervisors that granted the mayor's request for a declaration of emergency and the establishment of a curfew rescinded the approval on May 2. It was a lightning-fast reaction to an obvious mistake.

The police officials were obviously under strong pressure to prevent a recurrence of the April 30 riot, but it is one of the cardinal rules of the law that wrongdoing cannot be anticipated and acted on preemptively. Even a conspiracy to commit a crime requires a crossing of the threshold from thought to action. The actions of the police reflected careful planning and preparation.

I submitted a long, scathing report on the events and was prepared to testify accordingly. It was a bit of a wrench, given my admiration for Chief Hongisto, with whom I'd spoken on the phone but never met, and less of a wrench with a mayor I'd known as a police chief.

The city settled for $1 million. Mayor Jordan went on to lose the next election. Chief Hongisto got fired for another blunder (*Case 10: The Press*).

There's a reason they call it public life.

CASE 10: THE PRESS

"Were it left to me to decide whether we should have a government without newspapers, or newspapers without a government, I should not hesitate a moment to prefer the latter."

It took me a lot of years in public life to appreciate the wisdom of Thomas Jefferson's sentiments about the press, and I was grateful the discovery came when I still had the power of my office to do something with it. Almost all the "secrets" the bureaucracy guarded so sedulously were simply self-protective actions intended to mask human flaws. I came to see the press as democracy's foremost pillar. And I acted on that feeling, never hiring a press information officer, granting the media total access, restricting it only to protect an ongoing investigation or to shield a sex victim from being identified.

Once, a journalist called me from the scene of a crime—in this case, the third or fourth grisly outrage by a serial killer who picked up Native American women in bars and raped and sodomized them with a broomstick—and complained that the lieutenant in charge wouldn't talk to the press. I asked that he be put on the phone and I told him he had to talk to the press.

"Geez, Chief, it's an ongoing investigation. I don't want to screw it up."

"Fine," I said. "Say that."

That was the end of that, except that when the lieutenant finally arrested a suspect, he could charge him only with a violation of social security laws. He had a prosecutable but certainly losable case. Anathema to district attorneys, especially cautious ones. I pressed the case, even going so far as walking to the DA's office to strong arm him a bit, but he wouldn't budge. I said I'd go public. He blanched and countered. If I'd assign the lieutenant and another to him to work on the case another thirty days, he'd prosecute, whether additional evidence was gathered or not. The investigators worked, miraculously came up with a witness that clinched the deal, and the prosecutor got his conviction.

So when a lawyer and a group representing a committee for freedom of the press asked me to champion a First Amendment claim, I examined the facts and accepted. It looked to me like a case in which officialdom lent voice and muscle to long-nurtured resentments at the aggressiveness of the press.

It began when a small Minnesota town decided to hold a recognition dinner for retiring city officials on December 28, 1999, in a community center. There would be a social hour from 5:00 to 6:00 p.m. and a program of speakers from 6:00 to 8:00 p.m. Entrance fees of $15 each would defray expenses and gifts. The city manager placed his deputy in charge of the event, attended by elected and appointed officials.

A local cable television show dealing with town issues and officials sent two representatives, with a camera, to attend what they considered a newsworthy event. The representatives, who were not popular at City Hall because they were considered pushy and rude, arrived around 5:45 p.m. The deputy city manager admitted them, without charge, and allowed filming with some restrictions. As this discussion proceeded, an off-duty police captain and a uniformed lieutenant intruded into the talks. The conversation was not going well and the captain insisted the two journalists should "pay or leave" and pointed to the exit. The captain and lieutenant grabbed the cameraman and tried to lead him out, holding him strongly enough to cause a scream of pain. He put his foot against the wall to resist expulsion and to avoid being slammed into the wall or onto a table. Another lieutenant then joined what now were three other police officials and handcuffed the cameraman. Even the chief joined in, albeit late. The cameraman had surrendered the camera to his partner, who filmed this assault. The fifteen-minute video was forcibly confiscated by one of the lieutenants who later held he'd done it to prevent its alteration. A copy of the tape was given to the journalist who'd filmed it, two days later, preventing its use on a timely basis.

The cameraman was charged with trespassing, disorderly conduct, and assault. He was alleged to have brushed or bumped the captain with his camera and to have attempted to bite one of the lieutenants. The trespassing charge was dropped, but the other two charges went to trial. The cameraman was acquitted. In an action heralding the presence of a smidgen of common sense, the mayor put up the $500 bail on the night of the arrest. The other journalist was not charged but had to submit to the confiscation of the tape. He'd been forcibly ejected and one lieutenant testified he'd held the man "very hard." A lieutenant boasted of the incident to a platoon of cops at the next day's roll call.

The key question was whether this was a public or private event. If the latter, its operators could exclude the press because they were charging an entrance fee that constituted a contract in which they could dictate the terms of entrance, generally. When the person in charge waived the fee and permitted filming, the character of the event was transformed into a public function.

The interference of the cops was an untimely intrusion, probably intended to impress their bosses with their protective helpfulness against pests. That the city confiscated the tape, that the charges were maliciously prosecuted, and that the cops intruded into a situation in which they did not belong and had no legitimate role cried out for redress.

The captain claimed he spoke with the city attorney before taking the tape, but he had misinformed this official. He had said it was to be taken from the arrested person, which was not the case. Thus the permission's effectiveness was nullified.

The case was dismissed and we lost.

Both the cameraman and his partner sued in federal court on the basis of a violation of their First Amendment rights. The city responded that these were not "journalists." After I read a thick stack of documents, depositions, and reports and watched the videotape, I was confident we had a strong case and I prepared a tough report.

A state court judge held, during the prosecution of the cameraman, that the police had violated the Minnesota shield law in seizing the videotape, without issuing a specific court order. He ordered the return of the original to the cameraman.

The district court issued a summary judgment for the defendants, holding that the police had reasonably involved themselves in the situation and justifiably seized the videotape. It held that the plaintiff's constitutional or statutory rights had not been violated. This was a grievous blow and would usually mean the end of the affair. But I urged an appeal—a costly, tedious process—and the lawyer, with prodding from the freedom of the press folks, finally agreed.

A brief was prepared and, on November 21, 2002, the appeals court upheld the lower court. We'd lost again, and finally. I decided we all had fought the good fight, and we all should feel the pain. I never submitted a bill, but the bitterness of the loss, and the blow it landed on freedom of the press, lingers.

Richard Hongisto, the San Francisco police chief who had ordered the arrests in the aftermath of the Rodney King verdict (*Case 8: Rodney King*), and whose liberal actions I greatly admired, was fired over such an event involving the press. A free newspaper circulated a front-page photo of the chief, in uniform, holding his baton in a suggestively phallic position. Stung by a depiction he should've shrugged off, the chief ordered his troops to confiscate all available copies of the raffish journal. Predictably, his enemies in the ranks revealed his unconstitutional gaffe and he was fired when hundreds of copies were found in his garage.

CASE 11: "I'M ALREADY DEAD"

The primordial ooze of the ghetto nurtures avoidable tragedies, many of which can be included under the title of gang life. For the most part, these events are hideously complex, and well-nigh incomprehensible to middle-class observers. One such tragedy, described to me by my favorite activist lawyer in Minnesota, who tailored his offerings to what he knew would entice me, led to my painful involvement.

The events are propelled into motion by the shooting death of a black gang member on May 29, 1997. Two interchangeable black males are quickly arrested and jailed. The central figure in this case faces the bleak prospect of a long stretch in prison. He has a long criminal record, including an arrest on robbery charges flowing from a botched hold-up and shooting at a drug dealer's house. Self-preservation instincts kick in, and he reaches out to the police's Gang Unit for a discussion. He offers his aid on the shooting in exchange for help on his current dilemma.

It seems the police arrested the wrong guys in the May 29 murder. The informer not only can identify the real killers but he can lead the police to key evidence, including the guns used. On June 22, 1997, the informer correctly identifies the two killers and makes his own appearance in court on the robbery charge. The cops follow through, verify all the key points, secure the damning evidence, arrange for the release of the two wrongly held suspects, and intercede with the prosecutor to get the court's cooperation on clemency for their informer.

By March 18, 1998, the informer has testified before the grand jury and secured a release in court, with the documents sealed to protect him. He gets a long sentence, 250 months, but it is suspended. He will be on probation, has to cooperate with the cops, and the terms of probation are loosened to permit his leaving into the necessary oblivion.

The two shooters are quickly arrested. One of them calls a gang associate to ask if he'd accept and pass along a document the shooter had received. He was, it later developed, talking about a typed transcript describing the informer's discussion with the Gang Unit's cops. Although never definitively established, it seems most likely that the killer's lawyer had secured the document during discovery and handed it to his client. And there is no reason to believe the attorney would have suffered a moment's discomfiture over setting this tragedy in motion.

The killer writes his associate a letter and includes the transcript with the admonition "someone has to take care of this." All letters from prisoners are screened, and this one leaped out at the deputy scanning it. He consulted his superior, who called the Gang Unit officer who prepared the transcript. The cop says he'll look into it, consult with the prosecutor, and get back to the jailor. Only he doesn't. The jailor, a few days later, again calls the Gang Unit cop, who, shockingly, tells him, "Send it."

As this drama is playing out, the informer's role has been kept secret and he is desperate to get away, start a new life with his wife and son, and avoid the reprisals sure to come. He is not aware of the problem speeding toward him until the letter's recipient mentions it casually and guardedly, even while assuring his friend the informer that he won't forward it. But he does. During this period the cops do next to nothing to protect the informer, managing a couple of hundred bucks only. In protecting witnesses to a cop's murder a couple of years earlier, they'd lavished thousands on about a dozen individuals to protect their identities and provide mobility.

In short order three gang members coax the informer into an alley on promises of drugs and shoot him repeatedly. As he lay dying, he pleaded, "Please don't shoot me no more. I'm already dead." It is August 7, 1998. His last words are reported by the killers to their girlfriends.

Two of the three shooters are quickly rounded up and the transcript is found among the personal effects of one of them. The third is shot dead in Chicago in another gang murder. The two are convicted of murder.

The widow sued, in federal court, having hired Larry Leventhal, the one lawyer who'd fight the case and not dun her for payment. I was glad to be included. I prepared an acerbic report citing the contrast between this case and the same department's handling of the cop's murder; their obligations to protect key witnesses; the importance of encouraging informers; and the utter predictability of the tragedy of this case. I testified in a deposition that the forwarding of the letter was a death warrant.

The city's attorney hired, as its expert, my close friend and former protégé, a man I considered America's foremost criminologist, Dr. Lawrence W. Sherman. His report spoke of the statistical improbability of such an outcome as occurred here and other scientific verities.

It was clear that the city's best bet lay in securing a dismissal of the case in federal court, thereby precluding a trial. Settlement conferences usually wait on these outcomes since there's no point in paying if you don't have to. A judge reviewing our aspect of the case concluded we had sufficient evidence to warrant inclusion of possible punitive damages. A heartening harbinger, albeit a flawed one.

The federal judge overseeing the case, a former prosecutor I knew and respected, crushed us by granting the city's request for dismissal. The plaintiff had failed to produce a genuine issue for trial or prove that an official had known of the consequences of his actions or that there had been a violation of a clearly established constitutional right. It looked like both a tortured and a flawed piece of reasoning, and I urged the lawyer to file a costly appeal. Together we prepared what I thought a thunderous, point-by-point refutation of the judge's dismissal order.

The appeals court took months to decide to sustain the dismissal.

We had lost in federal court and again lost on federal appeal, but had the case transferred to the Minnesota State Court. The city again sought summary judgment, but was rebuffed. With inexhaustible resources they appealed the decision, won a partial victory, but faced trial on January 16, 2007. In all of these twistings, attorney Leventhal had to prepare briefs, appear in court, and absorb the costly process of these battles. This dedicated attorney kept alive a case that almost anyone else would have long since abandoned as hopeless. The widow was never importuned for any payments.

Leventhal finally secured a settlement on February 20, 2007. Minneapolis probably wanted to just be rid of the case. The settlement was small, but to the widow significant. She would get $10,000. An additional $10,000 would be set aside in an annuity for her daughter, born a year and a half before her father was murdered. The daughter would be paid on her eighteenth and twenty-first birthdays. An additional $1,200 would be granted for travel and dental expenses for the child.

Not a happy outcome, but a real tribute to Larry Leventhal's devotion, determination, and skill. This case perfectly illustrated why I much prefer working with selfless lawyers than their greedy corporate brethren.

What ultimately shocks me is the self-defeating stupidity of the police, who ensure a drying-up of sources of information that is the very lifeblood of policing. A *New York Times* headline, in 2005, referred to "Prosecutors Say Fear of Retribution for Testifying in Court's a 'Public Safety Crisis.'" The story describes a terrible retaliatory toll taken by criminals against witnesses in Baltimore. The city claimed lack of resources to offer protection, but neglected to report how quickly they find such resources to ensure the successful prosecution of cop killers.

CASE 12: LYNCHINGS

You might think a felony in progress, shots fired, an explosion, or similar emergencies would rank as a responding officer's top priority, but you'd be wrong. It is the prosaic-sounding "officer needs assistance." This will produce everyone around, and in seconds. In the event the cop has been killed, it produces a frenzy. The hysteria within the corps boils continuously until the killer is punished, not necessarily merely caught.

My experience with the first cop killing in the Bronx made me threaten to punish anyone who touched such a prisoner thereafter. The suspect was brought in battered and almost dead. "Resisting." Yeah. They almost blew the prosecution. Ironic that critically important principles so often come packaged in sordid wrappings.

So when a female attorney called me in 1993 to describe a cop killing, my consternation was great and I was genuinely ambivalent. This was a case of a popular, even loved, twenty-one-year veteran of a New Orleans police agency who had been shot and killed by a black thug. The criminal was a forty-year-old whose long list of arrests involved attempted rapes, assaults, and gun crimes and who had been sentenced in 1982 to ten years in prison as a convicted felon with a firearm. In the spring of 1990, while serving time for the minor theft of a few items from a market, he walked away from work detail, wrestled a gun from a security guard, and led the police in a wild foot chase through the central business district of New Orleans.

Cornered by the officer, who had holstered his gun, the criminal, pretending to submit to handcuffing, suddenly turns and fires four times, killing the cop. The criminal flees and falls as he escapes and tries to hide under a car. As he is discovered he attempts to shoot himself but the gun is empty. He is subdued and arrested and about to be taken to the hospital when the arresting officers spot a crowd of angry cops and decide to divert the prisoner to a police station.

The suspect had been shot in the right elbow and may have suffered a fractured skull in his struggle with the arresting officers. He had facial injuries. The accounts of struggles in the police district resulted in checkered and confused reports of the prisoner striking his head on the floor and similar injuries, all piously defended as mere responses to his aggressiveness. He is finally taken to a hospital, in a battered state, and dies in the early morning hours.

Thus both the cop and his assailant meet a fate neither could have anticipated, within thirteen hours of their encounter. And thus a heroic and selfless police action is fatally marred by the desire to be avenged. A classic outcome to a police tragedy.

The aftermath follows a predictable course of charges of brutality and bureaucratic explanations and exonerations of police actions. The black community's fear and hostility toward the police is not leavened by the presence of a black chief, who backs the cops pretty uncritically.

The criminal's family hires a forensic pathologist to do an autopsy. In addition to the gunshot wound to the elbow, the findings list a catalog of broken teeth, hemorrhaged eyes, and multiple head wounds, including a fractured jaw and skull. His ribs are fractured; there are abrasions on his legs, torso, and testicles; there is internal bleeding. He had been viciously worked over. Incomprehensibly, the suspect had a blood alcohol level of .05 percent—slight, but it indicates he'd had some drinks, somehow. While in the hospital he violently removed a breathing tube before dying. This was believed to have caused him to drown in his own blood. I was surprised the apologetics of the bureaucracy didn't include labeling this a suicide.

Instead, his death is ruled a homicide. The city coroner's original report ascribed death to a skull fracture from a probable fall. The resulting furor led to emendations and finally produced three autopsies, including the one by the medical examiner hired by the family. In the end it became impossible to ignore the obvious, multiple injuries caused by what was clearly a vicious stomping in the police station beyond prying eyes.

By late fall 1990, or six months after this sad incident, a grand jury decided it could not determine if the suspect's injuries had been sustained while in police custody. The DA said he wouldn't take the case any further.

Just three days before the first anniversary of the suspect's death, his family sued, charging that the chief and others conspired to cover up the case of the suspect's death. The family hired a tough lawyer, who promptly tackled the official versions. She hired me. The thought of confronting the cops in court was not one I relished, but the obligation was clear and inescapable enough. I'd do it.

My relief at not having to testify was great when the lawyer called to say the case had been settled. She followed the call with a letter that said, in part, "We did not get as generous a settlement as we hoped and had to make concessions on costs, but still it was a fair resolution of the case." I never found out the amount nor asked. I never met any of the principals, or even the attorney for that matter, a tough, white female who knew how to keep the case in the public eye. But I put in a lot of hours analyzing the material and developing an approach to it.

If there was one concern hovering over my imagination it was the prospect of a black riot. Police executives like me, who'd been burned (figuratively) by such events, grew chary of the pillaging and assaults that scarred so many American cities, leaving decades of neglect and abandonment in their wake. Now here was a combustible mix—a large black population outraged by a classic and horrifyingly brutal lynching. Why no outburst? The U.S. Justice Department, if prodded by such pressures as the Watts riots following the beating of Rodney King (*Case 8: Rodney King*), was capable of doing a tough inquiry, but allowed this one to vaporize into the mists of bureaucracy's haze.

The leaders fulminated, but the spark failed to ignite. My guess—and, despite all my experience, it is just that—is that the presence of a black chief, Woody Woodruff, whom I knew and who was an avuncular, lovable figure, helped. That a revered white officer, whose friends rushed to extol his virtues, was the victim also helped, as did the fact that the lynching victim was not a black youth cut down in the first blossoms of life, but a middle-aged thug with a long record.

The black community, supersensitive to the nuances, got the message and swallowed hard. This lynching went unremarked.

I never found it easy to take the high moral ground, having done enough stuff in my life to know that any of us is capable of anything. There was, however, in this case, a specific reason for eschewing ethical ascendancy. It was 1975, and I was in charge of the Bronx. I got an early morning call about a DOA (Dead on Arrival). We always had DOAs, so what was novel about this one? It was a prisoner. How had he died in custody? Perforated spleen.

I got dressed and went in.

The story was tangled almost beyond comprehension. Cops had responded to a burglary in progress. As they arrived at a tenement three guys scattered, throwing stuff under cars. While one cop collared one suspect, the other cops gathered the stuff—a couple of guns and a brown grocery bag full of bills. A great pinch, but where had the three guys come from? The cops did a quick search for a broken door and found none. The guy in custody said he'd come from a second-floor apartment. Going upstairs to check, one cop knocked on the door and, this being the Bronx in the 1970s, stepped aside with his handcuffed prisoner. Two shots pierced the door, whistling harmlessly through the dark hallway.

The cop hurriedly cuffed his suspect to the railing and, with his partner, went to the side of the door. Satisfied that the shooter must have gone back into the kitchen, the cop—one of the Bronx's really tough guys—smashed the door, burst in, tackled the guy, and drove him back about twenty feet, finally running into a small table and splintering it. The cop pummeled the shooter beyond the need to subdue him and had to be pulled off the man. The gun was quickly recovered.

The apartment held the shooter's wife and child. The kitchen table was neatly organized with a scale, glassine envelopes, measuring spoons, and a white powder. A heroin lab. The shooter, used to such events, had, in his verbal exchange with the guy in custody, said, in Spanish, incomprehensible to the cops, that he suspected his client had come to hold him up. The shooter was cuffed and led off to the station house.

Now the cops laboriously reconstructed events. The fact was that the three burglars had come from a top floor apartment they'd entered from the roof, lowering themselves to a window. A neighbor in another building saw them climbing down the wall and called 911. A check of the 911 tapes would've revealed this, but the guy in custody, seeing the fate of the drug dealer shooter, soon gave it all up. He'd been fucking a bodega owner's niece and she had confided that she and her uncle were going to Puerto Rico on vacation. The brown bag with a couple of thousand had been the week's proceeds and secreted in the oven. The thieves had gone out the apartment door, snapping it shut behind them, thereby leaving no trace of the burglary.

Mystery solved. The foray into the second floor had been the rather crafty attempt by the collared suspect to throw the cops off the scent. He now lapsed into the anonymity of small-time criminal life. He was booked, lodged, and submerged into the system.

The shooter was another matter. He was taken to the squad room for paperwork and interrogation. At first the sleuths helped, but as the fuming brute escalated the abuse he had started at the apartment, the room emptied of all but the cop and his prisoner. The cop spent the horror-filled night in visits to the cell where he'd angrily punch and kick the shooter. The screams and moans filled an otherwise quiet station house. Supervisors, never anxious to intrude between a cop and his would-be killer, found convenient escapes.

The bloodied mess of a prisoner lay groaning, foaming, and rolling on the cell floor. The cop finally called an ambulance. The prisoner waited on a gurney in the dark hallway of an ancient, defeated hospital. By the time a doctor got around to attending him, he was dead. The autopsy described an appalling series of bruises, cuts, welts, and contusions, but gave the cause of death as a broken rib whose splinters perforated the spleen. He'd bled to death. The injuries, at death, greatly exceeded those inflicted in subduing him. The autopsy report clearly indicated a homicide and would prove the lynchpin of any prosecution.

I launched an investigation. A supervisor working that night was a childhood friend and I exploited the opening. He came to the cop's defense. I threatened him with a possible perjury indictment, but he held fast. The inspector was not someone I trusted, and his report proved a predictable failure. I later had him demoted, but a weak and compliant police commissioner undid this act of simple justice.

Inwardly seething but outwardly serene, I bullied the detectives into reluctantly marshaling what bits of evidence they could or would muster. The silent, absent officials in the station house at the time suddenly realized they couldn't afford to come forward with alibis for the cop and lapsed into sullen silence. My trump card was the DA, a savvy politico who knew his way around and with whom I'd worked closely. I called him and convinced him I would go out on a limb if he would prosecute. It was a torture for him. The police union was an ally and they'd fight this kind of case, lavishing money and attorneys on the issue. Not to mention a lot of sidewalk TV rhetoric and tacit approvals of testilying.

The grand jury indicted the cop for the killing and a clutch of other cops and supervisors for perjury. The union quickly defeated me on the perjury counts, but these were tangential. Now we concentrated on the manslaughter charge, since it was clear we'd never convict the cop of murder. A talented assistant DA put together a tight case, the union pulled out all stops, and the trial became a bitter contest.

After many hours of genuine agony the jury came in with a verdict of guilty on the manslaughter charge. Within half an hour one of the jurors, probably reached by a relative on the force, tried to repudiate her verdict. The train, however, had left. The verdict stood.

The cop, so brutish that other law enforcers had asked he be kept off the roster of a pick-up football team, went to prison. The DA had a heart attack and died on his birthday. The shooter's widow never sued the police, although it was just the sort of case I'd have taken, years later. The case haunted me, prompting me to write a novel about it, never published.

As bad as the lynching was, it at least produced, with a little help from me, about as satisfying a result as it was possible to extract from the flames of a terrible tragedy. Yet hadn't we, the morally haughty NYPD, made this atrocity possible?

CASE 13: THE SWORD OF LITIGATION HAS TWO EDGES

What might have been the motives of an anonymous caller to 911 on October 5, 1992, summoning two white cops to a New Orleans corner, where a thoroughly described black male, even to the point of furnishing his first name, was alleged to be dealing drugs and to have a gun? Jealousy? Envy? A grudge? Racism? Simple good citizenship (a stretch in street culture)?

I never found out, but the call set in motion a series of awful events.

The officers arrived at the corner shortly after 6:00 p.m. and searched the black male, an eighteen-year-old of slight build, just under five foot ten and weighing 160 pounds. They claimed to have found marijuana and cocaine on his person. The suspect had been arrested several times previously.

Now a "struggle" ensued, in which the suspect was clubbed and shot dead. No one could produce justification for the act—no violence by the arrested teen, no threat with a weapon, no injury to the officers (although they complained of bite marks). The youngster did have a blood alcohol level of .18 percent.

It was revealing that on the same day a notification of a firearms discharge, required by police regulations, was recorded as "weapon discharge, no injuries." A witness on the TV news, who was never found, stated the "cops were beating him and he broke away and they shot him as he ran."

The mother of the slain youth had, a month before the incident, requested that he be committed to a mental ward for psychiatric evaluation. She was doing so for his protection. He had prior arrests for armed robbery, criminal damage to property, public drunkenness, DWI, and selling marijuana. There had been nine calls to his residence in eight months in 1992.

One of the officers was, remarkably, found guilty of having negligently killed the suspect and he was fired a year after the event. I was surprised by this outcome. I knew from experience that just about the toughest assignment imaginable is to convince mostly white jurors that a cop has committed a crime. Cynicism returned, however, as the conviction was overturned on appeal.

Though the shooter's partner tried hard to make the case for a justified shooting, the explanation seemed lame and forced. The mother of the dead youth sued for wrongful death. A black female lawyer called to solicit my aid. I took the case in January 1994, without hesitation, thinking it an unjustified police reaction and excessive use of force.

There was also a serious Fourth Amendment question over whether the initial search was justified.

The case proceeded predictably. I conferred with the lawyer in calls back and forth. I analyzed reports, documents, and depositions, including the mother's, which proved an unforgettable lamentation: "He was a sweet boy. Made a fuss sometimes. Not a violent person and he drank beer." She broke into uncontrollable sobs and tears throughout the day. She quit, moved away, moved back, and went through the listless paces of unwilling survivors. The tragedy was an internal weight she could not shed or even lighten. I thought her sad beyond imagining.

I was not surprised when the lawyer told me, later in 1994, that the case had been settled and my services would no longer be required. She never gave me any details nor did we ever meet. And that, to me, was that. The most one could hope for in the circumstances. At least the mother would have the financial wherewithal with which to cope with her grief.

Two years later, in 1996, the lawyer surprised me by calling to say the city had appealed the case and won a reversal. It was now set for trial. How could the city have appealed a settlement they'd willingly agreed to two years earlier?

I was away on vacation but hurriedly flew back to Minneapolis to study the file, which was about three or four inches thick. The lawyer sent additional material. I studied all of it feverishly and prepared to fly to Louisiana to testify. I delayed my return to Cape Cod, as the nearly hourly calls had me on and off the hook spasmodically. Finally I was told I wouldn't be needed. The lawyer said that my report could not be found, but she'd never asked for one. I hurriedly prepared one in longhand but it was not admitted into evidence.

I later learned that my police expert's report in the wrongful death suit had to have been submitted by January 7, 1994–but the mother's lawyer had hired me in February 1994, apparently knowing it was a sham, intending to bluff the case to settlement. Furthermore, although the lawsuit had been settled on May 2, 1994, for $1 million, in mayoral elections that year, a candidate accused the incumbent (who lost) of a sweetheart deal on this case, based on personal favoritism, and promised to appeal the settlement. The court vacated the settlement, setting aside the judgment as improper, and set a status conference for November 14, 1995, to set pretrial deadlines and a trial date.

The court required experts' reports to be provided no later than April 16, 1996. The lawyer's office wrote me on July 11, 1996, asking for another copy (none had ever been asked for or prepared earlier) of my expert's report. This set the whirlwind of flights, stand-bys, hand-prepared report, and other actions in motion.

I was excluded from trial because the lawyer had failed to provide the plaintiff with an expert report, characterizing my document as notes. The case went to trial and the jury found for the city. The mother's $1 million vanished. Her efforts and mine had been doomed from the start.

The most troubling aspect of this case was the lawyer, a black female who'd purposely betrayed a pathetic black client. Greedy and exploitative, she was just the sort of lawyer I hated working with, in contrast to the dedicated idealists who took these cases on belief, fought on faith, and occasionally emerged with a payment that subsidized future efforts. From then on I would evaluate the lawyers almost as thoroughly as I did the cases.

This case—the murder of a boy not yet nineteen—was another graphic illustration of the culture of Old World corruption of the New Orleans police department. Take, for instance, the New Orleans cop who was sentenced to death for ordering the 1994 murder of a female complainant in a brutality case against him. He'd brazenly pointed her out, over the police radio, to other officers who shot her dead. Or consider that hundreds of New Orleans' 1,450 cops went AWOL during Hurricane Katrina in late August 2005, leaving distraught and helpless citizens to their fate. Months later there were firings and resignations, all in the midst of official descriptions of the many "heroes" who came forward to help.

But it's the image of that weeping mother that I can't get out of my head.

CASE 14: RUGGED INDIVIDUALISM

Lawyers come in all varieties, but the ones I deal with most often and treasure are the devoted battlers who gravitate to the American Civil Liberties Union, the National Lawyers Guild—the people's law firms. But I don't restrict my efforts to this group alone. Sometimes the case alone draws me.

That certainly was true when a tanned and tailored Mercedes-driving lawyer asked me to take on a case of excessive force used on a rancher.

It was June 1990 in Southern California. The sheriff's deputies were engaged in a cop's ultimate cowboy dream: a high-speed chase of an escaped felon driving a stolen car over back roads and abandoned country. The chase, which had begun in the evening, concluded at 10:30 p.m. when the escapee crashed into a rancher's fence, fled, and was quickly captured.

The rancher, a feisty paradigm of the genre, had been admiring the sunset with neighbors over martinis. He approaches the deputies, who are converged over their prey, comparing notes. The rancher is irate over his fence's downing and demands help in rounding up his escaping horses. The rancher insists that the deputies, ten in all, form a human fence. His audaciousness borders on the suicidal. The deputies warn the rancher he might be arrested for interfering with the police if he persists. He is finally persuaded to see to his horses himself and secures two of them.

The vehicle driven by the felon is towed away. Late-arriving police kibitzers saunter in, mildly annoyed they've missed the action and have to play second fiddle to the front-liners who were in on the chase and capture. The rancher is described by the deputies as "extremely irate," often a prelude to a pinch. They "tried to calm" him.

Any cop in America could finish the script, as they could have done in the Rodney King case. Either the rancher backs off or he gets whacked and booked. The rancher's bellicose, flinty, pioneer spirit leads him to the wrong fork.

The cops' account describes an escalating scenario ranging from the rancher's confrontational "attitude" to the cops' fear of his "being physical." In these cases it is usually the thumpers who take the lead. They're not there to "take shit from assholes."

The rancher, in an escalating spiral of indelicacy, orders the cops off his land. They are trespassing. True, but risky.

Now he is described as "out of control," "screaming at the top of his lungs" and "getting into everybody's faces." The rancher's hands are described as clenching into fists. He is warned. In a report they quote the rancher's daughter as saying, "Just arrest him. He's being a jerk," in a general acceptance of the view, assuming she really said this, that jerkiness is a crime. Even disinterested witnesses describe the rancher as "excited," a perilous condition under the circumstances.

Cops wax creative under these circumstances, including such phrases as "neck veins bulging," "wild-eyed," "irrationally yelling," and other colorful descriptions. The incident quickly escalates and the rancher finally is subdued and handcuffed, but these are euphemisms for a mugging involving about eight cops. A female deputy falls back against a car, hitting her head. She is rendered unconscious. The rancher is struck with a flashlight and a melee kicks up dust.

Throughout all of this, the escapee is a vaguely interested onlooker, perhaps relieved to be reduced to a bit player's role.

The volume of police reports attested to the awareness, by the police, of the need to justify questionable actions. They described the rancher as intoxicated and belligerent in the face of "extremely patient" police response. His blood alcohol level was later recorded as .07 percent. The cops ungenerously speculated this may have been as high as .12 percent at the time of the incident.

The rancher was booked for battery with serious bodily injury and obstructing and resisting public officers. The resolution of the charges would, I believed, impinge critically on the outcome of any civil suit. He was freed on a $10,000 bond.

A host of neighbors wrote the prosecutor, commending the rancher as a pillar of the community. The police dismissed these as sent by people "not at the scene."

The criminal case went to trial and the rancher was acquitted of the more serious crime of battery, but convicted of the obstruction/interference charge. He paid a $500 fine, restitution to the three injured officers, was put on a year-and-a-half's probation, and served ten days in jail.

The rancher's wife filed a complaint of excessive force by the officers, resulting in a finding of exoneration for the accused. The rancher sued. The lawyer hired me, and I spent many hours on the case, got deposed, and was scheduled to testify.

The trial scene was memorable. About six deputies sat, resplendent in starched uniforms, at the defense counsel's table. My mustachioed, hard-bitten plaintiff accompanied the slick attorney who'd hired me. I testified as to the wrongness of the police actions and as to their mendacities. It seemed an apt illustration of the typical testilying and bonding behind the blue code of silence wall. A mostly white jury seemed uninterested. I left feeling I'd failed to connect, but the rancher shocked me by getting up and hugging me strongly as I left.

The jury found for the cops.

The lawyer later called me on another intriguing case. His client had been trapped and surrounded in a laundromat he was burglarizing. When the cops responded, a sporadic gun battle ensued. The burglar was wounded and captured. He sued over his injuries, a permanent ankle disability, alleging wrongful use of force.

This is what we, in the Midwest, call chutzpah. I declined the case.

To my astonishment the lawyer later advised me that the city had settled for $20,000. Not much, to be sure, and certain to be justified by a cost-benefit analysis, but I always thought cops should be supported when they're right. This was a sell-out and bound to result in a real injury to the cops' morale.

I thought it a great piece of police work, in stark contrast to the rancher's case.

CASE 15: LIFE IS A SPERM LOTTERY

You can't be too careful in choosing your parents. The wrong choice could wind up with a landing in Bangladesh, Haiti, or some bellicose Balkan enclave. And so it was for a screwed-up little girl in a northern Minnesota town.

The facts were not in dispute. The girl, six, was a handful. On her first day in a new school, in first grade, having moved a lot, she kicked, bit, and crawled under tables. There she would scowl, stick out her tongue, and refuse to emerge, and then run out of the room. In two scary episodes, she left the school and had to be found. Her behavior never moderated and it was noticed that it would be particularly severe after weekends.

A counselor was involved, and the principal was confident the child would adjust. She didn't. On occasions when the mother was called to the school, she invariably gave in to whatever demand her daughter made. On one occasion the girl wailed from 8:45 a.m. to 10:00 a.m. The school, unable to reach either parent, soldiered on, desperately trying to engage the child's interest and participation. They threatened her with the police.

Following a four-day weekend, the school staff saw mother and daughter on the sidewalk with the child sitting and the mother trying to get her to go in. An employee tried to help, but it was no go. Mother and daughter finally drove off. The school called, trying to get the child back for the afternoon session, but she didn't show up until the next day.

The mother dropped her off and left. The child ran off, but the counselor caught her and brought her to class and sat with her. The little girl "hissed like a cat and snarled." The principal arrived and physically removed the child to her office, where the girl was trying to bite and kick. The principal held the six-year-old in a "control position" on her lap. Efforts to contact either parent failed.

The principal called the police. The officer who responded took the child into custody, carrying her, and drove her to the police station where she was held. She lost a shoe in the struggle. Her father responded, got her out from under the chair where she'd scampered, and left with her. He said the school was terrorizing his child. The mother had referred to the child as "a little spoiled" and as someone who "likes to get her way."

The parents later claimed bruises on the child's body, but every time they tried to show them to the cop who responded, the child ran away and had to be carried back, only to run away again. The officer was unable to either confirm the bruises or photograph the child.

From the facts elicited from the female principal and counselor, and from the male officer, and clearly uncontroverted by either parent, the child was a holy terror. The cause of her behavior, whether medical or environmental, was not established. Her mother, curiously, cited a positive experience at her daughter's previous school.

In reviewing the record I was deeply impressed by the solicitude and patience of the school's personnel, from the principal on down. They made extraordinary efforts to calm and include the child. Their policy of calling the police when other measures failed and the parents couldn't be contacted was certainly questionable in its wisdom, yet I did believe they had a right to do so.

But the cop's lifting and hauling off the child was wrong, totally inappropriate police behavior that amounted to an arrest. It was the central reason I accepted the case. This was inexcusable practice, whatever good or bad faith inspired the action.

The parents, with utter predictability, lived in a condemned trailer with boiler problems, not a recommended practice in northern Minnesota.

When I called the lawyer in early 2004 for a status report, he told me the parents had split up, citing psychiatric problems, and had dropped the case. The lawyer had not been paid. As was my practice, although I never took these cases on a contingency basis, I sent no bill.

Why had the outcome failed to surprise me?

What must that girl's life be like now? What will it be like later?

CASE 16: DOIN' TIME

I rarely meet the plaintiffs, the persons whose causes I champion as an expert witness. This is mostly due to circumstance. They are the lawyers' clients and therefore look to them for the answers. Even clients who might know who I am don't usually learn of my involvement until the trial, when we all have to be in the courtroom together. Even then, there were plenty of times I didn't exchange a word with the plaintiff.

This distance often proved a relief because a lot of the clients were not people I liked or otherwise would have anything to do with. Criminal justice entanglements rarely snare pillars of society. The issue has been, and always will be, the principle at stake.

Such was the case involving a black male prisoner in an east Texas prison. He was alleged to have been mouthing off about the white guards in the day room, where inmates gathered to read or watch television. His remarks, as reported by the corrections authorities, ran along the lines of, "Them whores [meaning the guards] are bad as long as they're in here. I wish I see them in the world [outside], I'd put my pistol in their mouth and make them beg and then I'd blow their heads off." As the inmates gathered for this diatribe, he added, "They fucking over you all anyway." And so on.

It was 7:50 a.m., May 19, 1989. The screw (the inmates' label for a guard) ordered the inmate to sit down and stop trying to start trouble, whereupon the trouble, predictably, began.

"You can't make me shut up! I am twenty-six years old!" (Thirty-two, actually.)

The encounter was a classic of the genre: a black prisoner who feels his manhood is tested in every exchange with "the man" and a white guard who sees every comment in the context of an impermissible challenge to his authority, an act of defiance. The notion of conflict resolution, negotiation, or simply laughing off or ignoring the issue is unthinkably cowardly.

The words escalate to a point that is seen as demanding action. The inmate mouths off at being sent from the day room to his cell and tells the guard that he feels "the same way toward him." His talk is laced with "mother fucks" and graphic illustrations of what he'd do if they were on equal footing. That it is just talk is altogether lost on the guard, who splits the guy's lip. One inmate tries to help by pulling the riled prisoner off the guard, and another tries to restrain the guard. Fearing a riot, other guards rush in and subdue everyone. The fracas is quickly put down.

The inmate alleges the insults originated with the guard. The guard denies it, saying the inmate pushed him in the face and back into another inmate, who jolted him forward. The guard then punched the inmate in the mouth. An unlikely scenario. The inmate acknowledges that he struggled with responding officers and suffered a broken hand and other injuries in being controlled.

Interestingly, the guard admitted engaging in a verbal exchange that lowered him to the level of the inmate. Responding guards had to ask if the inmate was the one involved since there was no violence by the time they got there. They then took the inmate down by pulling his ankles and causing him to fall face forward, injuring him. By now the inmate, properly enraged, is spitting blood at the officers carrying him to the infirmary.

The internal inquiry mostly whitewashed the incident. However, stuck with the guard's admission of rising to the inmate's verbal bait, those conducting the inquiry had to find against him and issue a reprimand for his comment and for failing to call for help to handle the situation.

With utter predictability, the inmate was seen as a threat and disciplined. He lost three years of time for good behavior he'd racked up, got two weeks in solitary confinement, lost commissary privileges for a month, and had his status reduced to a level identifying him as a disciplinary problem. This would be certain to get him additional attention.

The inmate sued the guard and the Texas Corrections Department. A local firm was assigned the case by the court and hired me. My experience housing prisoners in the NYPD qualified me as an expert in custodial issues. My job was to explain to the jury the dynamics of the event, whether it constituted bad or good law enforcement practice, and why.

I had no illusions about our client. In less than one year around this incident he was disciplined six times for refusing to work, once for threatening an officer, twice for publicly exposing himself and masturbating, once for losing his meal ticket, and once for participating in disorders several times. He was what he'd very likely describe as "a bad ass." Yet at five foot ten and 137 pounds, he was physically unprepossessing.

I believe strongly in law and in order. There are bums and predators out there that we need to sequester from society for its protection. Yet our protection, yours and mine, lies in breathing life and meaning into the Constitution. This often places me in the position of trying to champion the cause of guys I consider menaces.

It looked to me, even from officialdom's account, that he'd been abused for mouthing off. There was no evidence of conflict mediation or attempts to de-escalate the incident. Quite the opposite: the guard's behavior appeared provocative and the injuries were much more consistent with the inmate's accounts than the guard's.

Added to this complexity is that, in the corrections field, everyone from guards to inmates is doing time, and everyone is locked into relationships that, in the style of a Jean Genet play, make it difficult to distinguish between the custodians and the criminals. Here, the keepers were mostly whites and good ol' boys. The kept were mostly blacks from the streets. Enmity ran broad and deep.

I met with the lawyers, submitted a report, and was called to testify. The state of Texas hung tough and fought. I did not feel I connected with the jury, whose collective attitude did not appear sympathetic to my view, but the case was lost when the plaintiff, my inmate client, was led into the courtroom wearing an orange jumpsuit, handcuffs, and leg irons.

We were doomed.

The jury found for the defendants, after two agonizing days of deliberations. One of the jurors later said the guard had struck him as a "big ol' Teddy bear."

CASE 17: DRUNKEN INDIAN STEREOTYPES

F. Scott Fitzgerald's pronouncement that "they [the very rich] are different from you and me" led me, more definitively, to realize how very different the lives of the poor are. They don't floss or visit dentists, taking their problems to emergency rooms when in serious pain. They spend a lot of time in line, not online. They take a lot of buses, drink a lot of beer, and wait around. Their lives are boring. Poverty has no saving grace, except perhaps in the way it impels those who've experienced it to avoid it. Poverty smells bad, tastes awful, and feels cruddy—and it doesn't look all that hot either.

One of my favorite lawyers, Larry Leventhal, a guy who regularly takes on good causes and loses money on them, called with a case I was glad to take.

The setting was St. Paul, Minnesota, in mid-November 1997. A group of Native Americans were visited by the father of a seventeen-year-old girl, arriving at around 5:00 p.m. after several bus rides and half a dozen beers. By around 7:00 p.m. the father had drunk another four or six beers and they'd eaten. His blood alcohol later registered at .16 percent.

The hostess had had enough and, in keeping with poverty's protocols, called 911 to have him and another escorted out. Two cops responded, checked for warrants and found none, and alleged (this was in dispute) that they'd checked with detox (a sort of medical facility for inebriates) and it was full. The other guy left but the father didn't, and his reluctance rapidly escalated into a not unfamiliar problem, now involving cops: he was "uncooperative." He claimed that he was handcuffed (which the officers denied) and maced (which the officers admitted). He was placed in a squad and driven off with the second officer following. Parenthetically and interestingly, a supervisor later disciplined one officer for failing to handcuff the guy when safety considerations required it.

The officers stopped, talked, and drove off again. The father asked for medical attention for the burning Mace. He was allegedly verbally abused en route, "drunken Indian" being among the routine epithets.

So far a pretty commonplace encounter, and not one that would inspire my outrage, although I'd have been happier if the cops had arrested the father on the hostess's complaint of trespassing or disorderly conduct. Callers have to step up too.

The two squads stopped at the St. Paul–Minneapolis border and, with difficulty, extricated my client. He was lightly clad. It was twenty-one degrees, and the wind chill was fourteen degrees lower. One officer said the other maced the father while trying to remove him. He allegedly spat on the officers. The man was deposited onto a snow bank and the officers drove off. The area is industrial and it was dark and deserted at the time. It was several miles from the man's residence.

The officers radioed in that the man had been "assisted" and went off to grab a meal. Caring neighbors, in a state where being stranded can mean death, helped him up, took him onto a porch, wiped his face of Mace, and called paramedics. He spent two days in detox. Neither officer prepared any reports in connection with the incident.

The victim had three misdemeanor assault arrests, all of which resulted in guilty pleas. He was thirty-seven at the time of the incident. A responding Internal Affairs supervisor reported him, three hours later (at 10:00 p.m. on November 15, 1997) as "extremely intoxicated," dressed too lightly for the weather, and emitting strong traces of Mace. This was the first appearance of a supervisor in this event.

Internal Affairs investigated on the basis of the neighbors' complaints and miraculously sustained the claims of excessive force. The officers denied most of the charges, relying on the protective mantle usually spread over these incidents. One officer had ten Internal Affairs complaints over three years, excluding this one. He also had four letters of commendation and a medal of valor. The other officer had three complaints over four years and had five auto accidents and an extensive sick record. He also had three letters of commendation. Both had two-year degrees and had served in the Marines.

One officer was recommended for dismissal and the other suspended for thirty days. Whopping penalties. The chief, Corky Finney, wrote a letter of regret to the victim, a rare and wonderful act. He was a decent guy, whom I liked, but his laissez faire approach to discipline contradicted my belief that the most direct and effective route to police reform is a determined chief. But as this case and too many others I reviewed illustrate, the signs were ignored: supervision, training, and control were absent and a reluctance to take on the police union, the invariable apologists for and defenders of police wrongdoing across the nation, led inevitably to such escalations as occurred here.

My report reflected the outrage I felt toward the officers' actions and toward the organizational climate that nurtured such responses.

A suit was filed in federal court involving an assault on the client: battery, false imprisonment, intentional infliction of emotional distress, violation of human rights, unreasonable seizure of a person, and others. He asserted the city had been negligent in hiring, supervising, and retaining the two officers. The case was settled for $92,500 plus attorney's fees in May 1999, almost two years after the event.

As if to prove that St. Paul's twin could match these actions, two Minneapolis cops responded to a call involving three Indians drinking in an alley on the night of January 24–25, 2003. They'd consumed half of a two-liter bottle of vodka and were drunk. The drunks were two adult males and a female. The cops said they'd checked detox and it was full. One of the males was left behind, picked up later, and dropped off (abandoned to his fate) by the two cops. Cops threw the two others into the back of the squad and drove across town to the Little Earth housing facility. They lied by telling the radio dispatcher that the three had been "sent" (on their way) and never checked female detox, which had space.

The temperature was two degrees above zero and when they arrived at the housing facility they hauled the two out of the back and dumped them in the parking lot. A neighbor reported seeing the cops linger over the fallen forms and then speed off. The neighbor emerged to see steam rising from the unconscious male, with a powerful odor of urine. He helped the female into an abandoned car nearby and covered her. Then they called security—two off-duty Minneapolis cops who were moonlighting—who took the male to Hennepin County Medical Center. They described him as wet and smelling of urine. The rescuers reported the urine to their supervisors and to hospital personnel but, as they learned the two had been dropped off by brother officers, the blue code of silence kicked in.

The supervisor, who'd written a memo mentioning the urine, now backed off and attempted to repudiate the actions, which the moonlighters also now denied. Still, there was also the hospital reference and a nurse's statement.

The female Indian shortly thereafter froze to death during another merciless Minnesota winter. The male sued. When a favorite lawyer called I took the case.

We needed to focus on the life-threatening nature of this abandonment rather than the "trickle on" issue. I wrote a tough report and the case wound its way through the system. The system closed ranks to protect the officers, who received a slap on their wrists. The union responded with a tortured locution claiming that the effects of the drinking must have escalated in the victim's system after the cops left him near his residence (he didn't live there). He couldn't have drunk more because the cops had poured his vodka out onto the ground—and he was unconscious anyway.

The twists and turns in the case were wondrous to behold. The main danger would be that some judge would grant a summary judgment to dismiss the suit. But there was another danger—that the plaintiff would dissolve into the mists of street life, which is what apparently happened here.

Not only was this an eerie echo of the St. Paul case, but probably emblematic of police treatment of, and scorn for, Native Americans in Minnesota. Both cases revealed organizational responses that were as reflexive as they were wrong.

CASE 18: COWBOYS AND INDIANS

I admit to being surprised, after moving from New York to Minnesota, at the prevalence and visibility of American Indians in the Twin Cities. That Native Americans shared the deracinating experience of blacks but on their own land—the ultimate irony—surprised me. I thought blacks were unique in the treatment they'd received, but they weren't. I soon learned that the racial issues attaching to one were matched by the other, and this dramatically included police treatment. Cops absorbed, through societal osmosis, the message that Indians, like blacks, were to be punished. When the opportunity included the mythic values surrounding calls for "officer needs assistance," the volatility spurted.

That's how an innocuous "check on the welfare of" call on September 1, 2002, escalated into assaults, arrests, financial outlays, convictions, and a federal suit. It began late one night when a fourteen-year-old Indian girl called her mother, who concluded that her daughter had been drinking, with other teenagers, at a party in a friend's home. The mother called 911 and a Minneapolis police squad with a female and a male officer was dispatched.

The cops arrived at 3:30 a.m. at a darkened, quiet house. No signs of a party, teenagers, drinking, or revels of any sort. They knocked and were told, by a visiting relative within, that she'd summon the owner. The owner, a thirty-seven-year-old male Indian, tells the cops there is no party or teenagers there and refuses them admission. He starts to shut the door and slams it on the foot of the female officer, who'd strategically placed it to prevent the door being closed in her face. Now begins a frantic attempt to gain entrance, in the name of extricating the captured foot. Her partner pounds and the householder resists.

The officers call for help and a sergeant responds. Perhaps forgetting that his supervisory role is to figure out the problem and its possible solution, he sprays Mace on the resisting homeowner. He then secures a sledgehammer and pounds away. The battering succeeds. The female officer retrieves her foot, reporting that she thinks her toe is broken, and six cops pour into the house, occupied by the male, his thirty-five-year-old wife, and their sons, nineteen and eighteen, as well as the visitor who answered the door, a forty-year-old female. They had been sleeping. There were small children in a back bedroom and upstairs.

Once inside the officers pummel and Mace the occupants, relying on the occupants' curses and outrage to justify their assaults. Blows and head slaps rain on the husband. The sergeant punches the man's wife flush in the face, which explodes into a crimson mess. She is kicked in the stomach and punched again. Wrist locks and pain compliance are applied as the occupants are cuffed and arrested. No mention or evidence of a party or underage drinking emerge from this encounter.

The parents were charged with assaults on the police and the sons with obstructing the legal process. They were forced to post a total of $95,000 bail in order to go home. The county attorney wisely demurred over the felony charges on the father and mother and all charges were referred to the more compliant city attorney for prosecution.

Now began the tortuous legal device ensnaring the resistant and innocent dwellers of an invaded home. The city attorney pressed the legal claims by the cops with uncharacteristic vigor. The father pleaded guilty to a misdemeanor, obstructing, and served no time. The mother was, surprisingly, convicted at trial of obstructing and received probation. The sons were acquitted at trial. The "broken toe" slipped into a "suspicious image" on the X-ray and vanished from legal view or consideration; no other officers reported any injuries.

The cops, although they'd sent one of their company to cover their backs, nevertheless added, on the record, that the fourteen-year-old they'd come to the house for might "have slipped out" in the "few minutes" between the cops' response and the coverage of the rear exit.

The family sued. A young lawyer contacted me, described the case, and I took it.

My four-page report would be critical. I called the event "a large police assault on unarmed and undangerous occupants protesting the invasion of their home." I criticized the police for failing to verify the bona fides of the original call. There was never an attempt to verify the authenticity of the call, the mother's relations with her daughter, the possibility that the daughter might have lied, or even that she had returned. I said the cops followed the assault with a determined effort to justify unconstitutional actions. I summed up a litany of police abuses and called it "malicious prosecution." It wouldn't be seen this way, but the truth was that this Indian family was doing nothing less than breathing life into the Fourth Amendment for the benefit of all of us. This case was a great example of "why restraints placed on the exercise of untrammeled power are so important."

The Minneapolis city attorney's staff were well aware that I'd buttress my report with tough testimony.

On the day scheduled for my deposition, January 26, 2006, Minneapolis settled the case for $50,000 and arranged for the family to meet with a black deputy chief of the Minneapolis Police Department, who promised an Internal Affairs investigation.

The settlement wasn't as much as I'd hoped for, and I had little faith in the IA inquiry, but the family was satisfied and I'd have to be too.

CASE 19: BEING AN ASSHOLE IS NOT A CRIME

So much of policing and so many of its errors reside in the assertion of authority, under some mystical rubric relating mainly to the dangers in loss of control, that it ought to be the subject of a long and profound study all by itself. This was proved by an earlier example of a home invasion that arose in early August 2000 in a northern Wisconsin city.

A female officer on patrol in uniform responds to a call of "suspicious behavior" in a driveway at almost midnight. She shines a light into a van registered to the house's owner and finds the owner's son, a thirty-year-old white male, six foot one and 225 pounds, apparently sleeping. She described him as glassy-eyed and smelling of alcohol. He answers her questions and attempts to get past her to enter the house, whereupon she grabs him and Maces him. He keeps going and is admitted to the house by his father, who denies her entry.

The officer calls for assistance, urgently, and four officers rush to her aid. The father, seventy-two, answers their knock but declines to admit them, closing the door in her face, but saying he'd see what it was all about.

The cop claimed that she intended to arrest the son for obstructing an officer, and said that the man's wife said it was OK to enter. The wife denied this later.

The son has gone to the basement to wash the Mace off his face and eyes. The officers rush in and there are now nine people there: the parents, the father's visiting sister, the son, and five cops.

The son does not want to accompany the officer, claiming he'd done nothing wrong. He is described by the cops not as drunk, but angry. The cop insists, and the son is described as assuming a hostile fighting stance and cursing—invariable preludes to action and a pretty lame excuse for official intervention. No one can report any violent act or physical contact.

This is usually the point at which the most aggressive of the cops surfaces, and he does, saying, "Let's cuff the guy and be done." Precursor to a melee, which predictably follows. The cop again maces the son, inadvertently spraying her fellow officer too. The cop leader, a likely "thumper" in my view, now strikes the son repeatedly on the knees, legs, and thighs with his baton to get him down. The five finally succeed in wrestling and pummeling the son, who is flailing about, to the ground.

The elderly aunt moves to protect her nephew's head. His father tries to stop the clubbing while the women plead for mercy. A loud pop shatters the scuffle. The son's left arm is broken, beneath the elbow. Yet the officers handcuff him, bring him to his feet, and take him to a hospital, where a nurse insists he be uncuffed, which the cops reluctantly do.

The son was charged with battering a police officer and resisting. The only injury reported by the cops was the leader's report that he'd been struck in his left ear. The father was arrested for obstructing an officer (for having tried to grab the lead officer's baton as the cops clubbed his son). Father and son filed a complaint of police brutality and ultimately hired a lawyer to sue for damages in federal court. Thus was the stage set for official resolution of the disputed facts.

I saw it as a straightforward case, an unconscionable home invasion without warrant or cause, and the terrorizing and brutalization of innocent citizens therein. The son's only sin lay in failing the cops' "attitude test." Officialdom responded in what I thought to be an outrageous fashion. The city not only vigorously prosecuted the criminal charges against the family, but, when they might have mitigated the damage by dropping them, even appealed when the case was thrown out as a violation of the Fourth Amendment's right to be secure against "unreasonable searches and seizures," the appellate court upheld the ruling. The city was rebuffed, but not repentant.

A police supervisor found the officers' actions justified, but damned the son as prone to violence when intoxicated. Yet no evidence of inebriation existed in this case. A supervisor's review of this whitewash found that the officers behaved "professionally throughout this incident." The department had, of course, a manual of procedures that eloquently described its total commitment to citizen rights and the need for procedures that adhere closely to the U.S. Constitution. Right. That no supervisor responded to take control of an incident in which five of their cops were involved reflects and buttresses the flaccid approach to supervision by the agency's leaders.

The city's leaders, despite news accounts contesting the officers' versions and even neighbors' support of the beleaguered family, all had escaped any accounting or responsibility for this outrage. Instead of confronting the issues they rushed to cover their asses. I was determined to capture their attention. I submitted a blistering report. Our lawyer wrote to tell me that the city worked very hard to exclude my testimony, including in his letter a copy of the defendant's motion to exclude me, along with the admonition that it would raise my blood pressure.

In a document dated March 24, 2003, the city held that I was "not qualified to give an opinion on any police practices." I had no "specialized knowledge, skill, or expertise" and my conclusions were "speculation about others' credibility and motives." I represented a menace by my "claims to be an expert on police policy and practices." I was no more qualified to opine than "any member of the jury." My resume showed "he is not qualified to pontificate as an 'expert.'" My employment history was found sadly wanting. I was "not an attorney, yet his report is full of legal conclusions." Mine were "improper statements." I was also "not a psychologist" yet offered "speculative statement" on an officer's "state of mind." They concluded with "he is nothing more than a shill for plaintiffs."

They devoted fifteen pages to my denunciation as a certified nincompoop. But their motion was thrown out and the city was now in a mood to settle. They clearly had little appetite for a trial. I was determined they'd pay for their misdeeds. I asked the lawyer if I could speak to his clients, a rare step for me.

When the father called me, I told him that an adequate settlement would constitute vindication. I would be happy to do battle, but any case was losable and he probably wouldn't recognize the incident through the officers' testimony. He'd now had some experience with the bureaucracy and was both chastened by the exposure and open to a reasonable outcome. He surprised me by reporting he knew of me, admired me greatly, and was grateful I'd taken the case. I suggested that a settlement of $300,000 or more should be acceptable. He agreed. His sister called and we had the same conversation.

The settlement conference proved a tough negotiation, but the city finally got the amount to more than what I'd suggested, and the plaintiffs accepted. This would be the only lesson the city government would receive in connection with this case.

I learned later that the father had died within a year of gaining this victory. I was very glad he'd lasted long enough to experience this vindication.

CASE 20: INDIRECT RESPONSIBILITY

"Indirect responsibility" is both an irresistible temptation to legislators and a swamp in which they frequently flounder. How they love to hold parents responsible for the predations of legally unreachable brats, only to discover the hideous complexities behind such rubrics as "family." In that vein, "dram shop" laws seek the very desirable goal—the ends always possess that characteristic—of curbing alcohol service to the inebriated. The phrase comes from the English unit of measure in which a dram equals an eighth of an ounce. "Dram" also is commonly used to denote a wee bit of whiskey.

The facts in this case, as they often are, were simple enough. An alcoholic, at its center.

The events took place the evening and night of September 29, 2001, in Minnesota. A thirty-seven-year-old white male is out drinking with friends at a bar. He wanders off around 10:00 p.m. The next report is fifteen calls, by alarmed motorists to the police, between 10:07 p.m. and 11:09 p.m., describing the male as staggering along a busy highway, being narrowly missed and needing help. A number of these Samaritans stop to try to help but are shunned. This is, after all, Minnesota.

Highway Patrol dispatches a squad but report they cannot find the man and get sidetracked by another drunk call. No one is looking for the man.

A sixteen-year-old enters the highway and within a quarter mile roars into the passing lane at speeds later estimated to be 59 to 71 mph. The teen hits the drunk and kills him. The boy, who is driving his parents' car with a license that permits him to drive alone at night, stops, notifies the police, and waits.

It's a Saturday night, 11:45 p.m. The lighting is normal, conditions are dry and clear, and the temperature is 45 degrees. There are no pre-impact tire marks indicating an attempt to brake. The blood alcohol content of the deceased is .24 percent and the young driver is sober.

The estate of the deceased sued the bar that, admittedly, served him drinks. Their lawyers contacted me. I was a bit torn. Clearly the bar was at least partially responsible for this death, but a number of questions finally convinced me to work on this.

First was to account for the gap, of about ninety minutes, between the DOA's exit from the bar and his death. Had he gone to another bar?

Second was the negligence and indifference of the police, who had been alerted by a host of concerned motorists and who had not really tried to find this man dangerously wandering a highway and being narrowly missed. The citizens had stepped up, but the cops had clearly failed. I thought they shared a large chunk of responsibility here.

And, third, why did this motorist hit him where all others had managed to evade him? Yes, he was licensed and legal, but he'd clearly crossed three lanes, into the left lane, in a short distance, probably speeding, and hit an object all others had seen and evaded. True, he was off the hook criminally, but I was sure he wasn't civilly.

I devoted all of three hours to this case.

I advised the attorney of the possible avenues of inquiry, but it was settled, by the dram shop's insurer, before it proceeded any further.

Both the driver and the police emerged unscathed. I never discovered the settlement details.

CASE 21: THE CENTRAL PARK JOGGER

A horrific confluence of events was set in motion as a young, single working woman set off on her jog just before 9:00 p.m. on April 19, 1989.

She launched into a city whose population had remained stable, at eight million, through decades of internal, racial, and ethnic shifts. The number of murders, though, had climbed from about one a day in the 1950s to almost six a day in the 1990s. The year 1989 was a lofty way station on the crime escalation, which featured similar rises in all levels of criminal acts.

At the same time a young man who had honed spectacularly murderous skills sauntered into Central Park in search of the city's nightly offerings of delectable prey.

A reign of terror was afloat in Manhattan's Upper East and West Sides and that night it would find its confluence just in between, in the park. And this reign produced horrendous crimes, only the obvious connections were not made by a police department distracted by levels of violence, social devastation, and drug addiction never anticipated.

So the hunted—single, young, white career women of the upper middle class—were unaware of a menace picking them off in terrifying profusion. They were, as consequence, not able to adopt even minimal precautions or avoidance strategies.

By April 19, 1989, New Yorkers were pretty hardened to the violence around them. They'd witnessed the Bronx turn into a moonscape and no one could park a car without a sign in the window reading "Door open—no radio." Some kiddingly suggested gift wrapping garbage to have it taken by the ubiquitous thieves from cars.

On that evening about forty black and Hispanic kids from Harlem decided to invade Central Park, engaging in an activity that produced a new word: "wilding."

Between 9:00 and 9:30 p.m. a man was accosted on a park path, taunted and frightened. Another was assaulted and robbed. A couple on a tandem bike were menaced but, in a surprising exhibition of delicacy, not seriously injured. The woman was groped and fondled. A taxi driver had rocks thrown at his cab and was threatened when he stopped to investigate. A series of four male joggers were set upon. Two managed to escape unharmed and two were beaten fairly seriously.

Cops on patrol responding to reports of these incidents managed to collar two of the marauders. They quickly gave up three others, who were brought in. The cops were in business.

One youth led to others and the police were rapidly developing the outlines of events and were identifying most of the participants, who were mainly friends, neighbors, and familiar to each other. The kids were around fourteen with a few on either side of that age group. As the day ended the cops had a fairly routine spill-over of Harlem violence into Central Park, a true social interstice, to be sure, but one whose risks were well known to its tonier users.

At 1:30 a.m. on April 20 everything changed, for everyone. An unconscious twenty-nine-year-old, 105-pound white female was discovered by two men walking a footpath in Central Park. She was off to the side, out of view, and had been brutally beaten. Her head was crushed, her face and eyes battered, scratches and abrasions everywhere. She was naked from the waist down and a T-shirt had been rolled into a ligature and used to tie her in a distinctive fashion. She was awash in her own blood. She had been raped and sodomized. She was quickly taken to the hospital in a coma.

The discovery electrified the press, with shock waves pulsing through the NYPD. The woman's life was ebbing fast.

The police carefully collected the evidence at the scene: clothes, shoes, tree limbs, and such. Semen, if present, would likely be the key to any solution.

And now began an ordeal of comings and goings into the station house. Kids, parents, families, detectives pounded in and out. More than three-fourths of the "wilders" were identified, questioned, or excluded. The cops poured it on.

Cops are well aware of the dangers in confessions. They frequently conceal key facts, known only to them and the perp, in order to verify essential elements. They seek evidence—guns, weapons, property, proceeds, clothing, fingerprints, DNA evidence, et cetera—to buttress what they know to be risky admissions. They're aware of scandals involving wrongly convicted murderers, child molesters, and other pariahs. And, typically, they are pretty careful to develop a case.

A North Carolina Law Review study (March 2004) supported an earlier University of Michigan analysis that questioned the efficacy of confessions. Those likeliest to confess falsely were the mentally retarded, the mentally ill, and juveniles.

All bets are off, however, when the pressure intensifies to the levels of the Central Park jogger case. Here careers are made and broken. The detectives work with the febrile energies of those moved by fear and greed. In the pressure-cooker of this inquiry, however, only results mattered.

Over the next two days the detectives drove hard. "Your buddy swears you did this and you know what that means."

The kids had, after all, been in the park and not far from where the jogger was found. The cops certainly convinced themselves, a form of self-hypnosis well known to white-collar criminals who convince themselves of their innocence, and simply needed to get the details. And the kids, many of whom, surprisingly, had no prior contact with the police—and some anxious to please and others too frightened to understand—soon began making inconsistent statements that the detectives wove into admissions. The kids weren't anxious to admit even the things they had done, since details of this crime were probably fed to them in dangerous tidbits, and so wound up in a labyrinth of their own construction. They would emerge confused, without knowing the import of their own words. How could they relate their comments to an event they were not aware of?

The kids had been coerced, intimidated, frightened, manipulated, isolated, harassed, deceived, and even promised rewards. They were deprived of sleep and their comments were reshaped into acknowledgments of guilt. They were not beaten or physically abused, which made their written statements a lot more acceptable, and the assistant district attorney helping on the case more comfortable. No tortured confession here. New York's police department, unlike Chicago's, had long since abandoned the third-degree.

No evidence was obtained connecting them to the jogger's assault, but a lot was made of one youth's assertion "I got mines"—meaning, in the context, that he'd gotten laid. This boast was later proved demonstrably false.

The police made every effort to connect the kids to the jogger. Clothing was collected and minutely examined, a pubic hair match was attempted, semen was gathered from the victim and matched against the suspects, and items missing from the jogger were sought. The scene was carefully combed for footprints and fingerprints and other clues. Not one factor was matched or discovered linking the kids to the jogger. Yet the detectives emerged triumphant, with written statements from the kids definitively tying them to this atrocious crime. The municipal air lightened with an exhalation of relief. The confessions clinched it in everyone's eager minds.

Now the gears of justice would mesh smoothly.

There were two aspects to the case, the jogger's (being central) and other crimes tied to the jogger's suspects and the other crimes by other suspects. The outcomes would prove ironic beyond anyone's imaginings.

Five kids—black and Hispanic, ages fourteen, fifteen, sixteen, seventeen, and eighteen—were charged with the other wilding crimes. All were convicted and sent to jail. Some of these, including the youngest, had been tied to the jogger assault by the others involved, but somehow cleared, either by the police or prosecutors. A surprisingly capricious process. The five convicted did their time, retaining the record and stain of that night forever. They drifted back into the anonymity and defeat of the ghetto. The five convicted must have been hugely relieved to avoid charges in the jogger case, but in the end, they were the surprising losers. Another fourteen-year-old's family stoutly denied all accusations and fought the case energetically, resulting in the dismissal of all charges against him on October 31, 1989.

Five young men were indicted for the attack on the jogger—who remained in a coma and was widely expected to die, having lost a huge amount of blood and suffered a crushing blow to the skull—and for other crimes in the park that night. All five were under sixteen but would be tried as adults.

The prosecution tried hard to introduce evidence and statements linking the five to the jogger, without success. The case, according to a prosecutor—later—"rested almost entirely on the statements made by the defendants." An understatement.

The kids repudiated their confessions and insisted on a Huntley hearing to establish the bona fides of the admissions. This was a rare and costly process, but the judge upheld the prosecution's version and admitted the statements.

The trial proved a hot contest, and the jury, despite the urgent demands for a conviction, tortured over the verdict. After days of deliberation that puzzled onlookers, they came in with the sought findings of guilt. All five were convicted of the assault on the jogger as well as on the easier-to-prove charges involving others using the park that night. The decision came on April 18, 1990, just one day short of the first anniversary of the attack.

This was not to be the end, as two of the youths, surprisingly, appealed—another rare, tortured, and expensive process. The appeal failed. A third never perfected the appeal, so it wasn't heard.

Because of their youth and because it was a rape/assault case, the convicted prisoners were sentenced to about ten years but wound up serving seven years or a bit more each.

Most studies of exonerations through DNA evidence use 1989 as the base year. By then practically all police agencies had come to employ it, and depend on it, to about the same degree as fingerprints. Semen had been collected at the scene from cervical swabs and the jogger's sock and, of course, matched against the five charged. Two amazing results followed: the test came back negative (no match to any suspect) months later, and the cops and prosecutors ignored it. One can imagine the dismay on receiving the analysis, but they managed to swallow it and carry on.

New York was seized by a pervasive hysteria surrounding the event and the communal thirst for the young men's blood.

The jogger, miraculously, gradually recovered. She'd go on to marry, write a book, and gingerly pick up the threads of her life. In a sense she was almost irrelevant to the crime since she had no recollection of it or any detail related to it. She could not have identified her attacker even though she very likely got a good look at him.

And the case sinks into the musty precincts of anthologies about great crimes of the century. The convicted were lost within the vast prison population, the jogger crawled back from the abyss, detectives went on to other cases, and families mastered bus schedules for visits in upstate New York prisons. By any standard or expectation this was "case closed" territory.

But life, which beggars the imagination of fiction writers, provided a stunning surprise.

A chance encounter at New York's Auburn Correctional Facility in the late 1990s led to the unraveling of the mystery. One of the five convicted, still in prison seven years after being sentenced, ran into an inmate who was surprised to discover this young man was still in for the crime—which this other inmate had actually committed— but fearing reprisal, had kept quiet about. His conscience, unexpectedly pricked, led him to seek counsel from other inmates, offering hypothetical circumstances involving a friend. They wisely suggested the friend should come forward.

The inmate, born in 1970, a dark Hispanic, had led a life of such turmoil, violence, and bizarre outbursts as to defy comprehension. The man had been in and out of prison and institutions. Employment meant hanging out in bodegas and doing errands or menial chores. He stole, robbed, and mugged. He had made a painful discovery as he meandered between the shoals of abuse, abandonment, institutionalization, and the countless blows rained upon the innocent heads of those who've made the mistake of being born to the wrong people. He had been shaped into a monster so gross as to cause him to lose the last vestige of hope remaining: a mother's love.

The man, certainly in 1989, was a latter-day Jack the Ripper, except, more menacingly, his victims weren't prostitutes but single, white, middle-class working young women. Among the crimes attributed to him was an almost identical assault two days prior, on April 17, 1989, on another of his favored Caucasian women in Central Park.

On June 11, 1989, he stalked, robbed, raped, stabbed, and beat a twenty-four-year-old white woman in her apartment in East Harlem. He characteristically battered her eyes, as if to frustrate any identification, through a sort of symbolic blinding.

On June 14, 1989, he raped, robbed, and stabbed to death a twenty-four-year-old blonde white woman in an apartment on 97th Street.

On July 19, 1989, he stalked, raped, robbed, and cut a twenty-year-old white woman inside an apartment. He tied her, and other victims, in the distinctive fashion he used on the jogger.

On July 27, 1989, he stalked, robbed, and punched a twenty-eight-year-old white woman in her apartment hallway. The crime was interrupted by neighbors.

On August 5, 1989, he stalked, raped, and robbed a twenty-four-year-old white woman in her apartment.

He confessed to other sex crimes for which he'd not been arrested but which were mostly confirmed in this inquiry. It is clear that, in 1988 and 1989, this rapist's rampages would, if known to the public, have created unprecedented levels of hysteria. The attacks were reported in the papers, but remarkably no connections were drawn between the cases.

By now he was an accomplished, calm, murderously effective stalker, rapist, assaulter, and killer. He was finally arrested for the 1989 killing. He pled guilty to the charges and was sentenced on November 1, 1991, to thirty-three-and-a-third years to life. DNA evidence had been central to the prosecution. The other cases drew little notice at the time. Little effort was made to link him to other assaults.

Inexplicably, prison offered a predictability, a stability, and even a rough sort of social structure he'd never encountered. In his troubled wanderings he provoked the attention of a sympathetic guard who became his confessor. It seemed to work a transformation. He, at thirty-one, seemed redeemed. The evidence for this lies in what transpired in the earth-shaking reversal of this monstrous injustice.

The district attorney's office was notified of the man's confession in early February 2002 and set to establish the facts. The man described the crime in detail.

The jogger set out for her run at 8:55 p.m. on April 19, 1989, from her 83rd Street apartment. She had a 10:00 p.m. appointment she meant to keep. The perp left the bodega where he worked and walked to the park with the preconceived notion of committing some crime. He first saw the jogger around 102nd Street and was attracted to her "butt." He began to follow her, intending rape. He anticipated her route and picked up a tree limb substantial enough to require both hands to hold it. He sped up to catch her. She was wearing a headset and oblivious to noise. He came up behind her and struck a heavy blow to the back of her head. She fell forward, conscious but stunned.

He dragged her off the road into a bushy knoll. She was recovering and protesting. He pulled off her pants and raped her. She broke away and ran, naked from the waist down. He chased, brought her down, struck her in the face and head with a rock, and punched her repeatedly. He took her keys and asked for her address. The violence escalated as she refused. He tied her, took her Walkman, key case, and keys and walked off, discarding keys and case on the way. He stopped to throw away the limb he'd used for the first blow.

She was bloody, unconscious, but still alive when he left, emitting a gurgling sound as if something had been broken within. As he was leaving the park he was briefly questioned by a detective he knew as "Blondie" and let go. A telling example of his sangfroid.

Every detail jibed with the facts, including the detective who was in the park that night. Here were two crime scenes, the weapons used, the jogger's route, the DNA, the mirror replication in other crimes, and on and on. The man set out to prove his lone guilt in this case and overcome the heavy opposition of the system. It was amazing how difficult his task became.

The cops resisted the startling news of a confession to this crime from an unexpected source and were thoroughly committed to the original outcome. They feared exposure of this neglect to detect a reign of terror under their very eyes. The perp's motives were less clear; he hadn't "found God" and he wasn't especially contrite. The statute of limitations had expired, so he faced no additional risk, but he seemed to have found a mysterious measure of peace in prison and appeared to be a little shocked at how decently he'd been treated, especially given what he knew of his own predations.

The Manhattan district attorney, however, set an investigation in motion that proved the man acted alone, committed the crime, and had no connection whatsoever to the "wilders." In the end he succeeded. By December 5, 2002, they officially moved to vacate (to set aside or annul) as improper all of the convictions of the five sentenced for the jogger assault, even including crimes they very likely committed. The motion was granted. The five were cleared and then they sued. I was hired by an attorney for three of them in 2003; he was working with the lawyer for the other two as well.

The reader may wonder what all the fuss was about. This was a happy outcome. But the

NYPD was totally committed to their original version. They knew they had failed to detect a latter-day Ripper in their midst. They hadn't alerted potential victims to the menace. The failure was clear and serious. In fact the killer had been frustrated in some attempts, several times by neighbors or passersby and at another by a woman claiming she had an infection.

By failing to discern an obvious and shocking pattern they'd deprived citizens of the possibility of developing defensive avoidance strategies. A serial rapist/killer of randomly selected young women is as dangerous as things get in urban life. The targets' vulnerability escalated enormously for their ignorance of his existence.

The police commissioner established a panel of three, led by a former counsel of the Knapp Commission to Investigate Police Corruption, with wide experience in police matters, to establish the adequacy of police procedures in this case. They issued a remarkable piece of sophistry that concluded that the jogger may have been attacked "successively" by the five youths and the serial rapist-killer. A tortured stretch. I was mildly surprised they somehow failed to blame her.

The one solid thing the panel had was that the presence of an assistant district attorney in the station house the night of April 19–20, 1989, both precluded third-degree methods and verified the absence of actual physical abuse of the suspects.

The panel issued its report on January 27, 2003, bitterly attacking the exculpation of the five; blaming the district attorney for securing a pardon; painfully constructing an alternative scenario implicating the boys; and finding no misconduct by the police. No mention was made of promotions or medals that may have flowed from the "solution" of the case in 1989.

The panel's report succeeded brilliantly in sufficiently muddying the issues so that the original failures to announce the menace, or even identify it or to prevent future assaults and a murder, fell through the cracks of public notice.

The *New York Times*, on February 2, 2003, wrote a tortured analysis that continued the confusion and rescued the NYPD from the consequences of its errors. The NYPD successfully confused the issues and escaped the charge they'd failed to detect a fearsome menace despite repeated, identical assaults. The serial rapist/killer was a genuine monster who'd earlier raped his own mother. Knowing the dark humor of the police—inventive, insightful, deep, cynical, and often cruel—I was sure they'd say this was a case involving, literally, a bonafide mother-fucker.

Yes, he was something out of a violent, bloody nightmare, yet he came forward to do the right thing. Eloquent testimony to the complexities of humans. Insight into such complexities as a murderer, rapist, stalker, burglar, and even incestor metamorphosing into unlikely hero, while the predictable rescuers, the cops, become mendacious, greedy, cowardly, self-protecting scoundrels, is the stuff of Shakespeare and Jean Genet.

Simple-minded, predictable analysis and stereotypes collapse under the weight of such real-life experience as existed in this case.

The case, worthy of a full-blown book and/or film treatment, instead slid into the muddy precincts of urban obscurity and confusion. The NYPD had dodged the bullet of disclosure. Now it would be left to a civil suit to establish whether justice would finally be done.

The only remaining hope for justice, besides the unlikely efforts of a poster child for capital punishment, lay in the lawsuit of the five who were wrongly accused. On December 12, 2007, after studying the case for years, the judge ruled that the plaintiffs could indeed sue the city for a violation of their civil rights. The case, I hoped, would now proceed to resolution.

As of late 2012, the city of New York had not settled with the five framed boys in this case. The NYPD is heavily invested in their grotesque construction of the case. No doubt officials were promoted and rewarded (seems to be a carefully guarded secret) and no one wants to lose the civil suit with the attendant publicity. So they kick the can down the road.

The police also failed to connect the series of atrocious assaults and one murder committed by Reyes. A serial rapist/killer and the potential victims were never warned. Hard to image a bigger, more terrifying blunder –and involving a really powerful segment of the population–articulate, well-off, politically connected upper middle class young women and their families.

As the band played on–somewhere, somehow some hapless official will be handled this can of worms to resolve.

CASE 22: NO GOOD DEED GOES UNPUNISHED

A society that lacks visible appreciation for social, economic, or racial justice is bound to view good Samaritans balefully.

In the early 1990s a group of doers of good fed up to one thousand homeless folks every day at San Francisco's City Hall Park. Over several years about 720 Food Not Bombs activists were arrested for conspiring to feed people in a public park without a permit.

The program began in 1980 in Cambridge, Massachusetts, that bastion of liberal left wingers, certain to evoke knowing nods from the program's critics. There were no arrests in the Harvard area. The cofounder of the group, a white male born in 1957, had, by 1994, been arrested ninety-two times and spent two hundred days in jail. He was also accused of using the hungry for his own political ends. Some liberals dubbed him an egomaniac pretending to Robin Hood status.

Civil disobedience has not been rendered more acceptable for its Gandhian practices of nonviolence. To some in our society such actions are violent.

The food was donated by restaurants, food processors, and homeowners. Opponents perceived health concerns, although no one was reported injured.

The San Francisco police dumped soup into a civic fountain, confiscated and threw the food away, and arrested the volunteers serving. The mayor was embarrassed. His successor, former police chief Frank Jordan, who I'd battled in another case (*Case 9: Post–Rodney Roundups and Sweeps*) that he lost, continued the harassment he'd led as chief.

One of those lawyers devoted to such causes took up the cudgels and sued. He asked that the law requiring a permit to distribute food on park property be declared unconstitutional and similar requirements rescinded; that the injunction issued against the food distributors be lifted; and that other restrictive actions be constrained. The suit also raised the outlandish claim that police officers needed to be held accountable for their actions.

The case petered out. I was hired but never learned the outcome, although my relations with the lawyer remained cordial to the end. It served as a fitting illustration of the ambiguousness of some of these litigations. I didn't always receive an answer; I didn't always ask the right questions. And sometimes these cases just fell between the cracks.

The illustrative point seemed to me to be how unexpectedly cold, or even brutal, our society could be toward the sort of actions Jesus practiced. It should come as no surprise that he was crucified, but we take that as commentary on the times and mores.

What does it say about ours?

CASE 23: EXTRACTING DEFEAT FROM THE JAWS OF VICTORY

My life, as a cop and as an expert witness, might be described as being constructed on preventable human folly. Amazing how much unnecessary grief people visit on themselves.

One such event began, as many do, at three o'clock on an October morning in 1992, when a twenty-five-year-old locked himself in the bathroom with a shotgun and threatened suicide. His panicked mother called the police in the small Minnesota town where she and her family lived, saying her son was upset over his recent marital separation.

Two deputies responded and spoke with the young man's parents and brother. Over the next three-and-a-half hours the deputies and the family, including two of his sisters, begged him to give up thoughts of killing himself. In the course of the evening he put the shotgun in a corner, emerged, and hugged a sister. The deputies quickly secured the shotgun.

So far a textbook example of how I'd have recommended handling the case.

The story now darkens.

The man and his family said he was forcibly and violently handcuffed, causing, he claimed, severe and permanent injuries. I should add here that misuse of handcuffs, usually by applying them too tightly, is one of the repeated refrains in policing. Allegedly he was not resisting.

The deputies told a different tale: that the man was agitated and cursing and had to be handcuffed to transport him to the hospital for psychiatric evaluation. No crime was alleged; the man was not then armed and not assaulting or threatening to assault anyone.

I thought the actions of the deputies exemplary, up to the last marring moment, when they overreached, and I said so in my report.

The cuffed male had imbibed five or so beers earlier but was thought to be sober, albeit sad and despairing. The moment of approaching sobriety is fraught and often accompanied by gloom. The cops, obviously frustrated and angry, finally lost patience and abused a person we in the NYPD would have called "an aided case." Some aid.

The issue of injuries—their extent, permanence, and even the loss of wages and such— were questions I never addressed. Those were the realm of other experts. I confined myself to the appropriateness, or lack thereof, of police actions. The police used a lateral vascular hold (which cuts off blood supply to the brain and renders a person unconscious) to gain control over what can only be called the patient. The man sued in federal court, alleging excessive force. The cops' expert found their actions appropriate and reasonable. In fact the actions weren't egregious and my report was not terribly critical.

The lawyer's concluding letter said it best: "I took your advice. My client took my advice. The case has been settled. My client will not be retiring on the settlement, but he is satisfied and thinks that the right thing was done."

CASE 24: PREVENTABLE TRAGEDIES

It is customary to expect inebriates to emerge into sobriety in a repentant state, often laced with self-disgust. This is a critical period in the custodial process and one every experienced observer includes in the monitoring approach to prevent such tragedies as suicide. Yet there are none so blind as those who will not see.

On May 11, 2002, a forty-five-year-old white woman, drunk and alone, drove a car into oncoming traffic in Minneapolis. It was a little after 1:30 p.m. She was struck by a car driven by a twenty-one-year-old man. Miraculously, no one was hurt.

The responding officer smelled alcohol on the woman. A later reading revealed a level of .297, or three times the inebriation level necessary for an arrest. The officer charged her with DUI. The other driver was not held.

The officer took her in to interview and book her. The taped Q & A reveals the woman saying things like, "I wanted to commit suicide" twice, and that she was "unhappy with my life" and "I am so much trouble right now" and similar expressions of despair. The woman was on depression medication because she'd been "arrested for DUI before." It was clear she had a serious drinking problem.

In filling out the forms, the officer, knowing she would be taken to the county jail and then transported to a detoxification facility, failed to record any of these warning signs or alert anyone to the risks she represented. He simply handed her off and didn't even check off the box labeled "to prevent bodily harm to the accused or another."

The county jail, which had experienced suicides and had taken strict precautions to prevent them ever since an inmate laboriously wove mop strands together and hanged himself, failed to elicit the information relating to the warning signs and fobbed her off to the detox center without a word to alert them to the dangers. The jail failed to check "suicidal," although they did check the boxes labeled "depressed mood," "confused, disoriented," "delusions," "chemical influence," and "upset/crying." This was a key link in the woman's chain of custody, but it was not connected.

The problem was compounded when the woman was admitted to the detox center. Personnel failed to secure relevant data on the woman. Under the center's own admission criteria (threat to self or others) she shouldn't even have been admitted. She was left, mostly unsupervised, on a four-hour monitoring schedule to wander TV rooms and such.

Approximately ten hours after the car crash the woman tied her robe's belt around a pipe in the ceiling and hanged herself. By the time she was found and cut down, she was dead.

It is customary among custodial agents to remove ties, shoelaces, belts, and other possible hanging implements during incarceration. To have provided the woman with a scaffold and noose is a blatant act of carelessness.

The bureaucracy hastened to cover its tracks. The handy pipe was quickly plastered over, and I assumed—waiting to discover the actuality at trial—they ceased giving out nooses too. The record was laced with references to how much she feared her husband and how anxious she was to avoid him. It was a tawdry exercise in blaming the victim's family, and there was nothing in the record to support the inferences of fear or abuse. Such comments would have put her in the county jail, where, chastened by previous suicides and attempts, they would not have provided her with the means needed to kill herself, notwithstanding their own failure to secure critical facts in her case.

So we have a case in which a drunken woman suicidally propels her car into oncoming traffic. She is on antidepressant medication. She is sure to emerge full of self-loathing from the binge. She has explicitly expressed a wish to commit suicide that is not communicated to those who most need to know these facts and is conveniently provided with the time, means, and opportunity to kill herself, which she seizes.

The failures by the arresting cop, the county jail, and the detox center are breathtaking for the reckless disregard for her safety that they reveal. That this indifference led to her death is not surprising.

The documents in the case were consistent with the lawyers' descriptions and I took the case. (I have had occasions where the reports totally contradicted the attorneys' views and those I not only rejected but usually declined to offer reasons.) I studied the written policies of each of the three agencies involved, which, if followed, would have led to a happier result. It was all too common, though, to pay lip service and honor the requirements more in breach than performance.

Given all the evidence of official responsibility for this tragedy I was shocked when the lawyer called to say a federal judge had dismissed the case. It was the same judge who had initially dismissed the case of the murdered gang member (*Case 11, I'm Already Dead),* in which we had appealed, lost, and moved the venue to state court. That lawyer was indifferent to his costs in pursuing his client's interests. The lawyer in this lawsuit would be discussing the possibilities of an appeal with the husband. This was what I thought of as a corporate case—that is, one involving well-heeled, almost always white lawyers and client.

The family decided not to pursue an almost certainly doomed appeal and the curtain rang down on this sad event.

The contrast between lawyers who calculated the costs and those who fought from principle could not have been more stark.

CASE 25: EVEN SCHMUCKS HAVE RIGHTS

The police are granted a ringside seat at the greatest show on earth. That show, unfortunately, is the human in disarray, homo sapiens (man the wise?) at his drunken, pathetic, psychotic, violent worst. Even so, we insist—and rightly so—that cops respond professionally and within the bounds of the law.

That was not what happened at an urban block party in Minneapolis on a Sunday in mid-August 1998. My client, a thirty-one-year-old white male, five-foot-nine and 148 pounds, attended and consumed a lot of beer, such celebrations being excuses to overimbibe and behave foolishly. His blood alcohol, tested hours after the event, clanged up to .27 percent. He staggered about and behaved badly—not especially violently or dangerously, but obstreperously. He went to the event with two friends, but they left before the following events unfolded.

The man attempted to enter a bar and compounded the error by refusing to pay a cover charge. Security stopped him. He left, but in the infuriating persistence of drunks, he returned. It was now 9:45 p.m. The drunk had to be physically escorted away, as he would throw beer bottles over someone's head. He now swung his arms and elbows—drunkenly and ineffectually, as described by witnesses, but threateningly, as described by security officers. A scuffle drew another bouncer to help and the man was led away. He reportedly swung at and missed a security guard, who punched the man in the head, knocking him to the ground. The security guard had to be cooled and was directed to leave.

More bouncers, from another bar, now joined an uneven fray. They hauled the drunk off, wrestled him to the ground with a chokehold, and sat on him. The guy was overwhelmed and offered no effective resistance. He had no weapons, and the bouncers suffered no injuries. Off-duty cops moonlighting as security for the event were summoned. They handcuffed the guy whose face "was into the ground."

It is a measure of the event that witnesses took the cops to task. The man was having obvious trouble breathing and was turning blue. A lot of blood was coming from around his nose and mouth. Having his arms bound behind his back added to his difficulties. At this point, witnesses reported the cops as "bullshiting" with the bouncers, ignoring the drunk's plight, and even arguing with onlookers.

As the witnesses pleaded for action, the cops, now recognizing the man's obvious distress and trying to placate the crowd, summoned an ambulance. The medics ordered the man uncuffed and administered CPR. They performed a tracheotomy. They took him to a hospital, where he remained in a coma and died almost a month later.

The man had inflicted no injuries, carried no weapons, and committed no crimes. One remarkable aspect of the case was the willingness of onlookers to step forward and testify in his defense. Yet no one was prosecuted, disciplined, or even discomfited in this atrocity. The cruel, callous behavior of the cops and bouncers would have, save for this suit, escaped accountability altogether. A man, however, was dead.

The family sued, and I was hired.

In November 1998, only three months after this tragedy, the suit—heard in federal court, as these cases almost invariably are—was settled.

I thought this a sovereign remedy for police wrongdoing. In truth, it seemed to be the only one available for such excesses.

CASE 26: PSYCHOS

Psychos and domestics—they are the most feared and loathed of all police calls. Domestics are messy entanglements involving men beating women in escalations of violence. Its apotheosis occurred when I encountered a case in which a man pounded his wife's head with an iron skillet until her skull was connected to her body by only a few strands of skin. The hair was matted with blood and brain tissue. While this horror was proceeding the couple's eight-year-old son sat on the floor in the next room and pretended to watch TV. I kept a thick stack of photos of this particular NYPD case to show doubters who questioned my department's tough tactics in arresting batterers.

Psychos are another matter altogether. Their menace lies in a number of factors: they are often violent yet innocent, and utterly mindless of danger or consequence. A psycho will plunge into a hail of police bullets with a kitchen knife with a frenzy that converts wimps into superhuman dynamos. And yet the world often fails to recognize psychotic behavior, mistaking it for eccentricity, orneriness, or stupidity. Among the many tragedies I presided over involving psychos, the one that stands out took place in the Bronx in the mid-1970s. A young man had gone berserk, cut up everything in the bedroom, including himself, with a terrifyingly large kitchen knife, and threatened his mother. Out of grief and fear, she called the cops, who, enclosed in a tight space with this maniac, shot and killed him. I cleared them after an inquiry, then faced the community at a meeting about the shooting. With TV, print, and radio reporters present, the self-styled community leader challenged me to explain events directly to the dead man's parents, who then broke into moans and wails. I could do nothing more than express my sympathies to them in their language.

These cases were much on my mind when an Albany, N.Y., attorney called me on July 6, 1993, to describe a lawsuit, funded by the NAACP (National Association for the Advancement of Colored People), that involved the shooting death of a thirty-five-year-old black male by the Albany Police Department.

The event began on July 8, 1984, with a 10:18 a.m. "man berserk" call to respond to the black male's residence, where the responding officer was met with broken glass. A neighbor expressed disappointment that the police hadn't responded to her many calls of the past two weeks over the man's violent and inexplicable behaviors. The situation now calmed, the cops leave, only to be recalled within the hour to another "man berserk" alarm at the same address.

A hare-and-hounds chase followed over the backyard, fire escape, and roof, and, finally, into the man's apartment. The cops talk to the man, six-foot-two and 185 pounds, through a closed door but soon secure a sledge hammer and batter it in. The man charges the cops with a knife and they shoot. He retreats into a bathroom. The officers kick in some windows, looking for the man. More shots by the cops and the man charges from the bathroom. The berserk male crashes to the floor and dies from bullet wounds of the neck, skull, face, and chest.

I accepted the case, believing that the cops behaved precipitously and unwisely. They should have contained, calmed, and negotiated the situation. Instead, their violence escalated events to the point of having to shoot the man. It was clear that the cops were, under criminal law, justified—or at least exempt from prosecution—in their actions, but their civil liability, and that of their supervisors, was equally plain. The man's former wife, perhaps sensing that some good might still emerge from a failed, bankrupt, and violent relationship, sued.

Now, almost nine years to the day of the tragedy, the case was coming to trial. The lawyer, a bit of a fuckup in my view, had hired me too late to participate in the trial, but I might be used as a rebuttal witness. In any case I could advise him on the aspects I thought salient and on which issues to pursue and which to ignore.

The lawyer notified me on October 5, 1994, that the case had been settled for $500,000. I'd put in a total of 20 2/3 hours on the case; he had sent a check for $1,000 and now owed me $3,133. I said I'd be willing to settle for $2,000. Despite an agonizing series of calls and letters, most of which were ignored or rudely dismissed, no payment came. I filed a claim for $2,000 in a small claims court in Albany on July 22, 1996, and drove the 250 miles from my summer place on Cape Cod and waited to testify. The lawyer, whom I'd never met but who looked like a Graham Greene Latin American police agent, approached me, introduced himself, and proffered his hand. I refused to shake it. I testified as to my work on the case, displaying a large box of material he'd sent and I'd reviewed, and smugly waited.

The judge, a kindly and receptive old lady who inspired my confidence, shocked me with her verdict.

"Judgment in favor of defendant, dismissing claim. No monetary award."

What I didn't know was that the lawyer had told her that he hadn't been paid yet, that there was an ugly family feud over the money, and that he would pay me when he was. On May 2, 1997, the lawyer sent me a check for $2,000. He graciously thanked me and said he regretted the "misunderstanding" with me.

I never regretted refusing to shake his hand.

Behind all this pettiness lay the tragedy of a dead and forgotten young man.

CASE 27: THOSE WHOM THE GODS WOULD DESTROY THEY FIRST MAKE MAD

The case was simple and direct, yet sensational. A man, in the middle of a messy divorce, shoots his wife, who dies a week later. He then shoots and kills himself. Pretty much the essence of domestic violence in America, simply escalated to its often inevitable conclusion.

The sensation centered on the man: the sitting chief of the Tacoma (Washington) Police Department.

Officials in Tacoma contacted me four months after the murder-suicide, in August 2003, for a teleconference. They provided the base outlines and I participated for a fumbling, stumbling hour, during which I offered a lot of experiential insights but precious little light on the specifics of their case. They paid me for my time and that, I was sure, was that. Even my imperfect understanding convinced me that I'd be more helpful to their opposition.

So I was taken aback when they called, two years later, and resumed as if we'd been under contract. Why hire me if I couldn't advocate their position? Their answer was unprecedented in my experience: they wanted my insights, the truth, and they knew they had a case with weaknesses. I agreed, and later learned that they had fifteen expert witnesses working on the case from whom they'd choose the most useful. The city would foot the bill.

I spent forty hours studying a stack of depositions, reports, correspondence, and news accounts. Usually I looked for the "aha" factor, the moment when I finally grasped the internal dynamics driving the action, but David Brame was a hard man to know. And this mostly because that's the way he played it. The key for me was figuring out just who Brame was and what drove him.

I was used to domestic homicides as the product of the drunken, desperate escalations of lower class strife. Brame, however, had been born in 1958 to a cop and his wife, an intact family. Brame's brother joined the force before him. His education was both desultory and indifferent, yet characteristic of a family that could afford the indulgences of sporadic study and work. He held a job as a stock clerk for five months, married a receptionist before his twentieth birthday, and divorced her nine years later. He was unemployed for well over a year, living with his parents, before he applied to the Tacoma Police Department.

A pallid background, more feckless than reckless, that got Brame through the investigative gauntlet easily except for one of those psychological evaluations offered in the name of science. This one said he was below average in aggressiveness and assertiveness and was defensive and rigid and overly cautious. He appealed the results, and after visiting his own psychologist, was found, miraculously, to be sound and a promising candidate. Buried among what look like idle speculations was the suspicion that he might be deceptive. In any case he was hired—and I'd have hired him too—and his field training officers could observe him more closely, and accurately.

Brame now began his climb to the top, starting in 1981. He led the sergeant's test and met a young college graduate, Crystal Judson, who was doing an internship with the police department, in May 1990. By then he'd been divorced three years. They married a year later and had a daughter in December 1994. David Brame performed brilliantly on promotional tests, ranking first or second on the lieutenant's and captain's exams.

An omen, however, had appeared back in 1988, when a young woman he'd been dating reported he'd raped her. The officer contacted was a friend of David's and he arranged a meeting during which David apologized for the "rough" but consensual sex and promised to seek treatment. When he failed to do so, she complained again, to Internal Affairs this time, which investigated and shelved it as "not sustained" (meaning it could've happened but couldn't be proved). Both investigators were convinced the date rape had occurred, but neither recorded it as a crime. It was not referred to a prosecutor. Still, a record had been made, although later expunged, and at least one of the players was deposed in an unrelated case and testified he believed the charge was true.

The Brames' marriage was a bit rocky and Crystal began to entertain serious doubts. David proved extremely controlling in her comings and goings. He'd dole out money to her in precise, minuscule amounts with reminders of "whose name is on the check." Crystal reported to her mother, in some desperation, her husband's oppressive behavior and his growing insistence on kinky, three-way sex involving a female police officer. By 1996 Crystal alleged a choking incident, being menaced by a revolver, and told "accidents happen" and "I'd rather see you dead than . . . " After calling 911, alleging threats, and consulting a lawyer, she decides on a divorce.

David Brame tells the local police department (not Tacoma's, since, strangely , he didn't live in the city) that he is a victim of his wife's physical abuse. "For informational purposes only," he has his mother photograph cuts, scratches, and bruises allegedly administered by his wife, and pointedly reports such incidents to his colleague. It looks a lot like a preemptive strike.

It is 1996–1997, and Crystal discovers she is pregnant and drops the divorce proceedings. A son, David Jr., is born in November 1997. The following month David makes captain and, fourteen months later, in February 1999, assistant chief. He is now poised for greatness.

The record includes a female police officer's account of David's persistent and cunning stalking for sexual favors. She reports being called by Crystal with invitations that never become explicitly sexual. This officer's promotional assignment is held hostage to her cooperation. She paints a tortured spiral of escapes and interactions, yet she couldn't complain to anyone since, as the single mother of a little girl, she couldn't quit her job.

The record contains other warning signals. In another suit, in which an aggrieved executive charges discrimination in 2001 in what is by then a largely dysfunctional department, testimony is elicited of the 1988 rape allegation against David Brame and the officer's belief that it occurred. In this suit he is described as "domineering, tyrannical, bullying, although he's not overt" and "quietly menacing"—and he isn't even the principal target of the litigation.

A shocked assistant city attorney meets with the city manager and, curiously, Assistant Chief Brame, to report this scandalous charge. The city manager asks a few questions and drops the matter, later insisting on including Brame with the two finalists for chief. He appoints Brame chief on December 28, 2001. Brame's stalking of the female officer is widely rumored in Tacoma.

So as 2002 begins, David Brame is at the top of his profession, and a happily married family man—at least externally. And that is the central point of his life: the duality of an external and internal life.

Brame's wife and in-laws described him as a dark, laconic, controlling figure with abusive sexual interests. His father-in-law later testified how David would attend family functions, eat and go off, alone, to a room and "pretended to sleep." He described his amazement at Brame's gregariousness when he observed him with his police colleagues at a promotional function. His mother-in law described how David would discipline his son by calling him into the bathroom and talking to him. The child would always emerge chastened and quiet.

Brame had learned how to keep his instincts mostly hidden from view, yet they popped up often enough to give an interested supervisor serious pause. Even the sparse and sanitized record reflected a failed first marriage, a rape allegation, rumors of sexual stalking, Crystal's recordings to 911 and contacts with a lawyer, and his colleagues' frightening descriptions of his management approach. And all this before the tragedy was even set in motion.

On February 24, 2003, Crystal moved with her two kids into her parents' home in a gated community. Brame remained in his home for a few weeks and got periodic custody, enabling him to spend time with his kids as the divorce proceedings marched forward. Bitterness escalated. Brame was described by associates as compulsively detailing the break-up, crying, losing weight, becoming disheveled—generally spinning out of control. One governmental memo even excuses a delayed report by an assistant chief because she was busy "holding Brame's hand."

On April 10, 2003, Brame appeared with an assistant chief and two police officers at a court hearing on his divorce. The next day he appeared at his in-laws' home with the assistant chief to deliver some clothes and pick up the kids. The documented incidents prompt an anonymous letter of complaint by Tacoma police officers citing Brame's improper use of police personnel. This was ignored because it wasn't signed. It was far from the first time, in my experience, that officials had hidden behind this convenient and spurious claim of anonymity to evade a clear responsibility to investigate. The charges were specific and investigation would have turned up wrongdoing by the chief.

Recovered records at Brame's apartment (he moved on April 17, 2003) indicated he'd had his subordinates call, on his behalf, Crystal and probably others, and hand him the notes they'd made on the conversations.

Crystal called 911 on April 11, 2003, on the issue of a possible restraining order on Brame. She hesitated over fear he'd lose his job and they'd all lose the income. She wrote her lawyer that she was terrified Brame would "come after" her because of the news accounts and media interest. It was hand delivered on April 23. The lawyer failed to act on her request for a restraining order.

The city's personnel director sought to have Brame placed on administrative leave and his weapons removed just before April 26, 2003. The city attorney warned the city manager that this wasn't "private, personal" conduct and that the city must be interested in its employees' conduct, on or off duty. The city manager, in the final weeks, was bombarded with warnings and did nothing.

On April 26, Crystal and her parents went to her home, which she now planned to reoccupy. They picked up some items and Crystal left for a parenting class, scheduled from 10:00 a.m. to 2:00 p.m. The parents lingered and went home.

Brame, who'd just returned from a training program in Las Vegas the previous night, a Friday, and picked up the kids, was in his car.

At around 3:07 p.m. Crystal called her mother from her car to check in. She suddenly reports seeing what she thinks is Brame's car three lengths ahead "but doesn't see the kids." She blurts out, "I gotta go, I gotta go!" Her mother frantically and repeatedly calls back. Nothing.

David Brame, police chief of Tacoma, shot his wife in the eye and killed himself at 3:11 p.m. in the parking lot of the Gig Harbor Shopping Center. When Crystal fell, her eight-year-old daughter tried to extricate her cell phone from under her mother's body to call 911, but couldn't. Crystal died on May 3, 2005, with tubes sticking out of her skull.

Crystal's estate sued the city for failing to act on all the warning signals to interdict Brame's actions. Her divorce lawyer will wind up in the legal cross-hairs for inaction. He reported receiving more than $10,000 in fees. One council member decently called on the city to "admit guilt" and the failure of process. Not bloody likely, or so it appeared.

I participated in a better informed teleconference on July 13, 2005, and sent my twelve-page handwritten report to my employer four days later.

How to understand the tragedy? I needed to resolve the dilemma. It meant analyzing Brame's life and actions. From these he emerges as a bright, talented man with dark instincts that must be repressed if he is to succeed, yet may drive him. What he needs is control and he masters it, to the point of reaching the pinnacle of his profession. The unraveling begins when a woman whose very weight he controlled escapes his domination—and with his kids.

Then follow public disclosures, through Crystal's court documents, which become freely available and which depict the unknown corner of his nature. Domestic violence, threats, and weird sex initiatives become items of discussion and titillation. A searing light focuses on Brame's Mr. Hyde psyche. In the end it is the loss of control, leading to unacceptable exposure, that triggers his actions.

In mid-September 2005, I was told I was no longer needed. The city had settled for $12 million, $11 million of which would be paid by its insurance. Part of the settlement was the creation of a domestic violence center to be named after Crystal Judson. Legal fees for the city, presumably including the cost of the fifteen expert witnesses, was judged to be $1.8 million. Strangely, the process would continue in the form of depositions to be taken, especially of the city manager, as Crystal's parents pressed the inquiry.

Why Brame didn't shoot his two children is a mystery buried with him. His parents sued for custodial rights. The kids, whose names were changed, live with Crystal's sister and her husband.

Everyone paid dearly for neglecting the glaring omens.

CASE 28: A MAVERICK'S ORDEAL

During my thirty-six years in policing, I was fascinated by the mysterious inner workings of the profession. I became a passionate student of its culture and practices and intra-agency maneuverings, and I earned some notoriety as an expert witness in the field. Yet I was flattered when Herman Goldstein—the father of community policing and a law professor and Wisconsin criminologist I much admired—recommended me to a cop in a Chicago suburb who'd gone to him to complain of an injustice.

I eagerly agreed to take the case.

One night in November 1995 a fellow cop informs my client that he observed a sergeant drive his personal vehicle in uniform. Half an hour later, at 11:30 p.m., the same cop tells my client he'd seen the sergeant pull garbage out of the trunk of his car and throw it in the department's Dumpster. The sergeant's hurried departure aroused suspicions.

My client decides to investigate, returning to the Dumpster to examine the sergeant's garbage. It contains documents, bills, personal stuff, and, strangely, a parking ticket for violating a handicap zone. The client then finds two more tickets (parking–fire lane $20) stapled together. The client keeps the records, believing them to be evidence of corruption: fixing parking tickets by discarding them. He shows his supervisor the evidence, along with Polaroid shots showing the Dumpster contents. A quick check shows two tickets stolen from the precinct files. One ticket had been issued to a known figure who ran a parking valet service and had close connections to the police administration.

The client now got the runaround from the supervisors he consulted, from "Forget it" to such homilies as "Take appropriate action." These were the contacts that would establish, for me, the organizational climate. This one was frigid to the notion of attacking internal wrongdoing. Not a shock.

One supervisor recommended that my client forward an anonymous memo to the chief outlining the circumstances. After he prepared it, he placed it in a supervisor's locker and waited hopefully. The chief received the memo and ordered the supervisor to deliver the evidence to his home, where he argues with the sergeant and refuses to sign for the documents as proof of service.

My client is later called into the lieutenant's office and advised that an internal investigation will be launched. The client, feeling the chill, asks for a lawyer and the interview is terminated. He is later called back into the lieutenant's office and is, this time, directed to answer questions. The client's request to have a police officer union representative present is denied, although it's OK to get a lawyer.

The chief refuses to see my client as the controversy escalates. The client is ordered to return to the lieutenant's office, which he does, and answers all the questions put to him. He is directed to turn over the evidence and declines, delivering the tickets to the police commission that oversees the police department.

The state attorney's office is contacted and they suggest this case be investigated as if it were any other criminal matter. The state attorney's office has a change of heart and asks to meet the client, who spends three-and-a-half hours responding to the questions of four of the office's staff.

A grand jury investigation is launched. The village manager initiates an audit of parking tickets. The sergeant who dumped the tickets confronts my client. The sergeant claimed he used the Dumpster for his personal garbage to save pickup fees.

The state attorney's office turns the investigation over to the state patrol. By August 1996, ten months after the start of this event, the state attorney's office announces, in a press release, that the state patrol had recommended no charges in this case. The chief resigned following the grand jury inquiry.

Now began retaliation in earnest. Phone calls and hang-ups come to the other cop's home and he quickly loses interest in reform, even though he was the first to observe the "ticket dumping." My client is harassed, threatened, and positioned for dismissal. An old-boy network of cronies closes ranks against him. The inquiries turn up ample evidence of suspicious cronyism, with characters whose records reveal penchants for cutting corners, extralegal arrangements, and favors—such informalities as selling raffle tickets and misusing the funds.

The case was not emblematic of serious corruption, but of an unholy friendship between high-ranking cops and streetwise guys who needed favors. There were Thursday meetings at a local restaurant, free meals, fund-raising for "charity," and pensions granted on favorable and questionable terms. The department reeked of a subculture sure to produce good outcomes for friends and unfortunate ones for enemies, or even strangers.

I was deposed over a five-hour struggle and clung strongly to the client's defense. He'd had a prior record in the 1980s for alcoholism and one attempted suicide, but he'd been dry for years. The culture had turned against him—another example of the blue code of silence, and hostility toward both informers and reformers.

The case was set for trial for May 15, 2000. The internal pressures on a cop transformed into a pariah are unimaginable. The culture that supports the blue code of silence is indeed a calling, not a job. Like an amoeba, a self-contained body like that knows how to reject a foreign body. The cop who dropped the issue succumbed. My client suffered.

Sadly, the case was dismissed before trial. I called the client to buck him up but he seemed depressed. The case dropped off my screen and I never heard another word.

CASE 29: THE CONSTITUTION HAS FEW REAL DEFENDERS—OR EVEN BELIEVERS

All that I ever learned about policing emerged from the agonizing mistakes I made or observed over my long career. I had a rich store of personal gaffes from which to extract knowledge. The Columbia University bust of 1968 in particular taught me an unforgettable lesson about crowd control and demonstrators.

Angry over the university's arrogation of precious Harlem Park land to build a gymnasium for its students, a group of kids had taken over some buildings in protest. These were rebels and ingrates, rich brats poking fingers in surrogate parents' eyes. Thanks to media coverage, one or two of them had gained prominence as bitter critics of society. The style didn't sit well with police administrators, who decided enough was enough. Although just a captain, I was centrally positioned in the decision-making ranks. We quickly steamrolled the university chiefs into compliance with a large police raid late at night, when things would be quietest. Using batons and tear gas, they quickly and brutally routed the sit-ins. Arrests were made, buildings cleared, order restored.

With the passage of time, I concluded I had responded angrily to the surface issues and ignored the substance. I'd forgotten the interests of the Harlem residents and misjudged the idealism of these student champions of their cause. I determined to learn from it. My chance came in 1975, when a statewide fiscal crisis prompted the layoff of thousands of New York cops. In an effort to find revenues, the city announced a tuition hike at its universities. Its hard-pressed students balked, and at Lehman and Hostos Colleges in the Bronx this took the form of sit-ins.

The president of Hostos was tolerant of the occupation. The president of Lehman demanded that I arrest and evict the interlopers forthwith. I needed his help in keeping the unrest from spilling over and out of the Bronx, so I labored to mollify him, unsuccessfully. I left, having made vague promises that I'd look into it and get back to him. Meanwhile, I assigned a trusted police commander to serve as my liaison to the sit-ins. He described my terms: destroy no property, assault no one, engage in no violence. In exchange I'd let them sit and warn them if and when I'd move against them. They were given my direct phone number, which they called fairly frequently, as did Lehman's president, who fumed at my temporizings as I strung him along. He lost patience and called my boss, a guy who had once worked for me and remained in thrall to my personality. I conned him along. The next call came from his boss, the NYPD's only four-star chief. He too had worked for me and had treated me with avuncular affection. I leveled with him about why I was stalling, and why I felt that every passing day made an undramatic outcome more possible. He let me handle it, warning me to be careful.

I received a notice that the Board of Higher Education would attempt to get a Bronx court to compel me to act. Having listened to both sides of the argument, the judge said, "The court recognizes the presence of Chief Bouza in the room. I am not going to issue an order compelling him to act, but I am confident he understands the issues and will respond appropriately." I'd gained the time I needed and the judge's decision spared me the humiliation of a court order to act.

I called the sit-ins at Lehman and told them that, after weeks of protest, their time was up. We'd arrive around 1:00 a.m. and arrest those who wanted to be arrested, charge them with trespassing, and additionally charge those who had to be carried out with resisting arrest. They were to refrain from violence and I'd ensure a peaceful outcome. We quickly removed and arrested some sit-ins, but most went home. The scene was repeated at Hostos. About thirty-four were charged from both schools.

So when an activist lawyer described the LAPD's handling of the demonstrations surrounding the 2000 Democratic National Convention, I again seized the opportunity to let lessons of the past continue to teach. The focal point was the Staples Convention Center, where Al Gore was to be nominated. The event would also draw President Bill Clinton and other high officials. Characteristically, the LAPD tried to place the demonstrators a long way from the convention site. Under court compulsion they set aside a large area for demonstrators adjacent to the center. They erected a thirteen-foot-high fence and a three-foot concrete barrier to contain the protestors.

The demonstrators were an eclectic mix of pacifists, enemies of capitalism, and social, economic, and racial activists. About six thousand to eight thousand of them gathered in the evening to hear a concert by Rage Against the Machine—a group whose deafening music the *New York Times* later reported among the tortures practiced on the Afghanistan War prisoners on Guantanamo. Another two thousand to three thousand protestors were marching through downtown Los Angeles. Mingled with these two groups were about seventy-five to one hundred black-clad anarchists. Some carried flags with an "A" circled.

Uniformed police in riot gear circled the demonstration area and monitored the marchers. A few plastic water bottles and small rocks began flying from the crowd toward the police, but they caused no injuries. The flurry stopped when the band began to play. Two males scaled the fence, exhorting the crowd to no effect. They were maced but this didn't seem to bother them much. Some street signs were torn and thrown at the cops, as well as other debris, and a few small fires were started in the demonstration area. The body of the crowd was, however, securely contained within the barricades.

Judging from their later depositions, Police Chief Bernard Parks and his command staff were exasperated and annoyed. They declared the assembly unlawful and dispersed the crowd with mounted units, mainly into the streets, where phalanxes of uniformed cops were stationed, probably at high overtime costs, to police these events. The cops moved in formation to disperse the demonstrators, most of whom complied. No real problems could be detected on the comprehensive videotapes furnished, yet the police began firing "less lethal weapons"—stingers, rubber pellets, and bean bags—at the crowd.

Less lethal weapons, like firearms, are intended to be used against persons committing a crime, such as hurling objects at the police, and as precursors to an arrest. (In all the LAPD training manuals the targets are described as "suspects.") Less lethal weapons are intended to be aimed at the ground, just in front of the target, so that the projectiles skip before striking, below the groin with any luck. Tear gas, in contrast, can be used against a crowd to disperse it without regard to discrete targets.

The firing of less lethal weapons at the DNC demonstrators was so indiscriminate as to cause the LAPD to suspend their use even before this case was resolved. Supervisors reported that as many as eighty rounds were fired by a single officer among the total of 167 rounds accounted for. Several demonstrators were struck and claimed injuries.

Depositions taken in connection with this suit reflected tensions, rivalries, and confusion within the upper reaches of the LAPD. The department showed hostility toward the press, little appetite for disciplining wrongdoers in the ranks, and a propensity for testilying. In this case, six officers claimed to have been struck by objects, though none seriously enough to warrant medical attention. In a bureaucratic bow to boilerplate prose, a bunch of cops were reported to have been "possibly exposed to a chemical irritant," somewhat hysterically supposed to be urine or a cleaning agent. Cops reported dramatic instances of "hand to hand combat" that, on examination, turned out to involve clubbing an unarmed demonstrator who was not moving with sufficient alacrity. The leaders repeatedly avowed that officer safety was their number-one concern. Funny. I always thought citizen safety came first.

A lot of the events were scheduled and the circumstances therefore anticipatable. My review of the LAPD's planning convinced me that the intelligence they developed was dismally thin. Why, in all their preparations, hadn't they assigned plainclothes teams to mingle with the crowd and identify and pluck out the troublemakers? This was not only constitutional, legal, and necessary, but it also constituted the very tactic I'd been imploring others to adopt. The LAPD's incompetence allowed the described "anarchists" to get away scot free.

The LAPD had the largest body of the crowd contained in a fenced-in area where they could produce little trouble, although it was clear the majority of demonstrators didn't indicate they wanted to make trouble. Yet the officers forced the group into far more vulnerable streets, which exponentially increased opportunities for violence and chaos and which led them to fire on the crowd without discrimination or justification. This was crowd management at its worst, and I was glad to say so.

Of the two hundred or so arrests, most were for sitting in at intersections. Most of the prosecutions failed or got dropped. In fact, of the seventy felonies charged, only four were prosecuted. About ninety demonstrators joined in this suit, claiming injuries from the police projectiles. The complaints of brutality were met with kudos to the prudence, restraint, and professionalism of the police, and the claims were summarily denied. Most of the injuries in these incidents were welts, bruises, and such—serious, but not disabling. One young woman, however, up from San Diego to participate and enjoy the concert, was blinded in an eye by a police projectile. She sued separately, and I heard she settled for $1.4 million.

The thing that struck me about this event was the degree to which police actions were driven by animus toward the demonstrators, and even to the press. I smelled the malign influence of the Secret Service in all the concerns over "security" and in the evil attempt to remove the demonstrations to a site that would render any protest a nullity. I looked, in vain, for some sense of appreciation of the virtues of the U.S. Constitution in the official actions, whether by the feds, the LAPD, or other bureaucracies. Their acts had, however, to be tempered by the courts and the watchdogs so often reviled in conservative circles.

I envisioned a tough fight and was surprised when my lawyer called, on March 5, 2004, to report that the case had been settled, without any restrictions on publicity. On May 10, 2004, the Los Angeles Daily Journal reported the settlement of $1.2 million for the ninety-one litigants. It took a suit by the American Civil Liberties Union to render the protest meaningful by establishing proximity to the protests' target without endangering the DNC.

The city did not admit liability, and the police "did a remarkable job of maintaining peace while protecting First Amendment rights," according to its announcement. The chief was cited as praising the police and was later elected to the City Council.

It didn't sound as if either the LAPD or the city learned much from this outcome, but I was certain that the fear inspired by this result would inhibit future abuses by the force. My aim was not to get them to admit fault, but to frighten them into behaving better.

CASE 30: THE IMPERIAL PRESIDENCY

The bloated expansion of the imperial presidency has resulted in assaults on citizen rights across the nation. An officious and self-important U.S. Secret Service serves as the avant-garde of this pernicious development.

I had had a lot of dealings with the Secret Service and heartily disliked them. A Praetorian guard, they had not only worked tirelessly to inflate the imperial presidency, but they invariably made demands on police agencies that were difficult, impractical, and sometimes of questionable legality. They didn't seem concerned that their insistences not only created huge inconveniences for the American people—highway closings, frozen zones, impeded accesses—but sometimes deprived them of their rights, especially of assembly and petitioning the government.

So when I heard that President Ronald Reagan was coming to Minneapolis in 1984, I steeled myself for what I knew would come. Demonstrators would demand their right to protest and the Secret Service would cocoon the president. Their concerns would go far beyond considerations of security.

I suggested a direct and simple route that the Secret Service could follow from the airport to the Leamington Hotel in downtown Minneapolis. Pretty soon a delegation arrived from Washington. They wanted a tortured approach to the hotel, through an unused and pretty inaccessible back entrance. I had consented to freezing the roads on the way, but only very shortly before the president's motorcade would approach. I could see the point of controlling overpasses and approaches and accepted a minimal inconvenience of the motoring public. But the approach to the hotel was impractical, and I demurred.

They were adamant. At first they tried a bit of a bribe. I could be included in the motorcade (not, I was certain, in the president's car, but close enough to feel the emanations of proximity). No, thank you. I wanted to be at the site of any protests. Visibly angry, they played their trump. Under federal law they could apply to the court to federalize a president's temporary residence and thereby gain jurisdiction. I'd be powerless to dictate any conditions relating to the hotel or its environs.

I was sure their game was to let others hold the bag and not assume responsibility—and liability—for direct policing. I pointedly told them I'd fight the process and they could count on seeing me in court. Their locals knew me and could report that they could rely on this maniac's word.

Their real motives became clear when one of them blurted out, "The president has never seen demonstrators before this." That was an epiphany for me. I hadn't been aware of that, or that avoiding the site—not maintaining security—was their first priority.

And so, President Reagan's motorcade drove past hundreds of shouting demonstrators protesting his aggressive policies without incident. My wife was there, behind the barricades, with her placard, proud to be among the only group of Americans Reagan had seen protesting his policies. I stood on the other side and led the cops in maintaining order.

Another example of the consequences of the imperial presidency could be seen in Portland, Oregon, in 2002. George W. Bush was visiting the city on August 22, and in deference to presidential security, traffic was blocked and detoured many hours (from 1:00 p.m. onward) before the evening's event—a commonplace "precaution" that utterly ignores the public's rights to its streets and has no practical relevance to the president's safety. To me it's just another add-on to demonstrate the Secret Service's concern and to prove, in the event of a tragedy, that they had taken a lot of measures, never mind their effectiveness.

For once the police did not attempt to shunt off demonstrators to a hopelessly remote location. The cops granted the protesters a permit and used metal barricades to seal off the area near the event hotel to pedestrian and vehicle traffic, affording demonstrators ample space while securing the president's safety.

About 1,300 to 1,500 demonstrators gathered near the hotel where the president appeared around 4:00 p.m. The group was protesting Bush's environmental and Iraqi policies with chanting, placard and banner waving, and such. One of the shocking features of the event was that the police had not made provision for guests arriving for the function. The result was a parade of spiffy Republicans snaking past a raffish, ill-clad bunch of rubbish-shouting protestors. It proved for me a telling measure of the demonstrators' civility that this gauntlet proceeded without interruption or even minor molestation. If any evidence were needed of the excessive nature of the police reaction, this would have been it.

So the arriving guests maneuvered through the demonstrators without incident and the crowd stomped, shouted, and hurled insults. In one video a cop makes the thoroughly unprofessional maneuver of trying, unsuccessfully but aggressively, to confiscate a picketer's banner.

The event escalated in raucousness with the police claiming that objects had been thrown at them, although there were no injuries. Things turned a bit chaotic as the police made the incomprehensible move of driving several police squads, slowly but surely, through the center of this large crowd, with predictable results. The surprising invasion prompted some demonstrators to jump on the squads' hoods.

It has to be said that the search by America's police for less lethal weapons with which to subdue suspects who may be armed, mentally disturbed, dangerous, or all three is a commendable initiative that needs to be encouraged. It is in the training and subsequent uses of those weapons that problems occur. Cops across the land have used these indiscriminately and wrongly because the necessary guides, controls, and training are woefully lacking. It is now clear, from experiences, they need close supervision.

As the noise and activity of the group escalated—although never to the point of either violence or danger—the police began to ratchet up their responses. By 8:15 p.m. a group of around fifteen protesters blocked one of the hotel's entrances. The police department declared an emergency and, without warning, began to fire pepper spray into the faces and eyes of demonstrators. The press generally reported that the demonstration turned violent when the police decided to push the crowd back, first with batons and then with pepper spray, rubber bullets, and bean bag rounds.

The police had little to no intelligence on what was a well-advertised event. Several police departments were working jointly to handle this demonstration and they plunged right into the orgy of less lethal weapons use with genuine abandon. A total of eight arrests were made during this incident. There were four hundred cops assigned. The police reported one squad car damaged and five tires flattened, and even complained of chalk graffiti. The mayor praised the police and criticized the demonstrators.

As was becoming increasingly common—to the growing chagrin of America's police— the event was widely videotaped. The scenes depict a peaceful if relatively raucous demonstration, made restive by the surprising invasion of police vehicles and following use of less lethal weapons of all types. Almost all of the misbehavior by the group, if it ever rose to such an incriminating level, occurred following the massive and spontaneous use of pepper spray on the crowd.

The cops had, once again, managed to clutch defeat from the jaws of victory. The crowd had posed no threat to anyone's safety, yet a contained, peaceful protest was demonized as a "police emergency" that necessitated harsh countermeasures. No element of officialdom moved to correct the cops or their leaders. No redress existed for citizens exercising their constitutional rights to assemble and petition their government.

If not for the energy of the aggrieved to sue, and the willingness of civil rights lawyers to follow through, this egregious abuse of demonstrating Americans would have gone unpunished and even unremarked.

I knew, from hard personal experience, that the imperial presidency was not about safety but about the Secret Service covering their asses and apotheosizing their leader to Augustan levels.

Only they lost. The city settled for $300,000, plus attorney fees, rather than face a trial. I felt a deep surge of satisfaction for what my lawyer described as my playing "a crucial role" in winning the case.

CASE 31: ATTICA PRISON

As governor of New York, Nelson Rockefeller committed two blunders that became deliciously, inextricably, but indirectly linked: tough drug sentences and the Attica Prison riot.

The first was Rockefeller's answer to the rising tide of drug use and crime in 1973, which resulted in a system overcrowded by toothless geriatrics who'd not exhibited any violent tendencies and who were increasingly expensive to host. The explosion of incarceration persuaded the nation to go on a prison-building spree. Within three decades, almost seven million individuals—overwhelmingly male and more than 40 percent black—were under some kind of control, such as jail, prison, parole, or probation. More than two million were incarcerated by 2007.

Rockefeller's philosophy was widely adopted to no visible effect, as treatment, prevention, and education sank into the mire of "being soft on crime." Soft-headed is more like it. Even the precipitous decline in street crime that began in the mid-1990s didn't slow the exponential expansion of the corrections system.

Rockefeller's other blunder was to pointedly ignore the pleas of inmates to negotiate when they took over Attica Prison on September 9, 1971. They'd captured a score of guards and held them hostage, complaining of abuse, overcrowding, receiving one roll of toilet paper per month, and other expectable grievances.

At the time the inmates made their request, nothing terrible was happening; the building was surrounded, and no one had escaped. But four days later, on September 13, a force of guards, state police, and other officers stormed Attica, producing the deadliest prison uprising in U.S. history. There were forty-three dead—thirty-two inmates and eleven guards (hostages)—and more than ninety injured.

The guards, hysterical over the deaths of their comrades and over rumors of atrocities, assaulted, brutalized, and tortured the inmates in an orgy of reprisal. The abuse extended far beyond the point of regaining control of the facility. The inmates were made to walk over broken glass in bare feet and run gauntlets of baton-wielding guards, and they were assaulted in ways made familiar by prison excesses everywhere—all of this with the tacit approval of supervisors and lasting over several days. The frenzy was stoked by the inevitable alarmists, speaking darkly of slit throats, castration and other mutilations, and sadistic practices on the captured guards, none of which turned out to be true.

A total of 1,281 inmates filed a civil suit in federal court in 1974, employing a young woman just graduated from law school. This would be her only case for the next thirty years. She contacted Dennis Cunningham, the lawyer who hired me in 1992 to testify on behalf of a former Attica prisoner. I was reluctant to champion the cause of prison reform in this case, but the governor's failure to respond to the inmates constituted almost criminal negligence in my view. I testified on the absolute need to negotiate as long as the situation is contained and no awful violence needs to be addressed.

I could not bring myself to shake the hand of the hardened criminal whose cause I was called to support and drifted into avoidance. The inmate, who'd gone on to work as a paralegal for that recently graduated lawyer for twenty years after emerging from prison in 1973, won $4 million in 1997. The extralegal assaults were held to be "cruel and unusual punishment." The state faced a staggering potential liability.

The state would appeal and negotiate with the surviving inmates; many others were now dead. The plaintiff, sixty-four in 1997, had been in for armed robbery and emerged as a leader in the uprising. That he was black seemed beside the point since most of the inmates were minorities. He died on July 31, 2004, vindicated. I was wrong to avoid shaking his hand.

The state had fought the case tooth and claw, with taxpayers footing the bill. Rockefeller was long dead. The $4 million verdict was overturned on appeal, the court ruling the inmate's case had to be included with the others in a class action. Sensing defeat, the state settled the case in 2000, granting $8 million to be split among the inmates and $4 million for the lawyers.

The retaking of Attica was a tragic mistake, occasioned by a governor's arrogance. The aftermath was criminal. I had no trouble testifying as to the wrongness of the assault and the breaches of law involved in the excess that followed.

A tragic echo of Attica occurred in Waco, Texas, on April 19, 1993, when federal forces stormed a compound thought to be a cult created for the sexploitation of minors. This after a fifty-one-day stand-off following a shootout between the feds and the Branch Davidians, followers of cult leader David Koresh, in which four Bureau of Alcohol, Tobacco, and Firearms agents died. An untried president and an unknowing attorney general combined to authorize a raid that left the buildings ablaze and about eighty-six followers of Koresh incinerated. As at Attica the situation was contained, the Davidians were surrounded, and nothing terrible was happening, if you discount the attorney general's alarmed reports of children being sexually abused. She went along with the jingoists impatient to avenge fallen brothers. These alarm ringers are an invariable feature of such stand-offs.

What such cases illustrate, with tragic force, is George Santayana's warning that "those who cannot remember the past are condemned to repeat it." There's nothing wrong with action, but it ought to be undertaken when the weight of the evidence clearly demands it. Negotiation, conflict resolution, mediation, and any other system of parlay needs to be exhausted first.

CASE 32: SPORTS RIOTS

Hooliganism is behavior that Americans typically associate with European soccer matches, but sports victories in the United States have been dotted with violent eruptions for years. Fans usually pour into the streets in celebratory riots that involve drinking, vandalism, fires, and, sometimes, looting and assaults. Police agencies throughout America have had to brace against these possibilities.

In 2002 the University of Minnesota hockey team won the NCAA championship and exuberant Gopher fans took everyone by surprise by erupting into the streets surrounding the campus—Fraternity Row, mainly—blocking traffic, vandalizing street signs, and setting fires. The police reacted as best they could, but it was a chastening, if brief, experience.

On April 12, 2003, the Gophers were to play New Hampshire in Buffalo, N.Y., for the NCAA hockey championship. The game would be televised. The significance of the date centers on the length and severity of Minnesota winters. We Minnesotans spend about five months pent up in our cubicles like hibernating rodents and emerge half-naked, bursting with energy and febrile from cabin confinement, into spring's first rays of sunshine.

Given the events that occurred the year before, it was obvious that problems would likely arise. The Minneapolis Police Department (MPD) had, however, been inhibited by the City Council for "overpreparing" for a trade conference that drew troublemakers—and trouble—to Seattle. That city had faced street disorders and near riots when the World Trade Organization held its meeting there. The council's concerns appear to have centered on turning downtown into a concertina-wired, Darth Vader–clad, garrison state that cost large sums in police overtime.

A deputy chief was quoted as having deliberately eschewed preparation as a result of this chiding, so the MPD held brief meetings with the University of Minnesota police and assigned six officers to serve as a "trip wire" to alert the agency to any problems associated with celebrations following the championship game. The university assigned its officers to the area, but at the first sign of trouble withdrew them from the streets to stand at the campus gates and "refused to come to our assistance," in the harsh words of an MPD lieutenant on the scene. A group of cops from various agencies were on campus working on a Safe and Sober program to monitor drunken drivers. Because they lacked riot gear they were used only to monitor and control traffic.

The game ended at 8:35 p.m. Minnesota time. University students along Frat Row burst into the streets, many in a drunken state. Pamphlets had been distributed about "the riot tonight" and rumors had been rife. The rampaging students tore up and down the streets, ripping apart signs, throwing objects, assaulting motorists, and setting fires. The apex was reached with the smashing of a liquor store's windows and the looting of contents. At the end the damage estimate was put at $170,000 to $300,000.

The police at the scene called in an alarm. Within an hour about 125 riot-equipped Minneapolis cops were ready to be deployed, but those sixty minutes enabled the rioters—sometimes numbering well over one thousand at given intersections—to generate a full head of steam. The streets were theirs and would have to be retaken.

In such situations one priority is to "protect the glass" (windows) and maneuver the mobs into dull side streets, where enthusiasm would be dissipated for lack of targets.

The inherently confusing scenario was rendered worse by the presence of a ranking officer—who also commanded the precinct in question—who said she "was not the incident commander." A responding deputy chief begged to differ, reported himself as unhappy with the state of things, and replaced her as incident commander. The Minneapolis Fire Department experienced great difficulty in extinguishing such fires as cars burning or a parking attendant's booth set ablaze because they were being pelted with bottles and debris. The first order of police business had to be to enable the firefighters to work.

The cops had a raft of less lethal weapons: stinger balls, chemical gases of all types, bean-bag rounds, and such. They formed into squads and began to disperse the crowds on the streets surrounding the university. Traffic was detoured and the fires gradually extinguished. The cops were required to report and account for every round expended, under a use-of-force policy in effect. They made liberal use of the weapons on hand, but scarce employment of documenting their actions.

Into this confusion stepped, individually and separately, two white males, a twenty-one-year-old student resident of Frat Row and a twenty-six-year-old carpenter. The student had consumed about ten beers and was likely abuzz. He wanted to see the action and wandered the streets. At one event, which involved two cars burning, he ran off, got chased by cops, and was struck in the back by a projectile. He limped home and had trouble breathing. Ice packs didn't help. Two young women drove him to one hospital, then to another, where he had emergency surgery to remove his spleen. The student had been bleeding internally and would've died if he'd taken to his bed. He required a second operation a few days later to remove a bowel obstruction and the incision leaked. In short order he was driven from robust to frail health. The carpenter also stood watching the riots and wound up being clubbed. His right arm was broken and required surgery.

Neither young man was arrested. No one alleged any violence or illegality. The cops—almost certainly from the MPD since no others had been trying to control the crowds—were not identified. No cop reported as having fired at the student or clubbed the carpenter.

A lawyer with whom I'd worked on a successful case in Superior, Wisconsin, asked if I'd take the cases. I read the material and agreed.

The odd thing for me was that I was an unapologetic supporter of police violence. Even after the LAPD had been pressured to abandon the chokehold, I permitted and encouraged its use, which is the policy even today. I presided over clubbings, shootings, gassings, and other assaults by the police. I saw violence as a key weapon in the police arsenal and trained cops in the full range of possibilities available to us. The only caveat was that the use of force had to be legally justified, measured, and appropriate, and that the weapons had to be in conformance with the law. I'd banned the use of sap gloves, lead-lined gauntlets in common employment yet legally forbidden.

I was struck by the confusion revealed as pervading the MPD. One supervisor reported arrests were not a priority, as if force could be used outside of the commission of a crime and to arrest the violator. He added that their number-one priority was officer safety. The problem was that the confusion wasn't theoretical; it got translated into actions on the street, as this case made abundantly clear.

When asked to prepare a report on this case, I abandoned my usual hyperbolic judgments and instead meticulously cited the confusions, omissions, contradictions, admissions, and complaints on the record. The lawyer even asked me for advice in jury selection. Expecting the cops to put the best color on things, or perhaps even testilie, I first thought of blacks for the jury, then of the better educated, then of people who had picketed, demonstrated, or protested. I felt that Joe Six-Pack, conservatives, religious folks, and blue-collar types would be sympathetic to the police.

Putting to rest the curse for the Bambino sent Boston revelers into joyous orbit as the Boston Red Sox improbably conquered the Yankees in the 2004 World Series, overcoming a three-game deficit to win four straight. Bostonians took to the streets. The Boston police's elite crowd control unit responded by firing less lethal projectiles. One struck a twenty-one-year-old woman in the eye, killing her on October 21, 2004. In 2005 Boston reorganized the unit and its approach and paid $5.1 million to the woman's parents.

In the Minneapolis cases the carpenter received a settlement for his broken arm. The spleen-loser awaited resolution of his more serious claim, which was settled for $412,500.

CASE 33: WAR PROTESTERS

There ought to be a training program for police executives dealing with mass protests. A sports celebration that turns to violence tends to be a spontaneous event that demands police planning, quick action, and targeted arrests. Ghetto riots, which usually emerge from flashpoints such as the shooting of a fifteen-year-old black boy by a white cop, require quick action to prevent fires and looting and preparation that creates credibility that the investigation to follow will be fair and thorough. Sit-ins require patience and deliberate actions that exalt process over speed. Labor strikes, which often result in violence, require protecting the rights of strikers to express their grievances and demands effectively while protecting management's rights to pursue its remedies—so long as these are enshrined in law. Each variation on the protest theme represents a unique challenge. Each requires planning, training, and effective execution.

If nothing terrible is happening at a mass protest, police should employ containment, negotiation, conflict management, mediation, and other techniques of persuasion. Resorting to violence has its uses and its limits. It should be used only when necessary and only to the extent permitted by law. Documenting all actions and decisions will inhibit freelancing and limit mistakes, as well as enable reviewers to judge the actions.

A lawyer with whom I'd dealt before and happily, called to describe the latest abuse, this time involving protestors trying to block military supplies to our forces in Iraq in the opening stages of what should be called the U.S.–Iraqi War of 2003.

The events of April 7, 2003, need to be seen within the context of bitter labor relations on Oakland docks, in which pier operators locked out members of the Longshoremen's Union and dozens of tankers lay idle in the harbor. The police had a comprehensive operational plan prepared before the events, but it failed to cite the protesters' stated aim to "picket, not necessarily (face) arrest."

Several hundred pickets showed up on April 7 before 6:00 a.m. at the pier gates, and a large contingent of cops in riot gear was there to meet them. Demonstrators blocked one gate for more than an hour. Traffic backed up. The police issued three warnings to disperse and gave them three minutes, at the end of which twenty-four motorcycle cops began bumping the pickets away from the gate.

The police began firing bean bags, tear gas, and wooden dowels (five to each shot) and throwing grenade-like sting balls that spray out and cause pain. Many demonstrators reported being injured by the projectiles. The graphic evidence of severe welts high on the bodies of many demonstrators proved that the officers were aiming high—strictly forbidden—and fired often and indiscriminately. Additional cops responded. The wonder was that no one had suffered seriously. No cops were injured.

The Longshoremen's Union, which had a resolution on record opposing the U.S.–Iraqi war, protested strongly when nine of their members were shot and injured on their way to work, and when a business agent "trying to protect his members" headed to work, was thrown to the ground, handcuffed, arrested, and held in custody eighteen hours.

The demonstrators were gradually dispersed, although twelve who had crossed a police yellow tape and knelt in front of a line of cops were arrested. A total of about thirty arrests on various charges relating to blocking ingress and such were effected. The use of force was justified by the Oakland police chief, who said, "The police had no choice but to fire when protesters failed to leave." He added he feared many more could have gathered during the day. The mayor defended the action of the police. Two council members demanded an inquiry.

An intelligence supervisor reported vivid scenes of violence in San Francisco, with the clear implication that Oakland would see a replica. Another intelligence report meticulously cited the protesters' aim to "shut down the war merchants," but omitted their references to avoid arrest situations. It was careful to cite a warning of "political violence." The reports were typically hyperbolic and unbalanced notices, reminiscent of the FBI's Counter Intelligence Program (COINTELPRO) of the 1960s and 1970s.

The news media covered the event extensively and were widely critical of the police handling. The union, unhappy with the city's response, hired my attorney and sued. Approximately forty injured people, many hit on the head or upper body, joined the suit. I was enthusiastic about the prospects for changing departmental behaviors through damages, punitive and actual, but tepid over the promise behind attempts to reform the agency's crowd control policy. Nevertheless, the lawyer sent me a proposed reform of the policy. I reviewed and edited it and suggested amendments.

An obvious argument can be made that we must, right or wrong, support those we send into combat, but an equally compelling argument can be made for the proposition that the hands of irresponsible leaders must be stayed when they stray into tyranny. The passage of intervening months had certainly made the position of the protestors seem more reasonable.

Initially, as was true in early Vietnam War protests, this was an unpopular, or maybe even unpatriotic, demonstration. Vietnam protesters proved prophets later. It was an object lesson of the value of gadflies and mavericks to a society heading in the wrong direction. Officialdom's lockstep justification of indefensible actions was just another demonstration of business as usual, even if it did, this time, involve Jerry Brown, a notably liberal mayor. That the action was aimed at organized labor only exacerbated the injustice.

In mid-September 2005 the lawyer surprised me with a call that they'd settled the case for an undisclosed amount and involving alterations in police policy I'd help to shape, without much hope for their effect. Her initiative took me aback because I usually had to inquire as to the status of cases.

The *New York Times* had the last word, when on March 20, 2006, the newspaper announced that Oakland had agreed to pay the injured Iraqi War protesters $2 million and to change its crowd-control policy.

The dissenters had, on April 7, 2003, been labeled unpatriotic troublemakers. As of the settlement they had to be seen as prescient.

CASE 34: POISONING THE WELLS OF JUSTICE

As an expert witness I usually encounter abuses involving stupidity, not calculated cupidity. This was one of the rare cases in which the law was twisted to accommodate personal, selfish ends. It seemed to me the ultimate in corruption.

The events unfold from a dispute over jurisdiction in a small California town. The city, in 1992, entered into a contractual arrangement to have its police functions performed by the local county sheriff, a common approach in towns seeking budget savings. It abolished its police force.

Over the years a black candidate was elected sheriff and the town became unhappy with his organization's performance. Service was deemed inadequate and the townspeople felt response to their calls was deficient. By 2002 the town had decided to let its contract with the sheriff lapse, under a provision of the agreement, and appointed a qualified white male as chief. The city manager, another white male, was the moving force behind these shifts. The sheriff objected, saying that he was still the police authority in town. His position was that, since the contract hadn't been formally abrogated, it was still in force and he was, as a consequence, still the city's police chief.

A pretty straightforward contractual dispute to which our court system is amply prepared to respond.

But this was not to be, as the sheriff muddied the waters with bizarre actions that are all the more remarkable for their having been abetted and supported by his subordinates. But then, one of the dolorous discoveries in public life is the surprising enthusiasm with which functionaries seize their supervisors' illegal orders and rush to comply. The resulting controversy ostensibly had nothing to do with the contractual dispute, except that the sheriff's actions can be understood only within that context.

The city's unhappiness with the sheriff's services grew and finally surfaced in press accounts. On November 1, 2000, the City Council passed a resolution authorizing the city manager to begin forming a police department and select a chief. The city manager was, on that date, appointed police chief and authorized to purchase equipment "as necessary for law enforcement." He was formally sworn in on March 20, 2002, and had two years in which to qualify for a license granted by the Peace Officers Standards and Training Act. The city manager appointed another white male as director of public safety and airport peace officer, on March 3, 2002.

In a brief dispute, the city manager resigned his chief's position on March 18, 2002, but, since it was not accepted by the council, he continued serving. Such missteps are one of the hallmarks of small town government life.

Now, in early 2002, the city manager/chief and the director of public safety/airport peace officer began to constitute and equip a police agency. They secured Bureau of Alcohol, Tobacco, and Firearms authorization to purchase otherwise illegal machine guns (two) and other firearms, like shotguns. Through a routine inquiry misdirected to that office, the sheriff learned of the purchase and was aware of the BATF approval.

While the city manager and director of public safety were attending a police-training seminar in Los Angeles on May 22–23, 2002, a sheriff's investigator prepared a request for a search warrant, alleging possession of illegal weapons intended to be used in the commission of a felony. The comedy of tragedies is deepened by this investigator's appending the city government's letter ordering the machine guns, the BATF form required for the purchase, and a firearm dealer's letter to the city attorney tracking the shipment of the firearms and asking for payment. Armed with all this convincing proof of the meticulous legality of the enterprise, the investigator secured the approval of the deputy district attorney, who reviewed these documents, and, incredibly, even a judge's signature authorizing the search.

The sheriff's deputies, accompanied by BATF agents who were quick to disavow their involvement (and who thereby escaped civil liability), barged into the homes of the absent officials and recovered two machine guns and other firearms from the locked safe of the city manager. The searches, which recovered other firearms, were conducted on May 22–23, 2002, and involved the residence and offices of both absent officials, later their persons, and even City Hall.

The fat was now in the fire.

The sheriff submitted the case to a grand jury, which refused to indict anyone. The prosecutor declined to charge as well. Adding further insult, the sheriff's assertion that the city could not appoint its own police chief was an unthinkable denial of the municipality's sovereignty. His chutzpah was breathtaking.

Remarkably the events all had been meticulously documented, making it easy to examine actions that, absent these records, would have seemed improbably bizarre. What the sheriff had managed to prove was how carefully the city and the two officials had followed the law. This was low comedy, officially sanctioned by trained officials charged with solemn duties. Gilbert and Sullivan might have resisted, since it strained credibility.

It was rare indeed to receive such detailed documentation of an official action being driven by personal animus and private gain. The case was important for its illustration of the value of outside review of officialdom's solemn acts, often accompanied by assurances of their legality.

In a later deposition, the sheriff, who had claimed to be the sole police authority in the city, admitted that the policing contract between his agency and the city had been "in suspense for almost a year."

Predictably and sadly, the episode still, despite the legal outcome, managed to destroy the lives of both the city manager and the public safety director. They lost their jobs and were unable to find others. The sheriff's deputies reportedly continued to harass the two officials and the sheriff's comments to the press inflamed the issue.

Desperate, the two sued the sheriff, who, to my real regret, since I relished confronting him, died before the case got to trial. I was glad to take the case. The lawyer, a woman, had been referred to me by a lawyer I much admired for taking cases with no regard to monetary issues. She, in common with many others, flew into spasms of urgent and frenetic activity between long periods of absolute quiet.

The case silently ticked away. A settlement conference was set for April 25, 2005. Since I was to be in San Francisco on the pepper-spray case (*Case 48, Swabs, Sprays, and Videotapes*) I called to see if the lawyer had any interest in meeting. She did and brought one of the plaintiffs along. I saw an urgent need to convince the former city manager/police chief that any reasonable settlement was a victory. We spent two-and-a-half hours discussing it over a splendid dinner at a Basque restaurant my wife had discovered on an earlier trip.

The case was settled for $400,000, with the plaintiffs splitting $280,000. Justice had been secured for two innocents snagged in the toils of bureaucratic machinations.

That the oppressor was a black official could be taken as a sign of the racial progress made in our society over the past forty years or so. An ironic measure, to be sure.

CASE 35: A VICTIM PERENNIAL

Most of these cases resided in a zone dubbed respondeat superior—the responsibilities of the employer for the actions of the workers.

As a police executive I screened employees by doing extensive background investigations on them, by training extensively and making records of it, by requiring documentation of police actions, and by promptly discovering misbehavior and acting against it swiftly. As a result we had very few lawsuits against my department in the nine years I served as chief in Minneapolis. Only one reached as high as $50,000, a case in which the cops had accidentally shot and killed a mugger.

All of this experience made me particularly sensitive, as an expert witness, to the responsibility of the higher-up for the wrongdoing of the officer on the street. I needed evidence that the chief and his cohorts were not complicit. Usually the reverse occurred—cronyism, cover-ups, indifference, recklessness, even perversity at the top. Indeed, if these cases proved anything, they demonstrated the corruption of many police administrators across the country.

Another egregious example was presented when an associate of a lawyer I frequently worked with described the plight of a Native American woman. A poster child for the defeated enemy, the woman in this case was thirty-five when the latest outrage took place on January 1, 2002. Her life's experiences to that point included physical, sexual, and alcohol abuse. Details behind these abstract phrases comprise such a vivid tableau as awakening in a truck's body with her panties off and the vague, drunken recollection of a series of males on top of her. Her arm was broken in a quarrel with her teenage son. She'd had six kids by four different men and, on the New Year's Day holiday in question, she was not only on probation for DWI but well known to the community's police for her drunken revels and exploits. Many observers would have condemned her as a hopeless fuck-up, but she was, to me, the very paradigm of the exploited female. This case would underscore the ugliness of her life.

She and a friend had been drinking heavily that New Year's Eve and were now, at about 2:00 a.m. on New Year's Day, stopping traffic on a Minnesota highway. The cops were summoned and the woman, known to the officers, was arrested for violating probation. The other was allowed to walk. The arrested woman was taken to a detention center, where she fell out of a chair and had to be carried to a cell. She refused to take a chemical test, but was clearly as drunk as a skunk.

The lady complained of chest pains, repeatedly vomited, and was "pretty sick." She was taken to a hospital in handcuffs by a male custodial officer, who was fifty-five at the time. She mostly lay down in the back of the squad car during the trip. The hospital staff reported inappropriate language between the woman and the custodian, characterizing it as "flirting" and even including a reference to "sucking cock" by the custodian. The nurse said his talk was of a sexual nature and out of character for a uniformed deputy to be engaged in with a prisoner.

Treated and released, the woman was again handcuffed and transported back. On the way the deputy stopped for gas, bought her a cream soda, lifted her sweatshirt, and sucked her breasts. She reportedly said something about "going into the woods" despite snow on the ground. The deputy drove behind the gas station, out of sight, and placed her in the back seat with the armrest down. She had slipped one handcuff and her arms were now free. She pulled down her pants and panties. He again sucked her breasts, felt her vagina (she had only just concluded her period), inserted his penis after making some comment about her ability to handle it, and ejaculated. He'd had a vasectomy so there were no sperm among his semen. He cautioned her to say nothing about this.

Both dressed, she was cuffed, and they went back to the jail. On returning, the woman encountered a functionary in the jail and, described as "kind of distraught," told her of the sexual encounter. She covered her face with her hands in profound grief. The entire episode occurred, roughly, between 1:00 p.m. and 3:30 p.m.

Officialdom now plunged into action with energy. A thorough investigation was launched. They checked the site and found the tire tracks behind the gas station. They recovered liquid traces from the back of the squad and examined the woman. The deputy's house was searched. Surrounded by a growing mountain of DNA and other evidence, the deputy admitted the sexual encounter, relying on the assertion that it had been consensual. Minnesota law, however, bans even consensual sex in such circumstances, assuming the inherently coercive nature of the crime. The deputy pleaded guilty to criminal sexual conduct in the third degree and was sentenced to forty-eight months in prison; his sentence was stayed pending successful supervised probation of fifteen years, six months to be served in the same county jail where he'd been employed. He was fined, ordered into treatment (presumably for sexual offenders), and faced other conditions.

The system responded to this abuse commendably. The problem now centered on the circumstances of the deputy's hiring, which revealed a much murkier picture.

The sheriff had hired the deputy on the basis of friendship. The job evolved into custodial functions. There had been no background investigation, not even a casual check with former employers, which would have scared off the most determined hirer. The hiring application was not only laughably sparse, but the few points made proved false. The deputy had been fired, asked to quit, or driven from a clutch of past employments. He had a bad driving record. His own wife distrusted him. The most cursory inquiry would have terrified even someone hiring him for a menial task, much less as an authority figure assuming responsibility for the custody of others. In addition to the recklessness of his hire, the employers tolerated the breach of regulations intended to prevent such tragedies as this one. Transporting a female for a considerable distance, by a male, is a taboo in law enforcement.

So this case represented two contrasting facets: the hiring of a misfit who placed all of his charges in danger and an investigation into wrongdoing that could have served as a model for others.

The county hired two experts, the first a doctor who conveniently described the victim's life, apparently intending to suggest that this loser was at least partially responsible for her plight. The graphic details, however, depict someone victimized since infancy— abandoned, abused, exploited, and arrested—who had developed a drinking problem by age eight. It would have been impossible to create a document surer to produce sympathy than this one.

The second expert, a police official, had been a protégé of mine whom I'd promoted, sent to Harvard, and offered to support as my successor but who refused because he couldn't bear to work with the Minneapolis City Council. I then helped and encouraged him to become another city's chief. His report, predictably, centered on the second half of the case: the investigation. He was, of course, right, and I'd agree with all of it. An honorable man, I expected no trouble from him.

In fact I thought both experts' reports bolstered our case materially and I used the doctor's extensively in my own analysis.

Now, as the prospect of a windfall loomed, the men who had abandoned the suspect earlier in her life were circling. I feared she'd let any hope for victory slip through her fingers and, since I never met her, counseled the attorney to make this a key provision of his effort. Ideally, if we won, I'd like to see her invest the money and live on the income it might produce. I feared the worst, however, given her track record.

The case was redolent of small town cronyism at its worst. It also illustrated the costs of such chumminess.

The courts fully recognize the need to give officials the benefit of every doubt in order to allow relative freedom to act in the messy world of street enforcement. Officials, only too mindful of this latitude, routinely press for dismissal of suits against them, and often get them. This is a critical juncture and almost always traversed before any serious movement to settle occurs. So I was pleased when, on February 24, 2005, a district judge essentially dismissed the defendants' pleas to get off the hook and firmly impaled them on it, even quoting me as justification for her findings. Now we could proceed with the knowledge that we'd get our day in court.

The county, faced with a scalding report from me—the employee's conviction in this case, their indifference to his history in hiring him—could and finally did give her $150,000, about two-thirds of which she'd keep. She decided to use her proceeds to buy a house off the reservation. I hoped she'd go through with it.

Next, the victim's devoted lawyers now concentrated on the abuser. He'd tried to sequester assets by transferring them to his wife, belatedly in terms of the law. He could have gotten off the hook for about $20,000 and an apology but, feeling judgment-proof, would have none of it. A trial beckoned.

On January 3, 2006, in federal court, I met the victim for the first time. She was crying uncontrollably. Her boyfriend, upset over her anxiety over the trial, had left her. Unable to stand this pathetic scene I gave her a new handkerchief (a perennial Christmas gift from my sister), which she gratefully used, mumbling what I chose to interpret as thanks. I told her she was doing the right and courageous thing. Her taking on her abusers would keep other women safer. Her children would be proud. This was a tough road and that's why it hurt so much.

I was, for once, reasonably satisfied with my testimony. I addressed my remarks directly to the eight male jurors, all white, and was brief but tough in my analysis. The victim followed me on the stand, a terrifying ordeal.

The trial lasted four days and the jury came in with a verdict of $60,000 in damages and $100,000 in punitive charges. Collecting it would probably prove to be problematic, but it would be attempted and the obstacles were not insurmountable.

I always thought, and said, that she was entitled to $300,000 for this injury and was glad I'd been close. The Minneapolis newspaper, the Star Tribune, did a great story, on January 7. Thus ended a modern saga. A woman who'd been, literally and figuratively, fucked over her entire life finally made them pay for this one. The guy should never have been hired and his claims of "consensual sex" were given precisely the hollow ring they deserved. The woman entered treatment, bringing the one virtue in Pandora's box of ills to bear on her plight: hope.

The lawyer later reported that the victim had given away most of the money in loans to relatives and gifts.

CASE 36: KILLER TOTS

After a long career in policing, extended through the analyses involved in expert witness work, I'd become pretty jaded about the escapades, gaffes, stupidities, abuses, and even crimes committed by our gendarmerie at all levels. Once in a great while, though, they were still capable of delivering a shock.

That was certainly the case with the Los Angeles Police Department. Despite its rigid military traditions and longstanding record of racism, sexism, and brutality, I thought the agency had kept itself remarkably free of any evidence of corruption. I was jolted out of that reverie on April 1, 2005, by a *New York Times* headline: "Los Angeles Paying Victims $70 Million for Police Graft." The LAPD's Rampart Division, under heavy pressure to crack down on gangs, had basically framed, shot, planted evidence on, or otherwise terrorized the bad guys they'd been sent to hunt down. The settlement involved more than two hundred suits. More than one hundred criminal convictions were overturned. The police chief was ousted and a reform chief hired, who assured everyone that this involved "a handful of rogue officers" and that new policies and programs would preclude a recurrence.

Sure.

Equally shocking were the egregious, cold, and mindless actions of the Chicago Police Department in a case involving two boys accused of murder—a case that would probably create more momentum for reform than anything I'd done in thirty-six years in the police business.

A band of "people's lawyers" with whom I'd worked on other cases sent the material I'd need to review. The surface facts were direct enough, albeit unspeakably sad. That the police compounded the tragedy was inexcusable.

On July 27, 1998, an eleven-year-old black girl was playing with friends and riding a bike near Chicago's notorious Cabrini Green housing projects. She was staying with her godmother, who noticed the girl was not in sight. Around 3:00 p.m. the godmother and a friend of the girl went looking for her but didn't find her. Later that evening the family organized a search party and distributed posters and reported her missing to the police.

The next day, July 28, at around 3:00 p.m., the girl's body was found, bludgeoned with a brick, recovered with blood and tissue on it. Her body was partly nude and she'd been sexually assaulted. A teenaged boy told the police he'd seen the girl at dusk the previous day with a tall black male. A teenaged girl supported the story of the victim being with a man of the same description. The police quickly detained a suspect seen in the area and conducted a lineup, but the boy could not identify him and he was released.

The autopsy revealed that the girl been killed through blunt trauma to the head. Her underpants were stuffed three-and-a-half inches deep into her mouth, forcing her tongue back into the oral cavity. There was vaginal trauma likely caused by a foreign object. Maggots had appeared. There was semen on her underpants, which were submitted for laboratory exam on July 29.

The case sent shocks of terror through a community mostly inured to the more commonplace crimes that dotted life in the ghetto. The police, in fact, had responded to the godmother's report of a rock-throwing incident earlier on the day of the murder between the girl and some boys, but the incident had subsided into just another skirmish of city life. The community expressed its anguish as pressure on the cops for results mounted, both from the media and officialdom.

The Chicago Police Department was aware of a pattern of violence and sex crimes against young girls in the area, and knew a suspect and his brother had been involved. On August 9, almost two weeks after the killing, a seven-year-old boy was brought to the police station with his grandmother. He was tiny (four feet tall, sixty-three pounds). The boy was about to start the second grade and had trouble speaking, not being understood even by those close to him. He regularly sucked his thumb. He was the third of four children and lived with his mother and father, both of whom worked. He'd never had any contact with the police. A diagnostic evaluation even included the boy's eagerness to respond to suggestions.

The police distracted the grandmother and questioned the child outside her presence. On this basis they now picked up a second boy, eight years old, and brought him and his mother to the precinct. Outside of his mother's presence the second youngster was questioned by detectives. Investigators shuttled hurriedly between the boys for almost four hours.

The detectives miraculously emerged with a statement in which the seven-year-old admitted throwing a rock and hitting the girl in the head and knocking her off the bike. Other detectives produced a statement from the eight-year-old corroborating the first. Detectives hurriedly announced their triumph, sweeping aside improbabilities, implausibilities, and even impossibilities in their rush to judgment. The wish was father to the thought and produced a grotesquely cruel outcome.

I had grown up in a system that defined the boundaries of police power: someone under age seven could not (period, under no conditions) commit a crime. Someone seven to twelve was presumed incapable of committing a crime, but the presumption could be overcome with evidence. Those aged twelve to sixteen were presumed capable. We all had been trained to check confessions and admissions carefully and to secure evidence to buttress the assertions. We had to be particularly careful about psychos who confess, the retarded, and juveniles who are vulnerable to suggestion. The time-honored practice was to withhold key facts on a crime—details only the killer and the cops knew—by way of establishing the authenticity of an admission.

A medical examiner, outraged by this outrage, insisted on telling the cops that the evidence contradicted their assertions. That the boys were incapable of producing semen seemed of little moment to relieved officialdom, all the way to the top. The cops prepared reports indicating the guilt of the boys and agreed to charge both with the girl's murder. They said the boys had held her down on the ground while they bludgeoned her to death with a brick. Now the department's brass began to discuss the possibility of accepting the investigators' recommendations that the boys be criminally charged.

On August 10, 1998, the police held a news conference to announce the arrest of the boys and they appeared in juvenile court to seek formal charges against both. The judge found probable cause and the boys were detained. Both the mayor and the chief supported the police actions. The boys were held in custody in a hospital. The next day, at a juvenile court hearing, the boys were ordered held and not allowed to return home until August 13, each with an ankle bracelet and confined to their apartments 24/7.

The chief announced the murder solved with these arrests and said the detectives had observed "the letter of the law." In two hearings in juvenile court the assistant state attorney pointed to one of the boys and called him "a brutal murderer."

The arrests proved an international scandal. The Chicago police had, at this point, clearly caved to pressures and seized on any way out, however absurd. The thought of a seven- and an eight-year-old boy committing a sex murder was logical and medical lunacy, no matter how willing America was to swallow incredulity in its embrace of the "feral child" imagery. This was a blatantly bankrupt act by a spooked department. Yet it got worse.

The girl's underpants were finally tested on September 3, 1998, and adult sperm and pubic hair were found. The panties had not been transported to the lab until ten days after the crime. The next day, September 4, the state dropped all charges against the two boys, over the strenuous objections of the Chicago Police Department and the mayor.

The bombshell exploded eighteen days later, on September 21, when, in connection with another arrest for a remarkably similar sexual assault, a suspect's DNA matched the semen in the girl's panties. The suspect confessed to the essentials of the encounter but attempted to dodge responsibility for the murder, unsuccessfully. The teenage witnesses identified him as the man they'd seen the girl with on the day of the murder.

This arrest was due, not to the interest of the police, but to an astute assistant attorney general's deduction. She had two cases involving girls eleven years old who'd been sexually assaulted in the same area where the murdered girl's body was found. She recommended that the suspect's DNA be matched against the semen found in the dead girl's mouth. On September 16, 1998, the lab informed the police of the match.

Even if the boys had been guilty—a demonstrable impossibility—the police handling of the questioning, arrests, and public statements could hardly have been more mindless. It would have been tempting to charge racism, but the chief and other key figures were black. On February 8, 1999, the New Yorker weighed in with a long analysis by Alex Katlowitz, titled "The Unprotected."

Officialdom clung to its hopes of the little boys' guilt, but the evidence gradually ground them to silent, begrudging acquiescence—but not concession. No apology was forthcoming and, since the actual culprit was safely and relatively permanently behind bars, they didn't rush to charge him with this one. Their obduracy was breathtaking, stonewalling their strong suit. Indeed, it was not until April 22, 1999, or nine months after the crime and eight months after he was identified as the culprit, that the perpetrator of this crime was finally charged with the murder. The Cook County state attorney now said the boys "should never have been charged."

Though the crime and arrests had shocked and terrified, the later arrest of the adult culprit required the abandonment of cherished myths. Yet the chief called the investigation the "greatest disappointment" of his first year, defined it as a tragedy within a tragedy, and refused to admit any mistakes or misconduct. The police department changed its procedures to require videotaping and the presence of a guard in juvenile investigations, but refused to exonerate the two boys.

The families of the boys had not been able to defend themselves against the assaults of the police. Now, the reluctant vindications did nothing to assuage their sense of violation. The litany of sad events following these accusations sound like the experience of a Salem witch, like a horror story of psychic and emotional turmoil. It has to be conceded that the boys may have stumbled across the girl's body and even touched it, guiltily, in the way of terrified but exploring little boys. This encounter, in their heads, might have led to confusions only too enthusiastically embraced by the investigators. This would be to place their involvement in the most damning light, yet never rise to a level dislodging them from the positions of witnesses in this case.

By 2004 one boy was having serious problems. The only hope remaining was the sort of vindication that might emerge from the civil process.

The case—or at least my side of it, involving the seven-year-old boy—ended in late October 2004. Not with a bang but a whimper, in a single paragraph on page 24 of the October 22 *New York Times*. Headlined "City to Pay $2 Million in Wrongful Arrest," the article vaguely described the event as the "slaying of an 11 year old girl" in 1998. No mention of rape. It described the culprit, gave no clue as to the fate of the eight-year-old boy, and added that the "city did not admit wrongdoing in the boys' arrests and has denied that detectives coerced them into making statements about the slaying."

One of the lawyers called me and we spoke about the events leading to the settlement outcome. The second boy had chosen a black former judge with good connections but no clue about handling a civil suit. Our lawyers had foolishly followed this guy out of the federal process and into state court to join forces, a move that ensured a less happy, less promising, less professional outcome. They were appalled at the prosecution of the eight-year-old's case. Failures to meet deadlines or prepare briefs or submit timely complaints became routine. My lawyers rued abandoning the federal court and, even more so, joining this incompetent endeavor.

In mid-October 2004, the trial beckoned. The sitting judge pressed for a settlement.

About $2 million per became the standard. Our group agreed but the others declined, even though their case had been dismissed for failure to prosecute it as required. They could still remedy this but continued to balk. Finally, at the eleventh hour, a city that desperately sought to put this case behind it by settling with both boys, had to settle with one, my client. He'd get about $2 million over several years, and needed it. My lawyer said he was in deep trouble without describing the factors. Shortly after the incident he came home and cut off all his hair.

The eight-year-old would continue his own struggle in the clutches of dumb representation. In all likelihood he'd get the same settlement as the seven-year-old in spite of his lawyer. The mayor and City Council would have to approve the agreement, more or less a formality.

And so, an internationally fascinating case highlighted by a twelve-page story in the New Yorker ended as a paragraph in the *New York Times*. I don't think the boys will ever receive an apology from the city's officials. Still, I was confident the outcome would concentrate officialdom's imagination wonderfully in the future.

Now the case really was closed.

Only it wasn't.

In one of many turnabouts that seemed intended to teach me more humility, the *Times* reported, on September 20, 2005, that the eight-year-old would receive $6.2 million from the city. So much for our collective sense of the prosecutor's feckless representation.

The true perp pled guilty in 2006 and received a substantial add-on to the life sentence he was serving on another atrocity.

CASE 37: TORTURED CONFESSIONS

Bad cases make bad laws.

What does that mean? They're all bad cases, more or less. The worst, though, involve cop killers. These tragedies drive cops to paroxysms of violence and revenge. The cops must be reined in dramatically or they'll apply street justice, which is not only wrong (in the sense of targeting an innocent subject) but dangerous to the desired outcome of the case when brutality is proved. I've seen cases lost because of overreaction.

Yet another case involving the Chicago Police Department—the widespread use of torture by cops to secure confessions to serious crimes—was so egregious that, at its end, it obliterated the ghastly crime that triggered it: the murder of two white Chicago police officers by two black men on February 9, 1982. Had an investigation of the abuses been launched at the time of the murders, most of the subsequent cases of torture very likely would not have occurred.

The tragedy began when Andrew and Jackie Wilson, black brothers in their twenties, were driving from a burglary when they were pulled over by two white cops in uniform, assigned to gangs. One cop came to the driver's side and asked Jackie, the younger brother, for his license; he didn't have one. Jackie was wanted for a parole violation; Andrew had two warrants outstanding. The cops checked the car. The second cop, on the passenger side, found bullets from the burglary in a jacket. Andrew jerked the cop's gun out and shot him in the head. The first cop found a gun in the car, pulled his gun, shouted "Freeze!" and, not knowing what happened to his partner, came around. Andrew then shot the first cop in the chest. Jackie said the cop was still moving so Andrew fired four more bullets into the officer. The brothers drove off, leaving the cops bleeding in the snow. The head shot proved immediately fatal; the cop who was shot five times died twenty hours later. It was February 9, 1982.

To say that an exhaustive investigation followed would be to seriously understate the case. Cops kicked in doors, rousted residents, pointed guns at innocents, shot a dog, and assaulted, arrested, and made the lives of black males in the area a dangerous misery. Mothers sent their sons off to live with relatives. The area was described as living under martial law, oppressed by an army of occupation. Black leaders protested, to no effect.

Strangely, a citizen offered a lead, but the suspect was the wrong one. In a world of interconnected criminal enterprises, he had, serendipitously, a connection to the killers. They'd divided the burglary loot in his house, next door to the pilfered dwelling. Anxious to evade interest he gave up the brothers and added they'd been plotting the escape of an associate who'd shot and killed a rookie cop on February 5. The two cops killed on February 9 were returning from that rookie's funeral. The killers had one gun, which they'd secured in an armed robbery of a house the previous day, but needed more. They got only bullets and other stuff in this burglary.

An auto repair man came forward and fingered the brothers after one of them asked to have their car painted and repaired.

The cops now centered their attentions on the suspects who were moving from apartment to apartment. The lieutenant in charge, who'd spend five days sleeping in the office between shifts, surrounded a building on February 14 and was the first through a crashed door, and arrested the shooter without firing. A minister offered information leading to the arrest of the younger brother, who'd been the driver. Both arrests were the result of the cooperation of a beleaguered black community that had every right to be resentful.

The brothers confessed, were tried, and convicted. Andrew Wilson, the shooter, was sentenced to death. His attorney demonstrated that his confession was coerced and should have been suppressed. The judges voted 3–0 to grant an appeal, citing fifteen wounds and injuries suffered in police custody. Both convictions were reversed on appeal and then were retried, separately, and convicted.

Seven years later Andrew Wilson sued Chicago, claiming that, at the station house on February 14, 1982, he was thrown to the floor, beaten, kicked in the eye, and had a plastic bag placed over his head. He nearly suffocated, but bit a hole in the bag. He was taken to another room by the supervisor and electroshocked in his ear. An hour later he was again shocked—ears, fingers, legs, testicles. He described it as agony. His teeth came loose, he clamped them so tight. A gun was thrust into his mouth.

After thirteen hours there, he confessed the murders of the two cops. He was still beaten thereafter. The jailor, though, refused to take an injured prisoner. Andrew Wilson demanded medical attention. Dr. Jon Raba, a Cook County jail doctor, examined him on February 15–16, 1982, and wrote to the police superintendent, calling for an investigation of the shooter's charges of torture. Wilson, with police encouragement, ultimately declined treatment. On being booked, though, the custodial authorities—protecting themselves from charges of brutality—photographed his entire naked body. His lawyer, a public defender, arranged for more photos, which showed clip marks of the electroshock devices attached to Wilson's ears. The police superintendent had sent the doctor's letter to Richard Daley, the state attorney, who did not pursue the issue.

An inquiry by the Office of Professional Standards, the police department's disciplinary agency, was ordered. A small file was compiled and finally given to an investigator to summarize eighteen months after the order to investigate. The investigator took almost two years to prepare a three-page summary that, with the ambiguous term "not sustained" (which meant it might have occurred but proof was lacking), cleared the officers.

The supervisor, who stoutly denied coercing a confession, was a war hero as well as a decorated cop. He looked to me like a "meat eater," one of those who set the pace in the ranks: first through the door, fearlessly facing guns down, making great pinches, and dispensing personal visions of justice before the admiration of colleagues. A cop's cop.

The shooter was a bum, one of nine children in a stable family. He registered 70s in IQ tests and couldn't read. Soon he got into criminal scrapes and did time, spending most of his life in institutions and prison. He fathered one daughter out of wedlock.

The bum became my client.

The photos of Wilson would be central issues in the civil trial of 1989. He testified graphically and so emotionally as to the third-degree methods that he frequently broke down on the stand.

The civil trial was a clash of cultures—the respectable overclass and the stained underclass. The jury was unable to decide, threw out some claims, and concluded in a deadlock. A mistrial was declared.

The case was fairly unremarkable except for a parade of suspects that followed, all of them making the same claims, with several suing and winning settlements. The attorneys, the People's Law Office of Chicago (PLO), had come up with four witnesses, persons victimized by the police in their search for the cop killers. A mother described the brutalization of a son who, with tragic predictability, died two years later. In this case he was held for three days, beaten, and released. She'd made no complaint. Another male described being pulled in, tortured, and threatened with being thrown out the window. He was so frightened he furnished information he knew to be false and was finally released. These witnesses invariably had checkered pasts and were pilloried on the stand.

During the civil trial the plaintiff's lawyers also had been getting anonymous letters from a likely police insider describing abuses in detail, implicating high-ranking officials, and offering leads. The PLO lawyers followed up on the charges of repeated and systemic torturing of suspects and pursued leads to others. A clutch of suspects—including another murder suspect in another case who had been arrested days before Wilson had—repeated details about the electroshock techniques of the supervisor, who had, in one case, been commended for "skillful questioning." Inventive, I'd have said.

The leads were received too late to be used in the civil trial, where the judge had repeatedly expressed his exasperation with the PLO attorneys. The court returned the case for retrial in mid-1989. The retrial now featured changed testimony by the police, a hostile judge from the first trial, and a witness to exculpate the cops. The contest was tinged with bitterness. The jury found that the shooter's constitutional rights were violated on February 14, 1982, and that the city had a policy of tolerating police abuses where cops had been killed. Yet they cleared the defendants of subjecting the shooter to excessive force. The foreman later said the jury did believe the cops had been understandably angry over the cop killings and overreacted, but not that torture to secure confessions was employed.

Wilson was convicted without the use of the confession and sentenced to life. The PLO attorneys appealed the verdict. He sued civilly for damages and received a settlement, claiming $10 million in damages. The suit would have no bearing on the criminal case, as he was serving a life sentence with no chance of parole.

In January 1990, the Office of Professional Standards launched an inquiry into allegations of a ten-year history of torture by the officer in this case and some of his subordinates. Amazingly, for as docile an agency as that of the Chicago PD, which had regularly exculpated members charged with wrongdoing, OPS came up with a report that concluded that "command members were aware of the systematic abuse and perpetuated it." Further, "the evidence presented by some individuals convinced juries and appellate courts that personnel . . . engaged in methodical abuse." The detailed report cited scores of abuses by the officers in this case.

The chief, a black, now had a dilemma. He solved it by sending the report for analysis to a black colleague, a former chief, in a think tank in Washington, D.C. This "thinker" recruited another former chief, also black, and together they concocted a pretty version. They found the data to be limited and in need of much more thorough analysis.

Amnesty International weighed in on the torture issue. OPS was asked to investigate further and came up with forty-seven documented cases of torture from 1973 to 1988 by the officers in this case. Finally the city moved to fire the supervisor and the two detectives involved in the cop-killing case.

The police union frantically searched for ways to fund the defense and provided moral support through demonstrations, newsletters, roll calls, and "rackets." The People's Law Office was described as defenders of "terrorist bombers." Their lawyers, who had represented such as the Black Panthers, finally contacted me in early 1992, as the attempt to fire the three cops in this case proceeded. I'd had other cases with them relating to police intelligence practices.

I reviewed the tangled web of reports, met with the lawyers—with whom I'd later work on the case of the two boys accused of a rape-murder (*Case 34: Poisoning the Wells of Justice*)—and spent about fifteen hours on the case only to have it end, inconclusively, with a call in October 1994. The case was treading water as they awaited the court's decision, and they were not able to use me.

An unlikely and unexpected hero, Illinois governor George Ryan cleaned out death row on January 11, 2003, by commuting to life terms the sentences of everyone on death row because of the demonstrated injustices surrounding so many cases. He also pardoned four death row inmates—Aaron Paterson, Madison Hobley, Leroy Orange, and Stanley Howard—because their confessions were found to have been extracted through torture. The courts rained down a flood of reversals of convictions on the basis they'd been secured through torture. Governor Ryan fared less heroically in his own trial as he was found guilty of corruption and racketeering charges and sent to prison.

From a tiny blurb in the *New York Times* headlined "Illinois Police Torture Accusations," dated August 30, 2005, I learned that the torturer, Jon Burge, a police commander, was fired in 1993. Still he receives a vested pension of about $40,000 a year.

Now a consortium of forty-six human rights organizations sought an investigation by the Inter-American Commission on Human Rights into charges that Burge and associates tortured 135 black suspects from 1971 to 1992 to secure confessions. The forms were, as in this case, electric shocks and burns. Recourse to an international body was a good measure of the suitors' desperation and determination to pursue this issue.

A special prosecutor who studied the charges in 2002, in a pattern of evasion characteristic of this controversy, still had not issued any report or asked for any prosecutions as of 2006. When he finally did, it proved a masterpiece of excuses for the powerful mayor's conduct.

I had lunch on September 13, 2005, in Chicago with lawyers working on the case. One had completely forgotten my involvement in the earlier (1982) case, and blurted out it had been settled. Well, I hadn't been paid and been misled as to the outcome. I said nothing and accepted the new cases (involving four of the released death row inmates) and now I'd plunge into the material. I'd simply table the issue of payment on the cop killer case.

This case, with its pressures, urgencies, emotions, actions, imperatives, and demands, forced the players into more intense pursuit of activities employed then and later, made more flagrant by the forces loosed by this atrocious occurrence. Others abused came forward. Anonymous tips (four letters) in 1998 came from likely Chicago PD sources. More suits followed. A blizzard of appeals fell and courts began to rule on the existence of torture by Area 2 detectives led by Commander Jon Burge, occurring before and after the Wilson case. Remarkable similarities were described, credible accounts given, arcane and esoteric devices were employed, and internal documents revealed the complicity of a series of police superintendents and mayors.

Daley had learned of the actions from Brzeczek's letter and should have learned from the deep and constant involvement of his assistants with these detectives. Remarkable internal documents reflect the organizational hypocrisy.

The detectives were extolled, commended, and rewarded even as they brutalized, tortured, and abused prisoners. And this to such a degree that they ultimately defeated the ends of justice by freeing or reducing the penalties of the guilty as well as the innocent.

The real torture appears to have reposed within the city government as they turned and twisted to defeat desperately needed investigations and actions.

Of particular note is a September 28, 1990, report by an OPS officer citing that the "preponderance of the evidence is that abuse did occur," that it was "systematic," and that it included "planned torture" by Area 2 detectives over a ten-year period. The Goldstone Report then named nine cases of shocking, two of hangings, and eleven of bagging. It identified fifty alleged witnesses from May 1973 to October 1986. These resulted in nine civil suits (five settlements, one mistrial, one dismissal, one summary judgment for defendant, one pending). There were serious injuries in five cases. The report was sent to Superintendent Leroy Martin who, clearly stuck with a very hot potato, fobbed it off to a "police think tank" for pedantic interment at some cost to the city.

Superintendent Hillard also testified that he learned of his counsel's "not sustaining" nine charges from 1982, 1983, and 1984 in which cops are accused of abuse, received from the newspaper account. This shelving was done because the cases were "stale" but neglected to mention the staleness emerged from the Chicago Police Department's failure to undertake timely inquiries. The cases involved Michael Johnson, Lee Holmes, Stanley Howard, Phil Adkins, Don White, Greg Banks, Lavert Jones, Darrell Cannon, and Stanley Ware.

The record is replete with references to the intimate personal involvement of the city's leaders in such notorious activities as to create citizen concern, press interest and commentary, judicial chastisements, and even some rare critiques from the police department's own ranks. The city's leaders commended, promoted, protected, and supported the abusers.

The widespread employment of third-degree methods spanned at least the years 1972 to 1984 by Area 2 personnel and Commander Jon Burge, who was finally fired in 1992 (although collecting a pension) and whose two key associates were suspended for fifteen months each.

Dr. Raba (after the Wilson letter) wrote of repeated incidents of abuse, on November 14, 1983, of Gregory Banks.

In incidents where officers sought to do the right thing (Laverty) and refused to participate in frame-ups, ostracism and pariah status awaited from Chicago PD associates. The blue code of silence is all over this case at all levels and documented by internal documents and testimony. All the victims of police torture are black. The torturers are white; the top administrators in complicity are frequently black. Interestingly, when asked if a code of silence existed, Superintendent Martin, on October 11, 1989, conceded "to some extent, yes sir."

The Chicago PD and city officials stonewalled, resisted, and funded continuous efforts to suppress exposure of these abuses. Millions of taxpayer dollars were expended in protecting wrongdoers. The taxpayers paid for extensive legal representation of accused torturers, and appeals, to the tune of, very likely, several million dollars, not to mention costs of defending the indefensible, the payment of judgments and settlements, etcetera.

Even when internal investigators sustain findings of abuse, supervisors reverse the findings and clear the accused officers. Where this proves unfeasible the administrators sit on the investigations or engage in such evasions as calling for better methods, closer study, et cetera, that are not related to the substance of the inquiries. Cheap, obvious, and practiced stratagems.

Ostracized black officers testified as to the abuses in Area 2. Police Superintendent Brzeczek, long after the fact, admitted torture and abuses occurred. Findings of wrongdoing were reversed, tabled, or shelved as inconveniences. The organizational messages were clear: the abusers were hard-working, dedicated officers doing the Lord's work.

What is altogether and consistently lacking at all levels is any evidence of a desire or attempt to get the Chicago PD to function in accord with the dictates of justice, its own pious assertions, or the U.S. Constitution.

Superintendent Martin on February 16, 1991, returned Goldstone's devastating report with criticisms and a request for more information. Later they send it to the Police Foundation for genuine entombment when the OPS report was returned to Martin on April 30, 1991.

Black officers complained to Commander Martin about Burge, but Burge chewed them out the next day. Aware of the bad treatment of Officer Laverty, low evaluations, exclusions, assignment of bad cases, reductions in rank, or transfers by Burge, they lapsed into coerced silence.

An Area 2 detective's sister's deposition describes the culture, the racism, the system wide cronyism, and protections relied on by Jon Burge. This occurred in a conversation held in mid-January 1987.

Even Superintendent Fred Rice received an OPS memo dated November 5, 1984, alleging electric shock methods employed over a twelve-month period. This was updated by another memo, citing more abuses, to Rice from OPS, on February 25, 1985.

The press dots the record with occasional accounts of police abuses, which are ignored.

Astonishingly, the Chicago Police Department in the twentieth-century was replicating the devoted endeavors of Spain's sixteenth-century Inquisition. How did a tight group of white cops frame, torture, and convict hosts of black males, most of whom were proved innocent or pardoned over two decades? They were led by a mawkishly devoted bachelor who was married to the job. His superiors, black and white, loved his solving of tough, hot cases. They were all reasonably careful to cover their tracks.

What blew the lid off was the hysteria surrounding a double cop killing that impelled the group into frenetic, reckless behavior that produced both the killers and evidence of torture. The revelation burst the dam holding back the information on other abusers.

A bewildering set of complexities that spanned decades of Chicago's life. What are the constants? The Daleys, pere et fils, were at the heart of it, having run the city's affairs for decades. Theirs was not a machine that took bribes, exploited sexual opportunities, lived lavishly, or was even resistant to some reforms. Theirs was an incestuous job-creating machine in which everyone was taken care of.

Rather than actually solving cases (the Wilson brothers' killing of the two cops being an exception—that one had to be solved, not just closed), the Daleys proved that the broad-shouldered city worked. They had no trouble finding cops happy to oblige. The commitment was to results, however obtained or even correct, as a practical matter. And these they got and they had a ton of closed cases to show for it. But the chickens would come home to roost.

What seemed evident, in 2005, was that justice had suffered and that the taxpayers would pay for their and their officials' myopia. How much they would pay became clear when a lawyer confided that the five plaintiffs in his case had turned down the city's offer of an $11 million settlement. On December 8, 2007, the *New York Times* announced a $20 million settlement for four men who had been wrongly sent to death row. I had worked on three of these cases, cases I was glad I accepted, despite my deep aversion to championing the cause of a cop killer. Andrew Wilson had, in the style of unlikely heroes, emerged as the symbol of outrage over police abuses and torture.

This case illustrates the human penchant for abuse when officials are allowed to function above the law. Just like lynch justice, it is not only brutal but misguided. You end up with innocents on death row.

What a lesson to a nation seeking to find its way amid a thicket of proposals for questioning terrorists. In 2006 America engaged in a fierce debate over allowing the Central Intelligence Agency an exception, permitting creative interrogation of terrorist suspects. In the Chicago case the nation had its answer. Yes, torture could work and produced useful results. The likelier outcome, though, was to create a band of criminals chasing criminals and to destroy democracy without adding to its security.

Bad cases do make bad laws.

CASE 38: SMALL TOWN TEENS

Among the chronic problems faced by police—domestics, mass protests, strikes, marches, sit-ins, riots, and other repetitive difficulties—are the behaviors of teenagers at loose ends who gravitate to popular hangouts. These loiterings often escalate into small problems, loss of business, and conditions inimical to commerce, property values, and other sacred beliefs.

Such chronic problems should have succumbed to analysis and training or, at the least, the development of principles that might guide actions that embrace the limits of the law. But in the police world action is frequently guided by prejudice, preconceived notions, myths, and treasured certitudes. Any prospect of reform seems to require the threat of terror, whether through a tough chief, the press, an FBI investigation, or a lawsuit. Appeals to the better angels of their nature seem to fall on stony ears.

But I digress.

A supermarket filling station complex in a small Minnesota town proved an irresistible magnet to the hamlet's teens. They clustered in numbers and flustered the management with congestion that looked menacing to cautious, unworldly, timid neighbors. Management complained to the police, often and insistently.

Such pressures are given voice at community meetings or rotary lunches, where the chief is in attendance or is called on to speak. The cops on patrol are fed general injunctions to "clean up that mess." Such instructions are a key source of problems for cops who don't want to challenge the chief and who find coping with the problem the lesser of two evils. Yet it is still ambiguous and can backfire.

My client was an eighteen-year-old on June 30, 2003, who was well known to the local cops as a sort of "hot-rodder in training" and they took a baleful view of his sulky attitude. The cops had long tired of these encounters. Now they were responding to the management complaint of teenagers hanging out with the usual embellishment of rough remarks, littering, loitering, and even possible drug dealing. Annoyed, the cops seized the eighteen-year-old, grabbed his cell phone, broke his expensive sunglasses, and administered scratches and bruises that produced spasms. The teenager had committed no crime and was not arrested—a serious police error, given the physical contact.

Two months later, on August 28, 2003, the cops engaged in a warrantless entry into the boy's home through the garage door, in what would be interpreted as a sort of wandering in with tacit permission and, with both parents present, ransacked the home. They claimed to be acting on a tip that the son kept an illegal gun in his car. Trying to repair the damage, the cops secured a search warrant, returned to the home, and came up with a couple of BB guns. They even involved a helicopter in this raid, raising great commotion. The "gun" in the car turned out to be a flashlight.

There was a history of previous contacts between one of the cops and the kid. He was served a trespass notice on August 9, 2003, for hanging out in an apartment house area. Now the father filed a request for the police reports, which the town at first resisted and then relented, but, claiming that the family were nonresidents, asked for a fee of $498 for the documents. The father proved residency, secured the papers, and sued.

The law provided a remedy for the police actions required: a trespass notice to be answered in juvenile court. For adults there were the ordinances relating to the same offense.

Why had the cops responded so aggressively when they would have achieved their ends without fuss or bother? Once again we encounter the ever-present "attitude test." The cops were going to show these young bums in their town who was boss. They were not going to tolerate the kids' surliness, laughter, or other derisions, real or imagined. This was the source of numberless police overreactions, many of which resulted in chastening suits.

The cops lucked out on this one, however, as the parents' heat cooled and they allowed the case to dissipate into a nullity. The police escaped justice only because the tenacity needed was lacking.

Case 39: Sex, Power, and Official Myopia

My cases have run the gamut of human experience—or folly, more accurately. Despite the variety there is a sameness that facilitates the path of evaluation. Yet each case has something new to teach me, which, in a real sense, appalls me. Not only is each discovery something I hadn't but should've known, each is also a nuance I should've but didn't bring to prior cases.

Such was the case involving sex in the trenches, where I thought I'd seen it all. The energy, persistence, single-mindedness, and aggressiveness of the hunter (male) of the hunted (female) was graphically illustrated by the stalking of a deputy sheriff by her superior in the hinterlands of Minnesota.

The deputy sheriff was hired in late 1995 and transferred to be an investigator eighteen months later. Her brief career ended with her firing in mid-2001. The five-and-a-half years between was a private, silent hell described dispassionately as "sexual harassment."

Her employment was not a frivolous stab at a job. The woman had gone through a police college curriculum and emerged with a B.A. Next came an entrance test, which she passed. She received good appraisals from her supervisors. She tied for highest score on a lieutenant's test. The sheriff, however, said the department was not ready for a female supervisor and passed her over. She tried again and was again put off.

She was dealing with a sheriff who was reported to have said that the plaintiff had "the best ass in the county" and was alleged to refer to some women as "cunts" and "bitches" and as emotional during their menstrual cycles. He was reported to be famously vindictive and to have an enemies list no one wanted to be on.

Prey and hunter had offices in close proximity. Sexual comments, advances, demands, and touching, as well as verbal abuse and threats, were constant offenses. "Are your breasts real or fake?" was one comment. When they rode together to county towns on business, the sheriff would touch her, hold her hand, touch her leg, rub her arm and breasts, hug her and pull her shirt up and pants down, asking for sexual favors all the while. He placed her hand on his penis, which she resisted, verbally and physically. She tried to avoid rides with him but he changed her schedule to force her to accompany him.

She was married but this proved no impediment to the sheriff. She was forced into such evasions as that she was menstruating, or any other excuse she could seize. She fended him off as best she could, hoping it would pass.

The aggression spilled into the office, where the sheriff grew more forceful. He asked for oral sex. On one occasion when he pulled down her pants, she struggled and pulled them back up. He attempted intercourse, but she kept her legs together and avoided penetration. He ejaculated on her pants and asked her if she was going to save them for the DNA evidence. After he called her into his office one day and made sexual advances that she refused, he called her "a cunt." Several days of nasty treatment followed.

The stalking went on over the years and escalated to a daily ordeal. The sheriff's behavior was obsessive and blatant, sexual harassment at its worst. He called her repeatedly, professing his ardor, and drove by her home to see if her husband was there. He attempted to entice her into a hotel. He humiliated her in front of others, yet no one interfered with the abuse. There was no let-up, yet she continued her silent, heroic resistance. She'd worked hard to be a cop and wouldn't surrender it easily.

But finally, in a car together and after gropings, grabbings, and exposings, he pushed her head down and she, resigned and frightened, blew him and threw up. The pursuit continued in earnest as did her evasions, escapes, and resistance. He "loved her" and couldn't stop. The department was wild with rumors and reports. As too often happens in police agencies the victim is ostracized, since no one wants to take on the predator, especially when he's the guy in charge and has a fearsome reputation. Her fellow workers saw her resistance as making things worse for everyone and counseled her to give him what he wanted. County officials were aware of the sheriff's inappropriate behaviors in past episodes. A trail of evidence was available for any examiner to see. None came.

The physical and mental toll on the female officer was enormous. Her health deteriorated rapidly. She was losing weight and getting sick. She started smoking more, sleeping less, even stopped showering in hopes of discouraging her stalker. She was depressed and anxious and took medications for it.

When she was fired in mid-2001, she finally complained of a hostile environment and the county hired a lawyer to defend against her actions. The assistant deputy was restored to duty, but she was frozen out by fellow workers and disdained by the sheriff. By the fall her doctor wouldn't allow her to return to work because of depression and anxiety. She took sick leave and sued.

The sheriff held a news conference to say he was "dumbfounded" by her charges, which he found "absolutely outrageous" and "unbelievable." As the lawyers approached settlement my services were dispensed with, having spent only four hours studying the documents and advising them. I was thrilled by the news that the beleaguered woman had won the astounding sum of more than $1.5 million from a county that had been willfully blind to her plight and that had determinedly resisted her cries for help. Characteristically the county admitted to no wrongdoing; it had settled merely to avoid the cost of a trial.

The sheriff resigned in April 2003, claiming back problems. Coincidentally, his resignation occurred a week after being charged with felony theft of public funds. He later pleaded guilty to the lesser charge of misdemeanor.

The case was an object lesson in the costs accruing from officialdom's deliberately ignoring plainly visible problems that, unaddressed, escalate into horrific personal and fiscal costs.

Where the husband was in all this I never learned.

CASE 40: RITES OF SPRING

Ah, spring. Its arrival produces an explosion of seminude, raccoon-like Minnesotans emerging from five months of artificial light and seclusion. Cabin fever is endemic but the warmth of spring carries hope even to those who hate the outdoors. No one would choose to live here for its climate.

The forty-four-year-old owner of a Jaguar is discussing its emergence from hibernation with a mechanic at a gas station in Golden Valley, a Minneapolis suburb. The Jaguar owner is black, big, even burly, but he is a sweet, gentle giant whose mostly white neighbors rise to his defense at his plight, which begins to unfold in a bank within a large supermarket a few hundred feet away. There, a thirty-two-year-old consummate fuckup is trying hard to capture the attention of a phone-distracted bank teller.

"Give me the fucking money," he says. "I've got a gun."

Finally, with the desperation of a Woody Allen character, he snatches a coin tray from the counter and flees. As he hurriedly exits, the teller presses the alarm and calls 911, describing the bandit, who is a scruffily bearded white male. The villain, in his hurried exit, pushes past a customer who follows him a bit and sees him throwing something into a black van with a black driver and then walking to the very gas station hosting our Jaguar-loving hero. The robber had sullied the pattern universally described as "Minnesota Nice."

This witness follows the action for a bit but gives up, gets into his car, and drives away. Within a short distance he sees the wailing police squads hurriedly converging and tries to flag one down. He fails, so he calls 911 on his cell and tells them where the villain is headed.

Police, bandit, and plaintiff all converge in the gas station. Three squads with five cops come from three directions, the cops bailing out with guns drawn. They were responding to a bank robbery by a white suspect with a gun implied.

The plaintiff puts up his hands to shelter his head and scurries for cover.

A cop chases him, yells "Stop!" and orders him to the ground. Our client slowly complies, but too slowly for the cop's female partner, who dives on him, kneeing him in the palm of his back and raising her knee to strike again at the upper back. His body and face hit the pavement hard.

"Give up your hands!" he is ordered. He complies as a handcuff is applied to his hand. The other hand is difficult to bring to the proper angle and an enormous cop, standing over the man and the officer, asks, "Shall I spray him?" She answers yes and he steps on the man's neck and blasts his eyes with mace from point-blank range. Not content, he sprays up the nostrils. The man claims he's been already handcuffed at this time.

The effect of the spray is to temporarily blind and choke, and the victim is now gagging, coughing, and spitting, in obvious distress. The recommended treatment is fresh air and heavy rinsing with water. He is hauled up and led and pushed and pulled to the squad, heaved into the back, and left there to stew for twenty minutes.

Meanwhile the bandit has emerged, given up, and told everyone he acted alone. The two blacks in the black van are cuffed and secured. The gas station manager tells the cop supervisor that the Jaguar owner had nothing to do with any of this and the sergeant agrees.

Now the Golden Valley Police Department sergeant faces a conundrum: what to do with a maced, cuffed, assaulted, and innocent bystander in custody? He resorts to the time-honored practice of concocting a charge—obstructing legal process with force—and our hero is driven off to the police station. His discomfort continues as he coughs, spits, wheezes, and blinks. The cuffs are too tight and cause a lot of pain, a not unusual form of deliberate police sanction against the unpopular. Finally, he is taken to a hospital for treatment. He is uncuffed and released, but he is still charged with a crime.

Now comes a startling development. The police department's deputy chief, on receiving the cops' statements of arrest documents, sees what any experienced executive would: a patently trumped-up charge that is not likely to be sustained if the accused balks—as our client seems certain to do. So the deputy chief calls the prosecutor and asks that the charges be dropped. The DA, sensing the need to cover his ass, complies and verifies his action with a letter, produced for the plaintiff during discovery.

The charges dropped, the Jaguar owner sues. The city hired private attorneys to defend itself and its cops—an economy measure that usually results in gargantuan legal bills. The lawyers who consulted another lawyer I'd just worked with hired me.

To me the case was about three things: racism, the lack of probable cause for the arrest, and excessive force. Having reviewed the depositions, court documents, and their expert witnesses' report, I prepared my own—a scathing denunciation of the officers' behaviors.

The city filed for dismissal of all charges, always a dicey process in a system that is more than tolerant of street actions by cops. The judge ruled that race was not a factor and that the cops had probable cause to arrest and handcuff the plaintiff. He held that there may have been excessive force and would leave it to the jury to decide.

Having partially failed to prevail, the city faced a trial, if only on a third of the factors. Approaches toward settlement heat up. Usually they'd want to know what I'll testify to and depose me, but they didn't bother. The trial in federal court would start September 4. I was scheduled to be the plaintiff's last witness.

Annoyed with the hassle of air travel, I drove the almost fifteen hundred miles to Minnesota from Cape Cod on September 8–9, 2007. I met with my two lawyers from 7:00 to 9:30 p.m. on Sunday, September 9. On September 10 I was in court early and met the plaintiff, who gave me a surprising hug. I learned that one of the victim's neighbors had tipped off the Star Tribune, inspiring front-page publicity twice and another prominent article within.

My lawyer took me through a boring and, I thought, ineffectual recitation of the facts at the trial and we broke for lunch. The plaintiff and his wife—solid citizens with three daughters—sat next to me. He surprised me with a question.

"Why did the judge throw out the issues of racism and probable cause?"

A toughie, but one that I thought deserved an honest answer.

"He's an idiot and doesn't understand the law." A look of shock came over him before I added, "But we need to be grateful he got us into court when he could've thrown us out."

I banked entirely on the opposition's cross examination to get my points in. I deliberately chose to label the cops' actions as "police brutality" and indirectly charged racial allusion.

Looking carefully and intently at the eight white jurors I made it clear I wasn't doing it for the money and emphasized I loved cops and supported their actions, usually. I refused to label this incident a real bank robbery. It was more like a petty theft involving about twenty.

The lawyer cross examining me then seemed to experience an "I gotcha" epiphany, pulling out annual reports I'd written, in which in more than two hundred charges (by citizens) of excessive force by my cops I'd sustained only two. I saw an opening clearly.

"That's because in those cases, as in this one, I always gave officers the benefit of every doubt." It ended, my testimony and plaintiff's case, on that point.

The defendants concluded the next day, a Tuesday, and the jury got the case. I heard nothing on Wednesday or Thursday and thought the jury must be agonizing over a dollar amount to give the plaintiff. It was either that or one or two held out. Still nothing when I bought the morning paper on Friday.

There, on the front page, was the headline, "Jurors: Officer Was Too Rough." They granted my client $778,000 in damages, plus legal fees.

And so, how should Golden Valley have handled a case I thought could've been settled for $100,000 and an apology? In a similar case—one involving a white plaintiff—the cops responded sensibly.

A *New York Times* story published July 25, 2004, and headlined "Handcuffed in the Woods of Scarsdale for the Crime of Beetlemania" grabbed my notice. I'd lived there for eighteen-and-a-half years, but that wasn't a factor. The story was a vivid account of attorney Harry Zirlin's arrest—flashing lights, cops running at him with guns pointed at his head—following a call to the police about a man in the woods with a knife. Seeing the only man in the woods who fit that description, police apprehended and handcuffed Zirlin.

But he was not "an armed menace to people in Scarsdale." He was a lawyer and coauthor of a nature book who was in the woods collecting beetles in a glass jar to add to his large collection of insects. He used the knife to pry the insects off dead logs. The prose was accompanied by a photo of the fifty-one-year-old attorney in a pensive pose in front of a bookshelf.

The cops checked his bag, verified his story, removed the handcuffs, and apologized.

Zirlin sued the cops, alleging false arrest and search and seizure. He confidently asserted that the cops must've known that anyone in those particular woods would be either a lawyer or a doctor. Richville Scarsdale, after all. He wrote a twelve-page letter to village officials, including an account of the event and a statement of his intent to sue. His key point was that there was no conceivable probable cause of a crime occurring. The newspaper article quoted thunderously from Zirlin's letter.

The village police chief wrote to the Scarsdale newspaper shortly after this December 21, 2002, event to say his cops had acted properly.

The story cited another police chief, a law school professor, and a civil liberties lawyer as saying the cops were on shaky legal ground in this case. A zesty quote from a New York Civil Liberties Union lawyer clinched the logic of abuse. It concluded with a paean to the lawyer's love of bugs and his passion for justice. No account of an effort to get the cops' or the chief's version. They might well have had no comment, given the bureaucracy's normal caution, but I did expect an effort, at least, by the reporter, to get the other side of it.

I read it and thought, "What absolute bullshit." The snide tone of the piece and the arrogance of the plaintiff pissed me off. Then I did something I'd never done: I initiated an offer to be an expert witness. I wrote the chief on July 26, describing myself. Two days later Chief John Brogan called me. He'd heard of me and wanted my take on the case. I wanted to make sure of the background and asked for more details. He told me that a woman had reported a suspicious man in the woods, with a knife, to a town worker, who called 911. They retained a tape of the call. The cops responded just as described in the newspaper story. No fudging, no attempt at cover-up—just a straightforward story of response to a suspicious-man call.

On no account, I told Chief Brogan, should he settle this case. It would be devastating to the officers' morale.

What should the cops have done on this call? Precisely what they did do: respond, investigate, undertake safe-guarding precautions, verify the innocence of the suspect, free him, release him, and apologize. As to the drawn and armed guns, cops are authorized to do this whenever circumstances appear to justify it.

Was the cuffing an arrest? Yes, but there was probable cause—a suspicious man with a knife (which he had) in the woods and a citizen's alarmed call. Ample justification for a stop-and-frisk and investigation.

Were the cops to ignore this call? Would the community's children be safer if they had failed to respond to such a summons? I'd have been glad to confront Zirlin—and the community—on the question of their children's safety.

On July 6, 2005, I called Brogan to get an update. Yes, Zirlin had pressed the issue. Depositions were taken—the chief's consumed about five hours of tough questions—and the case went to trial in federal court.

The jury deliberated about forty-five minutes and found for the defendants. Vindication.

New York Times

CASE 41: RANDOM SHOTS IN THE GHETTO

Some cases, despite favorable outcomes, end bitterly for me. I have to force myself to concentrate on the reasons I'd taken them.

Two black women are walking a street in a Chicago suburb at 4:00 p.m. People like them who are known to cops to be "wrong"—engaging in drugs, burglaries, or other street crimes—cannot undertake the most innocent transactions without attracting unwanted attention. The women are, in fact, drug addicts who would turn a trick or do whatever it takes for the next fix. They are noticed by three cops and a supervisor, on patrol in plainclothes, with their badges around their necks for quick identification. The women light a passing man's cigarette. One of the two has $6 in her hand, most likely to buy drugs. The cops see the huddle, guess a drug transaction, and double back speedily. It is a black neighborhood.

The cops quickly place the women by the car, hands on the trunk, and chase the male whose cigarette they'd lit. They catch him, put him on the ground, and handcuff him. He too is black and yelling to his grandmother to help him.

The cops find no contraband. Frustrated, they search nearby garages. An eighty-pound German shepherd charges them and they nervously jerk their guns and shoot, maybe as many as twenty times. They appear to be careful not to hit the other cops or their cuffed suspect, but the bullets fly about. The supervisor had to shout "cease fire" to get the cops to stop. The dog miraculously, or perhaps only ironically, escapes unhurt and retreats. The cuffed guy has a narcotics arrest on his record and his brother is a dealer, but today he is clean.

While all of this is going down, a bunch of guys who had been watching baseball on TV emerge into their yard for talk and beer. One of the guys is hit in the leg by one of the bullets. Not a serious injury, but a bullet wound nevertheless. The wild shooting had drawn an angry crowd of about twenty, who hurled imprecations at the cops.

The women and the cuffed male never sued, although they had cases. The wounded forty-six-year-old baseball fan did sue, and his lawyer hired me.

Ordinarily, race would be the first factor I'd look for, but it didn't apply here. All the cops were black. The uniform racial makeup of all participants probably served as an example of why it makes sense to have a police force that mirrors the society it attempts to control. White cops shooting an innocent black male is the classic precursor to a riot.

And the cops were right to investigate suspicious circumstances, but in cuffing the guy and searching the females without consent—a practice no doubt engaged in routinely without consequences—the cops were wrong and, in these circumstances, that was a real problem for them. Proper procedure would've been to stop, question, and quickly establish whether they had probable cause for search or arrest, or else release the suspects. But this wouldn't have accorded with commonly accepted standards of what constitutes effective police work on the street. Observing constitutional niceties is not the hallmark of tough enforcers.

This—an event that escalated to the notice of official inquiry—was the possibility cops have to foresee but don't. Any random act might wind up on front pages of newspapers or grand jury rooms, as this one did. Now all their actions would be examined, including trespassing onto the property guarded by the dog. That the grandmother had ordered the cops off the property compounded the problem.

The Illinois State Police investigated and found the use of firearms justified by the circumstances. It was another case in which officialdom, left to its own devices, ignored the police abuse of rights and illegal actions.

A straightforward, uncomplicated case, in which all the principals agreed as to the factual essentials even as they, in true Rashomon fashion, colored it with self-justifying hues. I developed an approach, met with the lawyer, prepared a report, drove to Chicago, and was deposed at great length. The city's attorney clearly saw me as the key to the case and toiled indefatigably to discredit my view.

And there the case, which had begun with the shooting in mid-July 1998, rested.

Finally, in early 2003, I called the lawyer. These issues often lay dormant for many months, even years, and now I sought an update. The case had been settled. He didn't say for how much, but I guessed, from his injured tone, for a smaller amount like $25,000.

The client, in any case and principally, at least emerged with a payday.

CASE 42: CONSTITUTIONAL RIGHTS VS. HAMSTRINGING THE COPS

The exercise of constitutional rights, such as to demonstrate against some policy or program, has put America's police in a conundrum. Citizens have the right to protest peacefully, yet demonstrations often contain criminal elements who exploit the larger body to hurl objects, smash windows, attack the police, and cause chaos. Police over-aggressiveness in investigating large protests has resulted in a reaction by literate and competent upper-middle-class types who often participate in peace, nuclear, environmental, or related protests. They've been joined by the American Civil Liberties Union in devising strategies to curb police excesses and have hit upon consent decrees as a major answer.

The ACLU is a stout defender of the Constitution, perhaps its only one, but it can also be a pain in the ass and go to extremes. These consent decrees often constrain police from performing legal and necessary functions. Unknowing chiefs—for example, civilian outsiders appointed to these posts—sometimes agree to these decrees and paralyze perfectly legitimate police operations. The NYPD had long been subjected to just such an agreement, signed by Robert McGuire, a police commissioner who'd never previously spent as much as one day as a cop. This agreement was rescinded in the wake of the 9/11 terrorist attacks.

Back in the 1950s and 1960s, however, the NYPD's Bureau of Special Services and Investigations infiltrated indiscriminately and widely—and legally. BOSSI had maintained extensive files on persons and organizations that had been active in protests and such, but who had committed no crimes nor had supplied any evidence that they had even contemplated a breach of law. The BOSSI files had been used in name checks—solicitation of information in our files by other government agencies—and these surfaced in official decisions relating, for example, to employment or applications for licenses or permits. This was not a crime, but it was a major mistake. The NYPD should have predicated infiltrations, investigations, monitorings, and the gathering of evidence on the existence of a criminal act, actual or potential. To prevent abuse of this power to investigate, record, infiltrate, or monitor, each inquiry needed to be documented and justified. There would have to appear evidence of purgings and deletions when the investigation failed to turn up evidence of criminality, at which point the inquiry would be abandoned.

The case I took on in 1996 centered on the Chicago Police Department's filming and photographing participants and speakers at an anti-nuclear arms race demonstration in Chicago on April 10, 1982. The event had been peaceful and no arrests had been made, but the police had failed to follow the consent decree they'd freely entered into with the ACLU in 1981. The decree, which had been prompted by graphic evidence of police overreach, forbade the department to gather information on First Amendment activities or to purge it if collected. The cops held that they needed to record the event to evaluate police handling of the protest. The judge held that, although they had not violated the law, the Chicago PD did breach the agreement.

I'd have trouble being useful to the ACLU in this case because my view permitted much more police aggressiveness than they liked. They needed me to testify as to the abuses they were attempting to correct, which I'd do, but they were anything but keen on my determination to keep the police armed with investigative tools that could be used against law breaches. Disruptive elements can and do swim among a sea of demonstrators to hurl objects, start fires, destroy property, assault cops and other targets of their enmity, and otherwise try to move the larger body closer to their illegal purposes. Cops cannot be disarmed against this threat.

Nevertheless, the ACLU hired me in 1996 to argue their side of it—that the filming was chilling and intrusive and that the evidence must be destroyed. I spent about five hours reviewing materials, conferring with the attorneys, and developing a strategy. As the matter drifted inconclusively, I was conflicted but content to let it evaporate into the arcane mists of litigation. Eventually, the cops lost the argument, were ordered to comply and train officers in the agreement, and pay costs.

Intelligence is tricky business. The power to pry inevitably leads to abusive intrusions. Controls are essential. Good intelligence is not good enough; it has to be acted on, and swiftly. Post 9/11/01 analyses all pointed to a plethora of leads and a dearth of follow-through.

The Patriot Act, adopted following the World Trade Center tragedy, is more a hunt for power than a search for effective intelligence approaches. The issue meandered onto center stage in 2006, as President George Bush attempted to justify the National Security Agency's wiretapping of Americans without securing a warrant, relying entirely on a nebulous concept of presidential power. I didn't think his view had legs.

The *New York Times* will rail over the infiltration by cops of the ranks of demonstrators. The media will wax hysterical over cops posing as reporters to secure evidence of criminality. Black leaders will object to crime-fighting tactics that mostly wind up netting black males (such as stake-outs, stings, and decoy operations). Yet all of the actions are not only perfectly legal, but wise, aggressive, and intelligent deployments of police energies. The American Civil Liberties Union will not agree, but they are wrong. It is the counter intuitiveness of some of these circumstances that leads intelligent observers to completely misread the issues.

I've seen intelligence interdict serious criminal plots. I've seen intelligence lead to chilling intrusions into the lives of honest citizens. I've seen intelligence used by such as J. Edgar Hoover to punish enemies, reward friends, and remain in office. If ever a delicate balance between power and need, criminality and intrusion, or effectiveness and abuse were needed, it is in the area of giving, using, and monitoring the use of intelligence by our government in its dealings with its citizens.

CASE **43**: LIFE AMONG THE UNDERCLASS

America's overclass (you, me) is never going to figure out that their differences with the underclass don't totally center on cash. Simple, taken-for-granted matters like phones and cars are often not available to the downtrodden—and the phrase is apt because we do tread on all of them. While our services are the professions trained to minister to our needs, theirs are whoever they can call to intervene in their lives. The underclass navigate different seas, full of menace. It is a lot tougher than commonly realized. And despite the best efforts, casualties mount.

In September 1995, a black mother (then thirty-three years old) who is worried over her impulsive son (seventeen) going out into the dangerous streets at night, tries to keep him inside. The oldest, most classic of ghetto struggles, if you except domestic abuse. The young man is not to be denied. The mother orders her daughter (sixteen) to go across the street to use a friend's phone to call the police.

It is about 10:30 p.m. in Minneapolis and the police respond to the address that came up on the 911 caller-identifier. Two white male officers arrive and are directed to the correct location where the mother insisted—and this is a measure of maternal desperation in the ghetto—they arrest her son for disobedience. Inside the apartment are the mother, her husband, two sons (including the disobedient seventeen-year-old), and three daughters.

The cops, with less than five years of service between them, refuse and turn to leave. Mother is pissed. Voices are raised. Versions diverge but familiar points arise, lending verisimilitude to such assertions that the mother asks for badge numbers (although Minneapolis cops had, by then, been wearing name tags for many years) and threatens to tell their superior they'd refused to act. She allegedly grabs one of the cops from behind as he exits—a real mistake, if true.

A predictable struggle ensues. The mother is maced, as are others in the home. A neighbor is thrown to the ground, fracturing his hip. The mother is handcuffed, seated, maced in the eyes, and dragged backward on her seat to the police car. She is described as irrational and out of control. The second cop said he heard but did not see the precipitating grabbing incident and didn't describe the mother as being on drugs or drunk.

And so the mother is the only person arrested. She is charged with obstructing legal process, assault, and disorderly conduct. In a system that requires that actions be followed with official responses, the neighbor's fractured hip becomes an unaddressed debit. A judge dismisses the first two charges and she gains an acquittal on the disorderly conduct in a jury verdict. Mother emerges vindicated, judicially anyway.

Neither officer reported any injury in this altercation, to use a favored term. The maced occupants did not suffer lingering effects either, although the mother complained of great pain in her eyes because of contact lenses.

It was clear that, though they may have been acting in reasonably good faith, the cops had mishandled the event badly, causing it to escalate into a totally avoidable fracas. To cover their mistakes they undertook the classic maneuver: a false arrest. The risks they faced were minimal and the use of Mace unwarranted. They lapsed into anger with predictably negative consequences. The mother had failed the attitude test and the cops fell into a robotic response. I took the case.

I reviewed the materials, offered a theory of the case, and prepared a tough report. This was now 1997, more than two years after the incident. Faced with what was, for the city, a negative disposition of the criminal charges, as well as a serious injury resulting from what should've been a routine police encounter, Minneapolis settled.

CASE 44: NO JUSTICE, NO PEACE

A willful girl ventures into dangerous waters and suffers an injury. Compounding the case are the cultural complexities existing in an exile culture, in this event Somali. The girl's father is dead, her mother works in another town, and the girl lives with her aunt and grandmother in Minneapolis.

The victim, an eleven-year-old Somali girl, in March 2000 defies her grandmother and goes off at night with friends in a car, ostensibly to get batteries for her CD player. She is taken to an apartment where she has a Coke and some juice. She falls asleep on a couch. She is awakened at 3:00 a.m. by a tall, thin black man who attempts sex and she resists. He punches her in the face, takes off her pants, disrobes, puts on a condom, and rapes her. She falls asleep and when she awakes, the occupants try to calm her, saying it's OK and not a problem and such. When she attempts to call home the female tenant pulls the cord out of the wall.

The girl is taken home and dropped off. Her angry grandmother had reported her missing and notifies the police of her return. At first the girl denies any sexual contact but the grandmother persists and she breaks down and describes the assault. The police file a report and secure a warrant for the suspect whose name has been provided but which is relatively generic and shared by many other Somali immigrant males. The physical description is of a tall man, six-foot-one, and very thin.

The cops recover the girl's torn pants, but the need for interpreters delays and confuses their inquiry. The use of a condom in the rape precludes DNA analysis.

The friends who took the girl to the apartment are identified, but the cops have little real interest and follow-through is spasmodic and indifferent. They never really investigate the case and the file reflects shocking neglect on the part of the cops. And, not prodded by knowing or insistent victim or family, they take the easier path of neglect.

The warrant, however, is out there.

A traffic stop turns up a Somali male for whom a warrant seems outstanding and he is brought in. His physiognomy is at total variance with the suspect's, but he is lodged and jailed for some time before the victim sees him. She immediately reports he is not the rapist.

In the meantime the record reflects no follow-up activity to locate the apartment where the rape occurred or its occupants, or to question the "friends" who took the girl off.

The arrest of the ersatz suspect occurred fourteen months after the rape. The man had the misfortune to reside in the same apartment complex as the site of the crime. The police took almost seven weeks to bring the suspect and victim together, at which time she quickly excluded him.

I thought it a clear violation of the suspect's rights. The arrest lacked probable cause, given the variance in physical description. The commonness of the name and any lack of evidence tying him to the crime compounded the absurdity.

I didn't much like the lawyer who sought my help. He seemed an ambulance-chasing hustler out for a fast buck, but I did like the case and took it, almost on the second anniversary of the rape. He hired me in March 2002 and we worked on it through that spring. I prepared a report, gave the attorney my theory of the case, and waited. And waited.

After seventeen months I wrote, asking for an update. The case was in federal court and the city had filed for summary judgment on the basis that the officer acted reasonably in securing and executing the arrest warrant. I responded with an affidavit countering this claim. I heard nothing and the lawyer hadn't answered my letter.

Now angry, I called the lawyer, who said the case had been thrown out on summary judgment over a year earlier. He whined that he'd lost money on the case, which was why he hadn't contacted me. I reminded him that our deal was not a contingency arrangement, and whatever the outcome, he owed me for time spent. He reluctantly agreed and groaned. I finally settled for one hour's work or $200, just to break his chops. The check arrived and I determined I'd never work with him again.

The plaintiff must have wondered at the twists and turns of justice in our democracy.

CASE 45: HIRING PRACTICES

Cronyism, favoritism, and nepotism within police departments have been evident in a lot of the cases I've worked on and the consequences of such hiring practices severe. The standard, for me, in deciding for or against an employee was whether I could justify the hire and defend my choice under withering cross-examination. Racists, bullies, bums, and other unlikely prospects got short shrift.

This case was a beaut.

One summer evening in 1998, a forty-nine-year-old black male, a postal worker for thirteen years and a military veteran, was in front of his home speaking with his friend and neighbor, also black. Two Chicago police officers, both white, drive up and one of the cops allegedly says, "What are you two niggers doing?"

It is a residential neighborhood and the officers did not seem to be responding to either a call or any discernible problem.

The postal worker questioned the cop, who flew out of the car, grabbed him, twisted his arm, and slammed him against the vehicle. The civilian offered no resistance. The cop then searched the man and found no contraband. The other officer, typically, just went along and helped his partner a bit, but was clearly discomfited.

On its face not a very credible charge. I was skeptical. There had to be more to it. What cop would use that language in 1998? Then I saw that the officer had twenty recorded citizen complaints, including brutality and racism. I could easily imagine this as the tip of a large iceberg of unrecorded abusive contacts.

Earlier in 1998 a fellow officer had filed a complaint against the cop, an unheard of act.

The cop had taken a leave of absence to work for the Federal Drug Enforcement Agency but had been terminated for a racist incident. Then he sought a reinstatement the Chicago PD should never have allowed. A personnel officer attempted to delay the cop's rehiring, but he was reinstated to the Chicago force. Had they refused to take him back, this incident wouldn't have occurred. The bureaucracy claimed to have been unaware of the call to delay his return.

The department--and this is typical—has written policies calling for intervention by personnel when "there are three or more not sustained excessive force complaints within twelve months" against an officer. Such glaring warning signs demand attention. But, also typically, the department did not act on its own requirements and the officer was tacitly encouraged in his pursuits.

A bomb, with a lit fuse.

Could there have been even one employee in the Chicago Police Department who would say this man posed no risk? Hard to believe such a fact pattern could exist. While I didn't get to examine the cop's pre-hiring background folder, I was sure it would be speckled with red signals.

I loved the case. I took it in 2000, or almost two years after the incident. I guided the lawyer through it, prepared a scathing report, and drove to Chicago to be deposed. I think my testimony curled the city attorney's hair. They now expended substantial energy on excluding my testimony.

On November 15, 2000, the lawyer wrote that they'd settled, that the terms would likely be confidential and constituted "a significant compromise, but one which the plaintiff wanted to accept."

I was glad for the man's vindication, angry over the retention of this ticking-time-bomb officer, and generally satisfied that a measure of justice had been done. I couldn't guess as to the amount, but hoped the aggrieved citizen cleared at least $25,000.

Curiously, a city that had taken not the slightest trouble to protect its citizens from an obvious menace expended real effort to keep the settlement a secret from the very people paying it. Another wonderful example of the "legitimate ends" of government secrecy.

Meanwhile the cop remains on the payroll.

Tick, tick.

CASE 46: ANOTHER FAILED ATTITUDE TEST

I sometimes navigate between feckless clients and greedy, insensitive lawyers. But it is the cases that matter – and the opportunities to change police behavior that they bring. This next case involved several distinct phases occurring in a St. Paul suburb on January 1, 1999.

A white male on the cusp of fifty is driving a country road at 2:30 a.m. and bumps a deer, a surprisingly common hazard in the Midwest. His car goes into an embankment.

An off-duty male officer, white, stops to help and calls an on-duty officer to respond. A female cop in uniform appears. The man calls his daughter's friend to tow his car out and the guy gets in and limps home in his battered auto. He is delivering that morning's newspapers and has to hurry. He transfers the papers to his wife's car and proceeds on his route.

At 7:30 a.m. he is observed speeding and pulls right over when he sees the police lights behind him. A white male officer emerges and gets the man's license information and returns to his squad to verify the data. The man has four minor convictions for speeding and receives a citation. As the cop returns to the driver, the paper deliverer makes a comment he meant as jocular, like he'd "put a bullet in my head." The car inches forward, the cop orders him to stop, reaches in over the driver, and cuts the engine. The cop tugs the driver out and places him in the back seat of the squad and calls for back-up, concerned about the "suicide reference."

Within twenty minutes another officer arrives and is briefed on events. The second officer goes to talk to the arrested driver, who attempts to run. The cop closes the door hard, slamming it against the man's elbow. The first cop describes a loud exchange between the second cop and the driver.

The first cop returns to the squad and tries to calm the driver, who is upset with the back-up cop's actions. He tells the driver he is free to go, but the driver, still upset, looks back angrily at the second cop. He raises his voice and waves his arms and asks for the cop's badge number. The first officer advises him to drop it and leave. Asking a cop for his name and badge number—a perfectly reasonable act and a citizen's right—is usually seen as an impermissible challenge to the cop's authority that must be met.

The driver persists, calling the second cop "rude," allegedly cursing.

The second cop decides to take the driver to the hospital, walks up, takes his handcuffs out, and says, "He needs to go to the hospital for a psych eval."

Now both cops try to cuff the driver, who resists and tries to walk back to his car. The second cop grabs his arm and the other cop helps. They tug, he resists. He is put down. The driver claims they kicked his legs out from under him and drove him hard, head-first, onto the ground, injuring him. He is cuffed, lifted, and taken to the second cop's squad car.

The driver is treated for cuts and bruises and released after the medical evaluation. His car had been towed and he had to go to the police station to retrieve his keys and car. There he met the first cop and they talked.

Another classic case of an asshole pushing the envelope until a tough cop decided to alter his attitude. Amazing how much unnecessary trouble people can produce for themselves. Still, I felt he'd been wronged.

The first cop was right to stop, cite, and safeguard the driver after the expressed possible suicidal intentions. His call for back-up was appropriate.

The back-up cop perceived the driver's behavior as disrespectful and determined to correct it. His approach caused an escalation of the action that led to the driver's arrest, abuse, and injuries. Even though he wasn't charged, the taking of the driver into custody and handcuffing would have to be justified, and it couldn't be in this circumstance.

The driver's request for the badge number was perfectly appropriate, but a challenge frequently failed by touchy cops. Taking him to the hospital after the first officer decided to release the driver was malicious.

The driver was neither armed nor physically aggressive, and the officers claimed no injuries from the encounter. His being upset was no cause for official action beyond the citation. The first officer was, however, complicit because he cooperated and assisted the second cop in his assault on the driver.

I got the case a year later and devoted about seven hours to meetings, notes, and the preparation of a long report. Then, a not infrequent development, silence.

The driver had been abused, without legal justification, and merited a defense. Such cases often came unattractively packaged. He was a fuck-up, but defending his rights is the first line of attack in preserving the rights of the rest of us.

I finally tried calling about eighteen months later to be updated. The lawyer's phone had been disconnected. I finally reached one of the lawyers involved, the one who'd originally hired me. He was apologetic and contrite. The driver had drifted away and the case had disintegrated through his loss of interest. The lawyer heard the guy had died in Mexico, a not altogether shocking development given his marginal approach to life and defiant attitude.

CASE 47: BLOWN COVER

The lawyer who called me on this case, and with whom I'd worked on others, was an earnest young graduate of Annapolis.

This case was a simple one. A street guy caught up in the drug culture in northern Minnesota offered to work with the local police on two conditions: that he be paid and that his identity as an informer not be revealed. As a practical matter, this meant he wouldn't be called on to testify against his targets. In such cases cops typically arrange to have an undercover agent make a buy or the informer sets up a buy-sale the cops can monitor and move in on.

The informer produced and the cops made several seizures and arrests. His identity was shared, in-house, with others working to combat gang and drug activities. One investigator put the informer's name on a search warrant and asserted he'd received the informer's permission to do so. Such documents are routinely available to defendants' lawyers under the rules of discovery.

The informer's activities quickly hit the streets and he was warned by friends and threatened by those he'd betrayed. It would be hard to imagine greater danger. His actions not only boiled the blood but served as a challenge to the thugs whose reputations and freedom were at stake.

The cops, in this case and others I was involved in, didn't seem to grasp that they had an equally deep, if obverse, interest in protecting informants to keep the vital information flowing.

The offending cop was detailed to a statewide task force working on gangs, so the city's curious defense was that he was a state, not a municipal, employee. I didn't think this premise would take them far.

The motions flew. The case was in federal court, where most of these cases, ideally, wind up.

The payments to informers were made by the city. One of its detectives reported that he'd had to lose a case rather than reveal the informer, who had adamantly refused to testify.

The informer's determination to remain unknown was clear in the record. There had been multiple investigations, arrests, recoveries of drugs, and payments. Over the next few years the warrants and busts all conformed to the original arrangement of secrecy. The precedent was broken by a different officer. And there was no record of the informer's willingness to be identified. He was a young, white man born in 1983. Curiously, the informer's recruitment occurred when cops were investigating the rape of his girlfriend in September 2001 by two males. Not surprising to me, but probably a shock to others, the payments to the informer do not appear to have totaled as much as $1,000.

The search warrant application, dated February 26, 2002, is the offending document. In it the officer shields the identities of others yet asserts that this informer "not only agreed to be identified, but has also agreed to testify in open court." A breathtaking assumption. Small wonder the city sought to get out from under. The document received wide circulation on the streets. It was axiomatic that action on it would be a point of honor with its targets.

The target of the search warrant on which the informer had been named attempted to run down the informer twice with his car. The snitch—for that would be the appellation used by both cops and robbers—first moved, then joined the army to escape, but he was injured and discharged. The problem is that these guys lack the resources necessary for the requisite mobility.

I'd had another case (*Case 11, "I'm Already Dead"*) in which an informer had been killed by angry associates while the police did nothing to protect him. No precedent was really needed because the actions invariably produced reprisals, as happened here.

The city attorney defending this case had previously handled that of another unhappy informer, a forty-eight-year-old black male who'd felt underpaid and who sued. He'd received several thousand dollars over the years but felt cheated. The attorney's approach alerted me to what we might expect in this case: a direct assault on the credibility and character of the plaintiff by way of discrediting his claims. This forty-eight-year-old had been assaulted as a result of his informing and was feeling aggrieved. The case went to trial. The informer hadn't paid taxes, had been shown to be a cheat and a deadbeat, and had received welfare payments fraudulently. He lost.

It became clear that a key point of strategy had to be, assuming a trial, for my lawyer to bring out all the negatives in this current plaintiff's background and attempt to explain them and balance them with positives. I didn't know what they might be, but I was pretty sure the city would be digging deep, assuming they didn't choose to settle. Of course, in the other case, the informer was not claiming "blown cover," only underpayment, which certainly suggested a measure of greed.

The city's position looked weak to me, especially if the first cop testified to the informer's insistence on anonymity. It seemed a prime case for settlement. In such cases, I frequently decide, internally, on a figure so I can advise the lawyer if he seeks this guidance. In this case about $300,000 seemed right.

I lost sight of the case, but the lawyer came to see me in 2006 with four new cases, all beauts. What happened on this one? His face furrowed, then a light. Oh, it'd been settled, for $4,000, many months ago. It wasn't much, but life is packed with minor victories.

CASE 48: SWABS, SPRAYS, AND VIDEOTAPES

Environmental issues usually pit ecological activists (frequently dubbed "eco-terrorists" by the opposition) against corporate interests ("polluters" or "despoilers"), with the cops squarely in between, but sometimes slipping into sympathy for the latter in meetings known as lunches with loggers. Politicians are sometimes viewed as siding with one or the other, with the magnetic pull of campaign funds sometimes tipping the balance toward the flush world of the suits.

In 2004 lawyer Dennis Cunningham asked if I'd serve as an expert on issues meandering about for more than seven years, a not unprecedented scenario. The issues in this case centered on three events, each involving objections to logging/clear-cutting and the preservation of forests and giant, old redwoods. Earth First is one principal participant. The events were:

1) Demonstrations on September 25, 1997, outside the offices of the Pacific Lumber Company and seven sit-ins inside linked by "lock boxes"—an L-shaped pipe into which an arm is thrust and into which a demonstrator locks onto a bar inside, lining up with a demonstrator who does the same. The larger outside demonstration involves placards, chanting, et cetera, and is largely peaceful, although at least two are arrested at its end for climbing onto a roof.

Inside, the seven demonstrators, starting at around 12:45 p.m., refuse to release. They're sitting in the center of the outer office floor. Members of the Humboldt County Sheriff's Office in Northern California read a notice and announce a warning of use of pepper spray. Upon the protestors' refusal to release, the cops hold their heads back by the hair and chin and apply pepper spray ointment, with cotton swabs, to the corners of their eyes and eyelids, seeking penetration. There is no resistance or violence by the demonstrators. Two females release and are cuffed. Water is applied to wash the eyes and face. The other four, still linked, are carried out on gurneys and cut loose with a grinder in minutes. The grinder is a cutting tool with a small part of the blade exposed. Cutting emits some sparks. No spray is used. All are cuffed and led off. It all ends by 2:45 p.m. A total of two hours.

2) An outside demonstration at nearby Bear Creek, in which two sets of couples link themselves between a tractor's tracks. It is October 3, 1997, at 9:40 a.m. They are warned as to the law and threatened with chemical agents. They refuse to release. Then two release, are cuffed, and led off. The other two are warned, refuse, and the head of one is held back

and his eyes are swabbed with ointment. Then he is sprayed directly in the eyes from a few inches away. The partner receives similar treatment. No resistance or violence. They chant. Water is used to wash their eyes, a grinder is brought up, and they are cut free and arrested.

3) A demonstration inside Congressman Frank Riggs's office, October 16, 1997, at 10:40 a.m. Four females are linked by lock boxes in a circle, sitting around a large tree stump. There are wood chips spread on floor. The police (in this case, sheriff's deputies and Eureka cops, with supervisors) arrive, issue warnings, and ask for voluntary release. The lock boxes are exposed and accessible but the cops speak of a "fire danger" (regarding the wood chips) and threaten chemical agents. All four women are swabbed with the ointment using cotton swabs, forced into eyes by prying eyelids. They are crying. Police threaten to use pepper spray. They are given five minutes (as in the other cases). It's impractical to carry out four linked women but not impractical to use the grinder. One releases and is cuffed. Others are held by their hair as spray is applied within a couple of inches of their eyes. Another releases and is cuffed. More spray. The third woman releases and then, at 11:02 a.m., the fourth. All are cuffed and led off. Eyes are washed with water. There are demonstrators on the sidewalk carrying placards and chanting and encouraging the arrestees.

All three events involved the use of chemical agents to secure compliance; the question centered on the appropriateness of the technique. The three events are videotaped by the police and those administering the ointment and applying the spray are calm, deliberate, and seemingly solicitous. Although most of the demonstrators are women, all of the cops dealing with them directly are men. There is a lot of physical handling, an approach usually disapproved of in most police agencies.

What confronted the police? A trespass, passively engaged in by environmental activists, with no physical resistance or violence and clearly intended to prolong the sit-ins and call attention to the logging issue. Passive resistance to arrest also constitutes a crime.

The police were there to enforce the law, which means to negotiate an end to the trespass or arrest the violators, charge them, and bring them promptly to court for adjudication. Additional charges of resisting can be added if they decline to cooperate.

Any attempt to arrest the protestors must be apposite to the circumstances. Police actions have to be measured and relevant to the objective sought. Torture cannot be inflicted to coerce compliance. The use of ointment and then spray are good examples of illegal use of force to secure compliance. The police have to engage in a good faith effort to solve the problem faced. The use of force by the police is circumscribed and widely known. It must relate to the objective sought, be measured and restrained, and can escalate only when the objective circumstances clearly demand greater force. The standards of reasonableness and appropriateness must be applied rigorously, as must be the law.

The police are clearly acting under orders from above. There are supervisors present. The events are filmed. The orchestration indicates thorough preparation and planning. They even wait about an hour for the TV camera. They're in no rush.

The use of grinders appears to be both logical and appropriate. It is related to the challenges faced and resulted in no injuries. If a mishap occurred the practice would have to be rethought and, perhaps, other measures employed. But we would not expect the police to hammer nails through protester's feet to coerce obedience or cooperation. Swabbing eyes with a caustic substance, and the use of spray in violation of the manufacturer's directions and their own departments' regulations, clearly constitutes torture. This is inadmissible. And besides, grinders had been used scores of times to good effect.

I expected to testify that the force used in these three cases—swabbing and/or spraying pepper spray—was inappropriate and in violation of the laws regulating the use of force, the manufacturer's own instructions as to the use of the chemical agent, and the police departments' (both) own regulations as to the level and relevance of the force used.

It is axiomatic that torture may not be employed to secure compliance. The use of "pain compliance" must be related to the objective sought. "Passive resistance" is not an oxymoron and is recognized in law and in the regulations of police agencies everywhere.

There are five interests commonly tied to a trespass: the victims, whose operations are being interfered with; the police, who must make arrests and do what they legally can to preclude a reprise; the prosecutor, who should apply the law and prosecute to discourage future breaches of law; the broader public interest of access to the interrupted services; and, of course, the rights of the trespassers.

The prosecutor has wide discretion, but the police can influence his/her actions by insisting on a vigorous prosecution of a lawful arrest. A determined complainant (victim) can buttress the police demand effectively. In a real sense the violation of the protester's rights was exacerbated by the prosecutor declining to bring many of their cases to court.

In fact, that only a few of these demonstrators were prosecuted makes it clear that the only intent here was to punish extra judiciously.

The actions of the police were wrong, the policies guiding them were wrong, and the outcomes prove it.

Because of the videotapes, widely distributed and used in court, the cases received national attention. The cops were stunned by the outraged reaction but hung on. Those swabbed, sprayed, and arrested sued.

Now began the torturous legal process. The police/sheriff defendants moved for dismissal on the grounds they were simply enforcing the law.

It must be said that the courts, federal or state, are mindful of the need to afford officialdom the freedom to act in street circumstances requiring split-second decisions. They bend over backward—mostly appropriately, in my view—to allow cops to operate. And juries, especially white, middle-class ones, are pointedly sympathetic.

So the case went to trial in federal court after the judge dismissed the charges against the low-level cops on the scene. They were clearly acting under orders, albeit illegal ones they could have resisted. The jury, confused by police assertions that passive resistance is "an oxymoron," and by the expressed concerns over the dangers of using grinders, the need to use "pain compliance techniques" to gain the demonstrators' cooperation, and a host of concerns and alarums that proved persuasive, declared itself hung. The judge, on receiving the mixed verdict, considered the issues and, after some days, decided to dismiss all charges against officialdom and the government bodies employing them.

The defendants appealed.

The appellate court held that the judge erred. He should have considered whether a jury might have found for the plaintiff if he'd applied the doctrine that their view might have prevailed if judged from the most favorable aspects. The judge had the case taken from him as it was returned for retrial.

The defendants appealed.

The plaintiffs, shaken by the defeats, hired Dennis Cunningham, who hired me. They were chastened by the inequality of the combat and persuaded as to the importance of experts in these matters. Some credible cop figure had to counter officialdom's confident assertions that this was totally proper and acceptable practice.

In my view it was torture.

I didn't doubt that the officials deciding the strategy thought, in good faith, that they were doing the right thing. Why else would they insist on, and even delay operations for, the arrival and use of videotapes? But they were wrong. They went counter to the laws governing the use of force, counter to their own regulations, and counter even to the manufacturer's instructions as to the use of pepper spray.

I supported the use of violence, even lethal force, but it had to be guided by the law, the standards of reasonableness, and the U.S. Constitution.

The case would wind its way back to court, but the reversal of the judge's dismissal was critical to what I hoped would be an outcome that would influence police actions in the future.

This case involved a small town in which police officials knew and socialized with logging interests. Imagine a juror's confusion as top-ranking officials solemnly testified as to the reasonableness of their actions—and with no one to refute their assertions. It was a case, whatever the outcome, that screamed for the appearance of a contrasting view. This was what my approach was all about.

As 2005 emerged the case was headed for denouement of some sort, either settlement or trial, in which we'd win or lose. At least we were afforded a shot.

I was deposed for five hours on February 2, 2005, and demolished the defendant's arguments. The case was set for trial on April 11, 2005.

I took an early morning flight to San Francisco on Monday, April 18, 2005, expecting to testify on April 19 or, at worst, April 20. I was forbidden to be in court before I testified and so sat with the plaintiffs and their friends in the lounge reserved for their use. I was impressed by the warmth, genuineness, altruism, and dedication of these sweet, natural youngsters. One breast-fed her baby in the middle of the room as if were the most commonplace thing on Earth—as it should've been.

Dennis asked me to make some remarks to them on Wednesday. I stressed the merits of their case and also the possibility of losing. They were obviously impressed by their conversion of this semi fascist.

Finally, late on Thursday, I was put on the stand. I was uncompromising—the practices were wrong, even illegal, the demonstrators presented no threat or danger and were under control; the obvious remedy was to use the grinder. The use of swabs and spray constituted cruel and unusual punishment, I told the jurors, as they were watching an act of police brutality filmed.

Everyone seemed pleased by my tough testimony, except the defendant's attorney.

A tiny squib in the *New York Times* of April 30, 2005, reported "Sprayed Protestors Win Suit" and went on to describe a jury award of $1 to each of the nine plaintiffs. In analyzing the case later, I concluded that the minimal grant of a buck each was probably predicated on my concession that the plaintiffs had broken the law. The jury was not inclined to reward illegal behavior.

Defendants had to pay costs, so I'd get more than $7,000 from Dennis. I asked Cunningham if he shared his legal fees with the plaintiffs and he said they'd get half, or about $8,000 each.

Typically decent behavior by a guy I admire.

CASE 49: WHY DO BLACKS RESPOND DIFFERENTLY THAN WHITES WITH COPS?

If any evidence were needed of the fascination police stories have for just about everyone, a brief review of the genre should scatter doubters. Even cops find the perch fascinating and citizens who go for ride-alongs, a hugely popular program, often find even everyday experiences unforgettable.

In this case a cop from Madison, Wisconsin, undertakes a busman's holiday and asks to go as a ride-along with a cop from Duluth, Minnesota.

It all begins when a twenty-year-old woman, three months pregnant, calls 911 to report some neighbors arguing over dogs. It never comes clear whether the dispute is over ownerships or behavior. This issue vanishes from the controversy.

The Duluth police officer responds, with the vacationing Madison cop as partner. It is around 9:00 p.m. on August 1, 2002. On arrival the cops immediately confront Thomas Matthews, a thirty-seven-year-old black man who's had minor contacts with the police previously and who is, very likely, at least verbally obstreperous. Cops are never able to distinguish this from illegal behavior and always seemed compelled to straighten the guy out. The precursor to endless police tragedies.

The Duluth officer quickly begins chasing Mathews, macing him, delivering baton blows to the legs and back, and forcing him into a fetal position. Matthews is cuffed after his attempt to get away and arrested. He is charged with obstructing legal process, which the prosecutor reduces to a petty misdemeanor. A year later he is convicted of obstructing a public officer and disorderly conduct.

I usually wince at such convictions, since they constitute the system's judgment of events in the cool and calm aftermath, but I took this case. The cop did not claim any violence or resistance nor any injury from Matthews and all agreed as to the outlines of the event. Matthews's attempt to get away and his stumbling, fumbling movements might have created suspicions of escape in the cops' mind. The scene is further confused by the events immediately following.

Seeing the roughing up of the neighbor on whose behalf she'd dialed 911, the twenty-year-old woman descended and demanded names and badge numbers. The Wisconsin cop ride-along tackled her, slammed her to the ground, kneed her in the stomach, cuffed, and arrested her, but not before she stumbled off, slipped, fell, and vomited.

About three Duluth cops are now huddled in deep discourse over the turn of events, a sure sign of perceived trouble. One ordered the ride-along to be taken from the scene. The young woman is taken to the county jail, where she is held nine hours and charged with obstructing legal process. The city attorney dismissed the charges against her and she received medical advice to abort her three-month fetus, which she reluctantly did.

Madison authorities disavowed their vacationing employee. Duluth was embarrassed that he'd not been asked to sign the requisite waiver of immunity and relied on the lame assertion that he was not a city employee and on his own in this complex transaction. The cops' version is laced with references to shouts and curses—certain precursors to baseless charges and lawsuits.

The case had the unmistakable whiff of a mud-wrestling contest. The citizens mouthed off, the cops overreacted, and the system was left with the problem of sorting it all out.

Another classic, with the cops unable to resist a challenge to their authority; citizens insisting on angrily asserting rights that, while they exist, cops don't much like; and no objective breaches of law. Yet there are arrests.

Citizens cowering, stumbling off, and being assaulted. Slips and falls. Opera buffa, with sad consequences.

These scenes inspired me to imagine a course I'd offer to black men on their encounters with cops. It would include such pointers as "A cop's bellowing commands are not a direct personal challenge to your manhood." And "Cops have a lot of power, and it is unwise to confront it." A posture of obsequious servility is actually the smart approach. Ours is what is called a statutory society—which means that cops can massage any situation into a breach of law embellished with perjuries that will bring swarms of unneeded, perfectly avoidable troubles. Still, I'd add, "If it is your purpose to provoke cops into reacting in ways that will give you ammunition for a winnable law suit, by all means carry on."

In this case there was no crime, no weapons, no assaults, and no injuries to cops. Still....

The case petered out into the vapors of neglect and disinterest. It wasn't all that promising to begin with and I guess it just drifted off. I never heard the outcome.

CASE 50: PROFILING AND ITS DANGERS

Lack of training—especially in conflict resolution, mediation, negotiation skills—bedevils police departments everywhere, but it absolutely cripples security operations caught between the Charybdis of order and the Scylla of low-level workers. The best cops learn to maneuver around tricky situations, but security workers don't get the exposure and enter service without having the educational backgrounds. The deficiencies can prove costly. Exacerbating the problem are the on-the-spot judgments that must be made in brief, touchy encounters. An internal system of profiling kicks in that is fallible.

It is a Sunday morning in November 1997. Following church services, a black man, his wife, and their four kids decide to visit his mother-in-law in a secure Minneapolis apartment complex. Admitted without difficulty, the man remembers a gift he'd forgotten to bring with them and returns home to get it.

Getting past the guards now becomes a hassle that rapidly escalates into an argument. The man asks to be escorted to the in-law's apartment, but is taken to the security office instead. Management has placed a video camera in the room to monitor its employees and justify the use of force when required.

The guards later describe the man as combative despite the unequal factors of size, weight, and strength. The visitor is roughed up. His head is banged against a wall several times, causing, among other injuries, a deep cut over his left eye. As he bleeds, he, being an African émigré, is told, "Welcome to America." The man is handcuffed behind his back and the Minneapolis cops are called.

The cops hear the guards' version, question the visitor, and quickly establish that the guards overreacted. They would not take the prisoner or charge him. Paramedics are called, ask the guards to remove the cuffs (an important fact demonstrating a false arrest), and treat and release the visitor. He is restored to his family. The guards, unhappy with the results, follow him to his mother-in-law's apartment and demand he leave. He complies and goes to a hospital, where he receives eight stitches.

The videotape of the beating is taped over, thereby erasing the account of this beating. Conveniently, the rest of the video, displaying innocent stuff, is preserved.

The CEO of security verified a racist comment by one guard and fired him. He was, however, rehired a few days later, but forbidden to work the apartment complex that was the site of the incident. The report of management reflects the guard's termination, but not his rehiring. He left permanently in December 1997.

The visitor, whom I never met, was, perhaps, an educated exile—as so many are—who grew up in an ambiance that didn't have the paralytic effect our racism imposes on many African-Americans. The natural assertiveness of those growing up, unselfconsciously, in a society that accepts them without cavil, prompted him to sue. The security company and its insurer fought the issue on technical questions of jurisdiction, applicable laws, et cetera. The Urban League pitched in for the plaintiff. The case wound its tortured way through the gauntlet of motions to dismiss, lack of jurisdiction or applicability, and such.

The plaintiff persevered. Finally, in 1999, or two years after the event, it was set for trial. It could not have been a case a defendant's attorney relished.

And, indeed, the case was settled, for $94,000 and legal fees, almost on the second anniversary of the event.

CASE 51: ROYALTY IN THE RANKS

Every case is a story. The major outlines rarely change, and even when they do, I alert the attorneys and invite them to discharge me if my testimony might prove harmful. But peeling the onion of complex, tawdry, painful human interactions always produces shocking disclosures.

It is January 27, 2002, in San Francisco, just after midnight. A thirty-six-year-old white male in a sunflower hat and hoisting a large brass drum is crossing a street. Props for stage production. Two cops allege he was stopping traffic, drunk, and banging his drum. Two housemates with him discreetly leave. The male is cuffed, arrested, and transported to county jail although he is injured and bleeding. The cops charge him with resisting arrest, public intoxication, and jay walking. He is released several hours later, after being cited. He is five foot three and 135 pounds.

I am always keenly interested in the prosecutor's response. These are usually elected officials with finely honed instincts. This one dismissed the charges to a community resolution board, which threw out the case entirely. A classic example of hand-offs of unwanted items.

The police report is redolent of disorderly descriptions: cars slamming brakes, going against the light, banging drum, failing to comply with police orders to desist, et cetera. The man even "reached into his waist band," presumably to extricate an AK47. A struggle and a takedown. Routine boilerplate to justify any actions. Yet curiously, no reference to any effects of alcohol (slurred speech, odor, staggering, et cetera) and no test for it in the blood; no injuries to the cops; no weapon found.

The man is described as violently kicking and spitting, necessitating his being kneed and placed in ankle restraints. The required entry into the use-of-force log was made by the responding sergeant. The drummer spent two weeks at home because of injuries to his legs.

The man sought my favorite advocate, Dennis Cunningham, who rapidly flushed out another case, occurring six months later, July 23, 2002, involving the central officer in the drum case—amazingly, a probationer. A cardinal rule of that status is caution. The aggressiveness in both cases defied logic.

The later case is another reminder that people act oddly, but odd behavior is not a crime.

A man is moving back to San Francisco with his goods in his car. He asks permission to park in a lot and gets it. He overstays his welcome, has lost his keys, is acting strangely, and the cops are called, around 6:50 p.m.

The offender is slight (140 pounds), white, thirtyish; the responding cops are, putting it gently, "large men." The offender is questioned and probably found wanting, attitude-wise. He is cuffed, for "officer safety," and protests. He has a driver's license, which he'd produced. He is placed in a bar/arm restraint and taken to the ground, face down, a painful business. He objects and reports his head is repeatedly pounded on the ground. He allegedly resists. He is gay. He is called "faggot" by the officer. The offender suffers severe cuts, scrapes, bruises, and a sprained wrist, as well as two broken ribs and a punctured lung.

The police report that he'd tried to go for the cops' gun. He was charged with the felony of attempting to take the firearm, assaulting a police officer, and resisting arrest. The Superior Court of California dismissed the first two charges. The man served three months in jail, although he had no criminal convictions in connection with this event.

In an amazing string of actions, the officer, while off-duty, assaulted two young males to steal their food, with other officers, in what became famous as the "Fajitagate" scandal just four months later. An incredible year, and a probationer at that. The investigation was notable for its failures and unwonted carelessness; the officers were not tested for alcohol until hours after the incident. And there were other incidents dotting the record. An incomprehensible spree. But these were the highlights triggering the amazing disclosures to come.

Typically, police events proceeded on a mangled but understandable path. Familiar territory. But a probationer acting in this outrageous manner, and repeatedly? That was new. As I studied the new case, its outlines came clearer, and, as often happened, Shakespeare had the answer. This was the young prince in Henry IV, cavorting with his Falstaffs. Only this guy was not destined for greatness. Still, he was a prince, the son of the SFPD's number two, assistant chief Alex Fagan Sr. Appropriately, the cop is junior.

With the two suits came a series of revelations that could be grasped only knowing Alex Fagan Jr.'s peculiar situation. So peculiar, in fact, that the alleged cover-up of "Fajitagate" led to the indictments of the police chief, the assistant chief (the cop's father), and other brass. It was an unsustainable charge but emblematic of the organizational realities the officer brought with him. "Bad news" was clearly etched on his forehead. The lieutenant first assigned to investigate Fajitagate was summarily transferred before turning over every rock in the case.

Officer Fagan Jr., it was revealed, had sixteen reportable use-of-force incidents in his thirteen-month tenure. Some of the persons he arrested had to be hospitalized. His probation was extended, but he was ultimately dismissed for failing to complete it—a fig leaf. He is a defendant in three other civil cases besides these two. His path is strewn with arrests, assaults, hospitalizations, and, finally, lawsuits. In a predictable aftermath, the officer was reported to have engaged in a violent altercation with his father in a Scottsdale, Arizona, hotel, on March 25, 2004, and to have assaulted the hotel manager as well.

Given the absolutely stunning actions of Fagan on the force, I expected a pre-police background dotted with warning signs. We fought for his personnel folder and finally received the thorough and complete document. Another surprise: It was clean, reflecting a possibly troublesome but not disabling drinking problem (he was cited for seeking to buy liquor with a fake ID as a teenager, and self-described as getting drunk ten to twelve times in the last year); an unprepossessing employment history of sales in sporting goods stores, et cetera; a driving record reflecting a speeding ticket, some recent summonses, and two accidents; minimal marijuana use (twice in 1994); no military service; one credit blemish; and about eighty college credits with poor grades. He was, apparently, a formidable athlete. He passed a polygraph, arriving ten minutes late for an interview with investigator. His psychological assessment defined him as "marginally suitable." Rated mostly moderate and "not significant" in scales.

I was taken aback by Fagan Jr.'s relatively clean slate. I'd have hired him.

Demonstrating the infectious nature of his actions Fagan managed to involve disparate officers in his escapades, many of whom are being sued, criminally prosecuted or both. He was, to his colleagues, a sort of latter day Typhoid Mary. But they did go along, didn't they? Ultimately his escapades enfolded the very top of the agency in his spider's web.

So we had a case of an officer whose sense of entitlement was such as to permit the thought he had carte blanche to pursue any whim or dictate of his volatile temper. And it appeared to surface only when he donned the uniform and holstered the gun.

One witness's deposition reflects rumors of Fagan Sr.'s drinking and run-ins with the California Highway Patrol. It isn't hard to figure where the feeling of having joined a fight club came from.

But the biggest jolt was a true anomaly. Up until the case's most traumatic development we might hold the assaults, mendacities, and abuses to be little more than the protected excesses of a favored child, albeit a little wild. All other police agencies protected their own, tolerated thumpers, and showered favors on insiders. What made this case distinctly different were the actions of a supervisor who actually thought her duty was to monitor and correct the behaviors of her charges.

Sergeant Vickie Joy Stansberry's four-and-a-half-page memo of September 19, 2002, to her captain proved perhaps the most surprising document I'd ever seen. That it was not ever really acted on simply enhanced my amazement. The police's very own "Zimmerman telegram."

Stansberry describes an incident occurring the previous day, September 18, 2002, at nearly 7:00 p.m., involving a man on a bus. Knowing Fagan Jr.'s history and worried over the tenor of the radio traffic (a call for an ambulance), she responded. She observed Fagan and his partner standing over a suspect with "a large bump, with an open laceration on his left forehead." Blood ran down his face. He was rear cuffed. The suspect chimed off. Fagan kicked him in the leg and had to be restrained from further assault. The officers claimed the man had to be escorted off a bus because he was drunk and combative. He stumbled, fell forward, and struck his head on a tree, according to the cops.

The sergeant observed a heated exchange between Fagan and the seated suspect. She ordered Fagan away and he said the unthinkable—"no"—several times. She called for the response of a lieutenant but the two working, correctly guessing the scenario, didn't answer.

The pacing and shouting and threats and refusals to obey continued. "I'm going to fucking kill you," Fagan said to the suspect. Another struggle ensued and the suspect was hobbled. Fagan refused the sergeant's orders and challenged her to "write him up." A crowd was observing this drama. More truculence followed as the sergeant fought for control over a charge who admitted he had "a problem with authority." In her car Fagan continued to shout at her. She counseled him as to the "inappropriateness of his actions." I had never seen a case of such documented insubordination. The sergeant reported the incident to her lieutenant and to the captain the next day.

In her devastating memo she describes another incident, on August 18, 2002, 10:50 p.m., in which Fagan's partner, in a mistaken response, shot a dog. Fagan again talked over the sergeant's commands and had to be reminded of his lack of respect.

Other supervisors reported to Sergeant Stansberry as to Fagan's lack of respect and officers who didn't want to work with him. This had to do with fast driving, poking persons in the chest with his finger, yelling, use of force, et cetera. She rode with him on September 10, 2002, and he made a number of gaffes, such as driving through a stop sign, showing reluctance to take a report, and other minor matters.

Failure to complete his reports was another complaint. Stansberry regularly reported these infractions to her supervisor. Then she recommended Fagan be retrained.

Huh?

Well, her depo makes the why clearer. Her captain, to whom she addresses her memo, had ordered her to recommend it when he learned she was pushing the issue and after consulting the cop's father. Imagine the consternation and conundrum created by that fateful, unprecedented memo. What to do? You couldn't, as would have been done in the past, can it, call her in, and tell her it never existed and go from there. This was 2002. People kept records and copies; there were computers and other retrievables. No, the captain did the next best thing: he ordered the retraining recommendation and kicked it upstairs.

This burning stick of dynamite exploded when someone (and the possibilities are too numerous to cite) mailed it, anonymously, to the San Francisco Chronicle, who ran a big story on February 13, 2003. I can't recall another such delicious piece of dirty laundry being aired for public delectation.

Stansberry, of course, became a pariah, a rat. She'd betrayed the code of silence. Fagan was transformed into the victim, along with his buddies. The unforgiving brotherhood in blue would never see the good she'd done or the harm Fagan and his buddies had contrived.

The lawsuits would focus everyone's attention. I later learned that the schmuck on the bus on September 18, 2001, sued. A "gold digger" of an attorney (the city lawyer's words to me in a September 13, 2005, deposition) had hunted him down and filed a suit. My examiner visibly crowed, "They lost."

Curiously the system knew just how to respond to both Sergeant Stansberry and Officer Fagan. It just had its priorities back to front. As if to confirm its instincts it had also defanged the one other supervisor seemingly interested in getting to the truth of "Fajitagate." Perfect consistency, but of a self-protecting sort that sacrificed the public's safety for the preservation of wrongdoers in the ranks.

The "parker" case wound its way through the system. By 2007 I'd submitted three reports, been deposed (six hours), and awaited the next step. The case eventually went to trial. I'd warned attorney Cunningham that the plaintiff needed guidance as to his behavior and testimony on the stand. No one took my advice. I testified forcefully. We lost. The jury found for the defendants and I could not bring myself to send a bill. I admired Cunningham enormously and the guy never got rich doing these cases.

CASE 52: BY STARTING WELL, ENDING BADLY

Hard experience and serious mistakes for most of which I escaped accountability through dumb luck taught me that police work requires flexibility. Fixed truths are few and far between. A plastic, creative approach, rooted in principles, often works best. This is a key reason that I advocated study of the classics rather than procedural manuals, although such exhortations brought no discernible adjustments.

Managing large crowds, demonstrations, parades, picketings, and such require massaging the challenges creatively. Concessions and restrictions should be guided by the circumstance, size of crowd, temper, number of cops, and other variables. Sloppy work and textbook results are neither achievable nor to be expected. The police planners need to be nimble. Minimize the harm; protect the glass; isolate and target troublemakers; negotiate with the leaders; try to anticipate next moves; remain flexible; and never pen in a crowd, allowing no escape. This has the same effect as sealing a pressure cooker; it generates tension and the potential for explosiveness. Society needs its safety valves.

America's March 19, 2003, attacks on Iraq came too late for protesters to organize and rally, so they concentrated on marshaling their forces the next day. And it was raining anyway, a cop's best friend after snow.

A polyglot group of students, workers, retirees, and militants gathered at Federal Plaza in Chicago in the afternoon for a protest rally. They had not secured a permit, but these were devices to allocate public spaces in an orderly, first-come, first-served basis, rather than hard, legal requirement. At its height, around 6:30 p.m., there were an estimated ten thousand demonstrators, many of whom began a march following speeches. An unpredictable and kinetic dynamic is thus set in motion, calling for a creative response from the Chicago Police Department. They met the challenge splendidly, halting and diverting traffic as they allowed the marchers to take over busy Lake Shore Drive. There was no plan or route and the marchers numbered in the thousands. They defined it as a peaceful protest, but the cops saw them as defiant law breakers. Still, a rough negotiation was maintained, enabling the marchers to protest and the police to maintain a semblance of order.

The denouement came as the marchers wheeled toward Michigan Avenue, Chicago's Broadway. The cops felt the need to interdict this plan and set growing phalanxes of cops to block access. I thought this was appropriate and would have given the police commanders sterling grades for their coping up to this time.

There is no doubt the marchers broke the law by blocking traffic and taking over the street.

There is some confusion as to whether the police originally acceded to a march down Michigan, but definitely chose to prevent it. Now came a blunder that the cop leadership actually thought was a brilliant ploy. How do I know? A police document.

On March 26, 2003, a detective was assigned to interview the commanders at the scenes to record an event in which 543 demonstrators were arrested. One police car and one private vehicle were damaged, and some few vehicles graffitied and no other violence or incidents reported, except for a few clashes initiated by cops as they walked into the crowd to make arrests.

And the comments of the generals at the scene?

One reported how he'd remained at the head of the crowd, anticipating and negotiating its routes, deploying officers and ordering arrests. He was clear in his determination to keep the crowd off Michigan Avenue. His remarks, as recorded by the investigator, are models of bureaucratic persiflage.

The next commander described being at Federal Plaza and how, unable to control the suddenly marching group, adjusted and attempted to redirect his forces. He described a hares-and-hounds chase in which willful protesters resisted police orders to comply. His intent, also, was to block off Michigan Avenue. He described violence, like kicking motorist's vehicles, tearing down a fence, spray painting cars, et cetera. He reported the crowd as "stopped" at Chicago Avenue, where the arrests began.

The next commander, John Risley, described his attempts to reroute the marchers. He painted a touching picture of crying children within trapped vehicles. A fire station and water-pumping facility were blocked. He offered a hint of police action when he reported that protestors "who ceased their illegal activities were allowed to leave the area in small groups." I found this quizzical. How could he possibly decide who should stay and who should leave?

The next supervisor reported the same chaotic scene, reiterated the complaint of others that the protesters lacked a permit, and directed his forces to block access to Michigan Avenue. Demonstrators with "anarchist banners," black and red, broke off and were followed by the police. His is the most extensive and complete account of the action. His big mistake came when he deployed his forces to block access to Michigan and sealed the escape route enabling his officers to initiate the arrest process. The fateful words, crowed to reflect a brilliant flanking maneuver, were, "The protesters were now boxed in from the East and West." He makes clear only those clearly innocent and caught up in the event were allowed to leave, and only after establishing their bona fides.

The next commander, Joseph Griffin, described how two teams "effectively boxed the crowd in."

The rest describe mayhem not observed on the four extensive videotapes of events produced by news organizations and the police.

Much is made of such comments as "Fuck the police" and "We're taking the streets."

The descriptions are at odds with recorded vandalism or injuries, as well as with the videotapes—an invaluable recent adjustment to these inquiries. One lieutenant reported being struck on the back of the right thigh.

The approximate 543 arrests (plus detainees) were divided into three categories:

200 to 225 detained one-and-a-half to three hours and allowed to leave without charges. Not arrested according to police.

225 seized, detained, arrested into custody, released without charges.

300 seized, detained, arrested into custody, charged with reckless conduct. Charges dismissed in their favor.

Not one was charged with resistance to arrest or any act of violence and not one was convicted of anything. The police clearly lacked probable cause for arrests and used the tactic of seizure merely as a means of illegally controlling a crowd that was penned in, by the police, with minimal opportunity to exit.

What began as a very large, peaceful protest of the Iraq War declined into a police-inspired debacle.

The police handled the demonstration at Federal Plaza very well, permitting the expression of grievances by about ten thousand participants, listening to speeches. The launching of a march upon the city's streets represented a major challenge for the police commanders, which they met splendidly. They adjusted, deployed, and massaged the march to constitute minimal disruption while protecting protestors' rights. The question of permit got raised later by police commanders, but it was never really a factor.

The descriptions of the marchers' actions and the police responses convinced me that the cops were handling this just right. The police sensitivity to a march along Michigan Avenue was well founded and I supported their view and blocking actions.

Now began the two major and impermissible police blunders: boxing in of demonstrators and the indiscriminate and unjustified arrests. The first trapped peaceful demonstrators and passers-by in circumstances that might easily have stirred a panic or worse. Releases were few and measured. It was a miracle that a disaster didn't occur. I've never heard of corralling a large crowd like this with virtually no release of pent-up tensions.

The bankruptcy and insincerity of the arrest process becomes clear from the outcome. The Chicago PD made no effort to tie any arrests to a specific act of criminality. Arrests were made simply to remove demonstrators from the scene. There were neither orders to disperse nor opportunity to do so. The extensive videos depict peaceful scenes totally at odds with police alarms and reported incidents (or non-incidents) of violence or vandalism. There is no notice to disperse nor any visible effort to allow the crowd, now clearly exhausted, from dissipating.

It is possible that elements within the crowd—a small minority, masked, carrying red and black banners, et cetera, a group that caused problems in the World Trade Organization meeting in Seattle years earlier—were there to create mischief. The cops were certainly right to be concerned and to monitor the group's actions.

Police deployment at Federal Plaza and the march that followed were excellent. The penning in of a large group is unprecedented, in my experience, and dangerous. The mass and indiscriminate arrests cannot be justified, as their resolution makes clear. Many innocents were swept up in this round-up.

The police started well and ended badly. A classic case of turning a victory into a defeat.

In another irony the city hired an expert who'd been a high-ranking member of the Seattle Police Department and very likely involved in that city's disastrous handling of another protest march that cost that chief his job. This expert finds the police actions "reasonable and proper." He cites they had no permit, and divines that the marchers "intended to march on Lake Shore Drive" without offering any evidence of this motive. He reasonably concludes that Michigan Avenue should be protected and describes police movements to preclude it. He applauds police reactions, the orders to arrest, and the need to preserve access to a hospital. He cites such breaches of law as disorderly conduct, blocking traffic, reckless conduct, and "perhaps others."

He somewhat fudges, but ensnares himself when he holds that "it was proper for the police to then contain this group of marchers" and release them slowly. No comment on the arrests ordered or of a "corral." He commends the lack of violence and the absence of damage to public or private property—in sharp distinction with police hysteria over the dangers faced.

The expert then genuinely decries the failure to follow the Chicago PD's own "mass arrest procedures" but chalks it up to "part of the circumstances." C'est la vie. The police, he adds later, "did not do a very good job of documenting criminal violations, so that arrestees could be effectively prosecuted." But, he failed to add, "not even one?" He did add, however, that this "doesn't mean that the arrests were improper or that they lacked probable cause."

At his report's end I felt he'd made my case. Why hire me when they had his analysis?

Why did the Chicago PD begin ordering mass, indiscriminate arrests when the demonstrators were "contained," exhausted, and unthreatening? Well, probably because they could, and probably because they were pissed. A rather large and unnecessary example of the brass—one of whom became chief—applying the attitude test.

The demonstrators sued and the people I'd worked with on the "Killer Tots" case (*Case 36: Killer Tots*) took it on as a cause and contacted me. As of 2007, more than three years later, the case percolated along in the federal courts. The city inexplicably, spent a huge amount of energy battling the class action status of the suit, subdivided into the three groups described earlier. Was this the legal equivalent of the battle of Korea's Pork Chop Hill, where American commanders finally deduced that the Chinese were testing America's will to fight by taking and retaking a meaningless military objective, at great costs?

I met with three of the lawyers from the People's Law Office for dinner on September 13, 2005, as I was in Chicago for a deposition involving the bad behavior of a rookie cop

(*Case 51: Royalty in the Ranks*). They were puzzled that arresting officers invented fictitious names for officers on the police forms prepared on each prisoner.

Two reasons: first, no cop is going to defy a commander's orders to arrest the demonstrators, yet they knew they were asked to follow illegal orders and feared they'd be sued and lose their homes. So they resolved their dilemma by obeying the orders to arrest and escaped legal responsibility by putting false arresting officers' names on the arrest reports.

As of 2007 the case crept toward resolution. I thought the defendant's battle over classifications a smokescreen. The real question usually centered on their motion to dismiss. These skirmishes lay ahead.

The case was fought hard by the city. When they moved to dismiss on the basis that the cops have a tough job to do and need the court's support, it was granted. The case was thrown out.

The People's Law Office appealed. I urged them strongly to do so.

American's smartest judge – in my opinion – Richard Posner – reversed the decision and sent it back for trial.

The city faced a very embarrassing possibility. I was poised to testify that I'd never encountered – or even heard of – police officers falsifying their names on arrest reports – a sure sign they knew they was making false arrests.

The City of Chicago caved and agreed to a settlement of $ 6.2 million, to be paid in 2013. They owe me $12,000.

How sweet it is.

CASE 53: TREE HUGGERS

The most important case I worked on, from every perspective, was *Bari v. Held*, which ostensibly began on May 24, 1990, when a bomb exploded under the driver's seat of a car occupied by Judi Bari and Darryl Cherney. But the roots of this incident go back many years and need to be understood in order to grasp the meaning of the events and their aftermath.

The issues, from the first, were clear and consistent: preservation of thousand-year-old redwoods in the Pacific Northwest versus logging interests. The strike came to be known as the Timber Wars. Earth First versus large corporate interests. Each side hosted a full spectrum of elements, from the accommodating to the adamantly, and sometimes violently, opposed. An understanding of the factors and forces required insight and sophisticated analysis—qualities among the first to be sacrificed in these controversies.

Earth First was regarded as a radical group of tree huggers, but even within these there were deep divisions. Judi Bari, for example, was engaged in a vigorous debate supporting peaceful resistance against militant elements demanding violent reprisals against loggers. In March 1990 she had publicly renounced tree spiking—embedding spikes in trees that would snap chain saws and send the pieces flying, often seriously injuring loggers. Her arrests had been of the civil disobedience sort rather than involving violence.

Darryl Cherney had been arrested for trying to place a banner on the Golden Gate Bridge. The group undertook such actions as surrounding a truck loaded with logs, with some chaining themselves to the timber. And corporate offices were bombed. So there was violence as well as hot rhetoric driving the polemics. And within Earth First there was a lively debate centering on the forms of protest, but broadening also to include economic theories of preservation, exploitation, and distribution.

In August 1989 Bari's car was rammed from behind by a logging truck that sped off after her car hurtled off the road. Her car was totaled. Three activists, including Bari, and four children went to the hospital with minor injuries.

An outside observer—the FBI, for example—might be excused for suspecting Earth First of criminality given the 1990 pamphlet signed by Darrell Cherney (misspelling his name) and containing boasts of sabotage, stealing, and doing whatever possible to "fuck up the working of the mega machines." This pamphlet may well have been the work of a not-so-clever forger and serves to illustrate the confusion occasioned by the plethora of documents flying through this controversy. Another Earth First notice, dated April 13, 1990, speaks of their intent "to spike trees, monkey wrench (any form of sabotage), and even resort to violence if necessary." It was signed "Arcata," presumably meaning one who prefers a simple, rural life.

Attracted like flying iron filaments to a magnet, fringe elements on both sides enthusiastically joined in with threats, anonymous abuse, and assaults during confrontations. A deeper layer occasionally surfaced, also cloaked in anonymity, but apparently willing to join violence to the threats. And, to add to the cassoulet continuously aboil, there were charges and countercharges of forged press releases, pamphlets, letters, and documents. Winding one's way through the labyrinth required an expertise and objectivity few possessed. When married to the predispositions of those to whom wishes fathered thoughts, it is easy to see how and why the mistakes made in this case occurred.

This was a case driven far more by political conviction than simple malice. The consequences, though, would not be mitigated by these truths. A shadowy figure got Bari to pose with an Uzi in her Earth First shirt and the photo wound up being sent anonymously to the Ukiah, California, police. Among the ideological inspirations for Earth First were the International Workers of the World, the mythic Wobblies of socialist–anarchist–trade unionist ideals. There were violent elements on both sides. The most blatant included such clashes as Bari's car incident, blows exchanged at demonstrations, the nearly fatal chainsaw accident on a logger who struck a buried spike, and a bomb explosion outside a lumber company's office in Cloverdale, California, on May 9, 1990.

It was a time of militant, radical, sometimes violent activity. Power line towers were toppled on the notion that radiating electricity was harming livestock and humans. Animal rights activists poured blood, freed laboratory creatures, and invaded experimental laboratories. Environmentalists camped high-up in trees to frustrate loggers. Local police agencies responded to or monitored their events but the only official body developing a national perspective on these activities was the FBI. It was natural and inevitable that police agencies would look to the feds for a perspective and for guidance.

In 1990 Redwood Summer loomed. It was to be a series of nonviolent actions of civil disobedience, concerts, picketings, road blockings, sit-ins, and related events that would result in some arrests but which were planned, by such as Judi Bari and Darryl Cherney, to be passive and safe enough to attract pacifist elements. Bari and Cherney had been pleasantly surprised by the appeal of the issue to nonviolent protesters who were passionate about the environment. They saw Earth First as broadening its appeal beyond its radical image.

Bari, a divorced mother of two girls, had been romantically involved with Cherney, but that was now over and they were loving friends. Cherney, a bachelor, was a sort of balladeer/troubadour who composed lyrics for the ecology movement. Bari joined him on stage with her violin. She was a radical feminist who had little faith in the nurturing instincts of the human male, but who awakened to this aspect through the tender care and concern of males following this tragedy.

So, as Bari and Cherney drove south to Oakland on May 23, 1990, their intention was to enlist the support of Seeds of Peace, with whom they'd have an evening meeting. Seeds was an organization of dedicated young activists who provided logistical support at demonstrations. They'd worked together in the past but this was to be an attempt to secure their aid for Redwood Summer. Seeds would provide tents, tables, water, food, monitors, and such. They would participate only if reassured as to the peaceful nature of protests.

And so they met and discussed that summer's actions and their participation. Sympathizers put them up to save hotel costs and such. They met up on the morning of May 24, 1990, rehearsed, and decided to return to the Seeds of Peace house to play some more. Judi's play was rusty. They didn't know the way and were led by a friend in another car, who remained back as they got on the route. Bari was driving her 1981 Subaru when, at 11:50 a.m., a bomb exploded under her seat. The car rolled slowly and stopped.

Bari and Cherney were removed to the hospital. Her pelvis was crushed and she suffered internal and external injuries. Cherney had only minor injuries. The Oakland police had little knowledge of, or experience with, Earth First. In any case the use of a bomb made it a federal, as well as a state crime. Now began a series of official actions that can only be understood as the panicky embracing of a solution to a serious problem. Pressure built. The press probed. Answers were needed.

The FBI knew Earth First, or thought they did. Rarely has the dictum "a little knowledge is a dangerous thing" proved truer. A meeting was held that evening in which the FBI told the Oakland PD that they knew this group. Earth Firsters were ecoterrorists, engaged in crimes. Bari and Cherney spontaneously uttered incriminating statements about "it was a bomb" and "someone threw a bomb in the car." The feds said the bomb was behind the seat and in plain view, and a bunch of nails in the seat (Bari made her living as a carpenter) were "identical" to the ones placed with the bomb.

The Oakland police arrested Bari in the hospital, that same night, charging her with possessing an explosive device. They charged Cherney with the same crime the next day. The announcement of the arrests produced a sensation. Headlines shouted; anchors solemnly intoned the official version. Citizens were relieved. How the res gestae (spontaneous, incriminating utterance) comments amounted to a confession would remain a mystery. The bomb was under the seat and covered with a blue towel and not visible. The nails were of a common variety and could not be definitively matched to the bomb implements.

The terrorist label set a series of actions in motion in which events were interpreted conveniently and made to fit preconceived notions. No one questioned the evidence, except the people asked to present it in court. The district attorney did not want to enter a forum all that naked. The police pressed. Additional evidence was needed. Two visits availed nothing. The cops then secured search warrants.

I have always been grateful for whatever legal requirements mandate documentation. There is nothing quite like examining a written account of an event to establish legitimacy of actions. In my view this case turned on the Oakland Police Department's application for a search warrant on May 25, 1990. In one warrant (and they are all similar) for the complex occupied by Bari and her estranged husband, the document promises to find evidence of explosive devices and their accoutrements. The first evidence of incrimination offered is Bari's statement that "a bomb went off in my car." Cherney is cited as saying this was an assassination attempt on him, but the guilty admission offered was, "We are political activists with Earth First and they threw a bomb at us."

The sergeant requesting the warrant added that he responded to the scene, examined evidence, and "was advised by these FBI agents that the bomb/device was on the floorboard behind the driver's seat when it detonated." The sergeant was briefed by an FBI expert at the scene who examined the bomb's remains and said that a "separate bag of nails was discovered in the vehicle that are identical to the nails taped to the explosive device." The expert also described "a large hole in the rear seat floorboard immediately behind the driver's seat."

Much was suggested by an elaborate description of a violin and two guitar cases carried to Bari's car the morning of May 24. That there are prior references to their having sung a song before leaving doesn't seem to inspire exculpatory thoughts. The judge would be left to guess as to the content of these cases. Shades of Al Capone! There is a reference to Earth First's reputation "of violence and sabotage."

The sergeant "believes that Bari and Cherney are members of a violent terrorist group involved in the manufacture and placing of explosive devices." He also believes that they "were transporting an explosive device in their vehicle when the device exploded. Cherney's explanation of the incident is inconsistent with the physical evidence found at the scene." (This was true; a bomb had not been thrown at them. What a damning admission.) The sergeant further believes they will find material "used for the manufacture or storage of explosive devices" if the warrant is granted. Night service was requested. He also requested the power to search Seeds of Peace house.

The warrants were granted and executed. A top-to-bottom search for explosives, wires, nails, or anything that might tie Bari or Cherney to a bomb produced nothing.

The flaws were egregious and deliberate. The Oakland Police relied on the FBI's misplacing the epicenter of the explosion by moving the impact core backward, to the floor board, rather than under the seat. The damage to the seat itself was conveniently ignored or fudged. Even Bari's injuries—direct impact in the pelvis—confirmed the falsehood. Holding that the nails were "identical" was another proof of federal malice as well as the blanket imputation of terrorism attributed to Earth First.

The search warrants proved the case of malicious prosecution. It would be the second leg of my rationale for taking the case. The first was the arrest of Bari and Cherney without a trace of probable cause pointing to their guilt. In depositions the Oakland police made clear they didn't know anything about Earth First and had been fed incriminating tidbits by the Iago-like federals. In such cases "advisers" frequently fade into the background when the shit hits the fan, but this time the Oakland cops kept the FBI at the center of the case.

By the end of May 24, 1990, the FBI had sold the Oakland PD on the menace presented by Bari, Cherney, and Earth First. Amazingly, although they swayed a judge to sign a mendacious search warrant application, they weren't able to similarly spook the DA, who felt the need for some kind of evidence before proceeding. A quaint idea.

The idea, though, became so fixed that even after the bankruptcy of the theory linking Bari and Cherney to the bomb was definitely established, the federal and local authorities did nothing to detect the actual terrorists who tried to murder the car's occupants. The investigation began and halted with false arrests and malicious, fruitless searches. The importance of the lesson—to secure evidence and proceed methodically—cannot be overstated, yet officialdom often succumbs to the temptations of pressured moments.

Caught with their hands in the cookie jar, the FBI expressed shock, shock, at the thought that they had anything to do with the arrests and searches.

My task was simple: to determine whether the actions of the Oakland Police were reasonable and how reliable was the basis of their beliefs. A familiar position. How many detectives had I thrown out of my office for wanting to act against wrongs, but, inconveniently, lacked evidence?

By the time I testified I had a box about 9 x 20 inches chock full of documents, reports, depositions, articles, and such that reflected the entire case from beginning to end. Conspicuous by its absence was any record of the sort of careful investigation such an atrocious crime should have inspired in any agency remotely interested in pursuing justice. They had their theory, and by God they'd not be diverted, whatever the evidence.

The case was bizarre beyond imagining, yet weirder elements kept popping up.

The Lord's Avenger, for instance. A letter postmarked May 29, 1990, and addressed to Mr. Geniella, Press Democrat, 215 W. Standley St., Ukiah, CA 95482, and signed "The Lord's Avenger," contained remarkable assertions. The two-page, typewritten letter was to become the central mystery of a complex case. It begins with the claim, "I built . . . the bomb," interlaced with biblical bombast aimed at the poisonous, satanic abortion views of Judi Bari. The anti-abortion harangue continues, spewing venom at her blasphemy and spreading to the lumber issue. And so concludes the first page, a routine, religious rant of little special significance.

On page 2 he describes the Cloverdale bomb at a lumber office, claiming to have placed it (exploded on May 9, 1990, with no injuries). It is then that the letter takes on special importance as the writer explains, in knowing and excruciating detail, the precise makeup of that bomb, even to its failures and the reasons there for. The precise mixture of gas and oil, as well as every component, were patiently described. The work reeked authenticity and every element matched actual events and circumstances.

Then he describes putting the bomb in Bari's car and when. This is about thirty-six hours before the explosion and throws into question his/her veracity, but the precision and accuracy of detail, down even to the blue towel covering and concealing the device, could have come only from the fashioner of this complex time bomb. The Avenger ascribes the delay to the hand of the watch inexplicably stopping and somehow starting again two days later, probably from the car's motion.

The note concluded with hell-fire admonitions, dread, and triumphalism. The writer promises to destroy others of Judi Bari's ilk and concludes, "I have spoken. I am the Lord's Avenger."

Remarkable document and almost surely the work of the actual bomber.

The date, five days after the explosion, makes it possible that Bari or an ally could have written it, but the vituperation is sulphurous to the point of raising doubt. What is indisputable is the importance of a document whose author was never identified and in whose identity very likely lay the key to this mystery. Typewriter analysis would've helped, but it wasn't employed. No real effort was made to link the missive to a series of suspects provided by Judi Bari. She was clearly not seen as being of any possible help in identifying the culprit. My view was that she ought to have been central. Feisty, intelligent, knowledgeable, and determined, she would have been a great asset to any inquiry. The authorities didn't think so.

I'd worked with Bari's lawyer, Dennis Cunningham, on the Attica Prison case (*Case 31: Attica Prison*) and others and greatly admired him. He took on unpopular cases, drove beaters, wore threadbare suits, and generally looked a step or two removed from homelessness. I liked his thorough-going, bulldoggish, yet seemingly distracted approach. He'd stand by the lectern, drop notes, seem ruffled and confused, and stumble about in his questioning, but all of this concealed a laser focus that bore in on the key issues. I'd had lots of dealings with Dennis Cunningham, and he just seemed to be no form and all substance— my favorite combination.

Judi Bari with Darryl Cherney sued the FBI and the Oakland PD for the public humiliation and disgrace attendant on the arrests and searches. I was hired in December 1995 and had lunch with Cunningham and Bari in San Francisco, having already agreed to take the case. (I never met Darryl Cherney.) Her involvement was both crucial and central. It also illustrated the value so cavalierly cast away by the Oakland PD.

In later months I was shocked by Judi's active participation in the questioning of witnesses during depositions. I never saw any client so immersed, and so usefully, in a case. The remarkable thing was how patient, tolerant, and accepting was Cunningham over behavior almost any other lawyer would have found offensively interfering. I suggested approaches, focused on the arrests and searches, prepared reports, and awaited being deposed.

The FBI and OPD fought hard. The case was in federal court. They sought dismissals, introduced motions to limit or exclude testimony, and fought my involvement. The briefs flew so fast and furious that I wondered as to their meaning. I finally concluded that no assistant U.S. attorney wanted to lose this case on their watch because of the attendant publicity and fought to delay a trial.

The case was redolent of COINTELPRO, the Counter Intelligence Program, a thoroughly discredited initiative of J. Edgar Hoover in the 1950s, when he was director of the FBI. COINTELPRO was the apotheosis of Hoover's assaults on actual or imagined subversive elements. How its existence was discovered is of the stuff of Le Carre novels. It began with a burglary—what the FBI would've called a "Black Bag Job," if the positions were reversed—only this time the break-in was of an FBI resident office in Media, Pennsylvania, on March 8, 1971, by what were believed to be antiwar activists.

The burglars were particularly selective in their thefts and provocative in their actions. They went for the security files. And they waited, undoubtedly creating consternation among Hoover's minions. After two weeks they began mailing selected photocopies of documents to senators, congressmen, and journalists. They revealed the scope and breadth of the FBI's reach, mainly into legal, innocent political activities. Trusted employees were revealed to be FBI informants. Black student unions and a Boy Scout leader were targets. Wiretaps on Black Panthers were revealed. A "dovish" Congressman's daughter was investigated.

The missives dropped like a Chinese water torture, revealing the full scope of the FBI's broad interests. It showed the agency expending huge energies monitoring the actions of citizens engaged in democracy's business. This was Big Brother revealed. And they couldn't solve the case. The revelations proved a devastating blow to the FBI's image and continue to haunt it to this day.

This case demonstrates that old habits die hard, as the FBI painted Earth First with the broad brush of subversion without bothering to distinguish the disparate elements within the environmentalists. And this was almost two decades after COINTELPRO's exposure and eighteen months after Herbert Hoover's death. It was the spirit of Hoover's COINTELPRO that guided the fatal hand behind the abuses against Judi Bari, Darryl Cherney, and Earth First.

The case staggered through the court system, piling pages on pages of briefs, a legal steeplechase in which the feds adopted every stratagem short of trial.

I was deposed on December 11–12, 1995. By then I was outraged at the FBI's Mephistophelean tactics and Oakland's gullible acceptance and willingness to follow this evil counsel. My testimony reflected my outrage. I was scathing in my criticism but concentrated on the arrests and search warrants. The attorneys for the defendants, representing the FBI and OPD, tried to tempt me into expanding my charges. This would have led me to indefensibly shallow shoals. I resisted. Yes, this was the only basis for my sense that they had acted inappropriately.

The transcript is dotted with Judi Bari's intercessions, patiently accepted by Cunningham. They made a great team because of her sharpness and his forbearance.

Cross examinations by the opposition, whether in trial or deposition, are fierce combat. The other side's lawyers work on diminishing your stature, credibility, and qualifications. Who wants to defend his status as an expert, on anything?

As to the location of the bomb in Bari's car, I said the FBI agent "told Sergeant Chenault something that was factually incorrect at the time, and that he should have known was factually incorrect." Later I added that "characterizing the separate bag of nails as being identical to the nails taped—I find that wrong." This was "complete overreach" by the investigator trying to secure a search warrant. I went on: "I'm not prepared to say it was based on good faith, either. I think it's an attempt to secure a warrant without a basis for it." I questioned the "attempt to persuade a judge that you're dealing with terrorists and criminals." I said that saying Bari and Cherney had a reputation for violence was wrong and "irresponsible." I thought they'd led the judge "down the primrose path."

The deposition centered on my testimony that the cops had had no basis for the arrests of Cherney and Bari and this was confirmed by the prosecutor's repeated declinations to charge them. But it was the search warrant application that I attacked as being "simply outrageous" and "a figment of his [the applying detective's] imagination and an invention. . . . Before you can secure a document to which you must swear, it ought to be true, and it ought to be based on evidence . . . neither of which is the case here."

I resisted their attorneys' attempt to get me to go beyond the few specifics I was attacking. To succumb would have mired me in a series of questions I'd certainly flounder among. By focusing on the factors I was confident about, I kept the battle within an arena I understood. At the end I think it was pretty clear to the defendants that I meant to take them on to the limit. They'd been unable to shake me and I'd gotten my views fully and dramatically on the record. The defendants then set to further delay, combined with continued efforts to exclude or limit my testimony.

The lawyers continued their appeals, motions, delays, and strategies, thereby postponing the day of judgment by years. It would be a dozen before vindication arrived. And the case dropped me.

Judi Bari died on March 2, 1997, of breast cancer. She was forty-seven and was survived by her daughters Lisa, then sixteen, and Jessica, then eleven, as well as her sisters, *New York Times* reporter Gina Kolata and Martha Bari, as well as her parents.

Her *New York Times* obituary described a feisty and determined environmental activist. She was credited with likening Earth First's efforts to the civil rights movement of 1964, broadening its appeal beyond the more radical, monkey-wrenching, tree-spiking elements. The *Times* further described her—and this was before the civil trial—as a moderate and a pacifist. She'd been a labor organizer and relocated to Northern California in 1979, working as a carpenter. Her interest in preserving trees lit up when she was casually told that the siding on a house came from a thousand-year-old redwood. The car-bomb explosion was treated neutrally in the obituary and the civil suit was described as being "in progress." Right.

Civil suits, however, like corporations, don't die with the demise of principals. Bari's death dissolved a partnership with Dennis Cunningham that seemed indissoluble. Other forces, confusing to me, came into play. I was contacted by a lawyer who said he was taking over the case. The executors of Bari's estate, which had control over the suit, seemed to be on the outs with Dennis.

I said I wouldn't work with anyone but Dennis, who had, after all, hired me. The lawyer said this was all OK with Dennis and I should carry on. I needed to hear this directly. Dennis called and asked me to continue my work and he was fine with it all. In later years and other cases Dennis usually remarked on how I'd "looked after his back." He returned to the case as his replacement relocated to New York. But the months and years continued to pass and a succession of U.S. attorneys dodged this bullet and escaped judgment. Finally a trial date was set for April 9, 2002, or almost a dozen years after the event.

I entered this presumably final phase with no sense of triumph, being well aware of the sympathies of naïve white jurors for officialdom. I warned Dennis to try for blacks and others who might have had some real experiences with the system.

I wondered that the feds and locals had made no attempt to settle the case. It seemed to me they could mitigate the risk by offering $1 million, with two-thirds going to Bari's estate and one-third to Cherney, and they might also wring the concession of confidentiality and avoid brutal publicity if they lost. They hung tough.

The trial lasted two months and scores of lawyers battled. The defendants, knowing from my deposition how positively rabid my testimony would be, worked hard to limit it and succeeded. A judge I developed less than fondness for severely restricted my answers and frustrated me totally. She'd instruct the jury on probable cause for arrest and the sufficiency of the warrants, the two central points of my testimony. So I spent a couple of hours on the stand trying to respond as the defendant's lawyers repeatedly leaped to object and the judge proceeded to warn me sternly. I felt bound in a legal straitjacket and left the stand believing that my testimony, which I thought crucial to the case, had been thoroughly diluted and suppressed.

Cunningham had wanted me to testify to the existence of a conspiracy between the feds and locals to deprive Bari and Cherney of their freedoms. I disagreed and held strictly to the premise that they'd been falsely arrested and their persons and effects unjustly searched. Bari participated via a video, taped shortly before her death. Cherney stunned onlookers by performing his song "Spike a Tree for Jesus" from the witness box. His lawyers later apologized to the jurors, in closing arguments. On the stand the defendants pointed to each other as precipitating the rush to judgment.

I awaited the results, and waited. I went to Europe for five weeks, returned, and the trial was still on. Finally it was given to the jury, who amazed me by deliberating and deliberating. Day followed day and three weeks passed. They weren't hung, just discussing the issues. Finally, after seventeen days of agony, they delivered a verdict. It was a stunning and very public defeat for the defendants. Bari's estate was awarded $2.9 million, Cherney $1.5 million. The award received nationwide publicity, from the *Los Angeles Times* to the *New York Times*.

Hugs, tears, and even placards erupted in the courtroom. The case developed into a symbol of official abuse of leftist causes and I thought the interpretation correct. It was a real blow that affirmed the rights in the Constitution.

The feds and locals expressed disappointment and considered appeals. They could not understand how the jury came to its findings considering "the evidence." The blame fell squarely on the shoulders of the FBI leaders pushing the case and the OPD leader silly enough to follow. A bulls' eye.

Cherney and especially Bari were vindicated heroically. The single-minded obsessions of the investigators allowed the bomber(s) to escape justice altogether and the authorities never got it that, even conceding the possible involvement of Bari and Cherney, they still had deep responsibilities to follow other leads.

The case had haunted me, particularly after Bari's death. It seemed important yet losable. The result could not have been more personally satisfying.

The curtain of secrecy surrounding the unexpected, happy outcome was pulled when a juror spoke out. In early July 2002, the judge lifted a gag order she'd imposed on the jurors and one immediately took to the electronic superhighway. The juror's e-mails said that the lies of the defendants were obvious and surprising and that they had to cover up the mistakes of their investigation. She was the only juror who spoke publicly at first, as four declined and five could not be reached, of the ten-member panel. But she was a beaut.

The jurors had quickly agreed that Bari and Cherney had been wronged and spent most of the time sorting out the charges, responsibilities, and awards. The trial was held in the shadow of the 9/11 terrorist attacks—a big hurdle to overcome given the defendants' charges of terrorism by the plaintiffs. Another juror later joined the public discussion, adding how unanimously all felt that the officials had violated the rights of citizen-victims in this case. Interestingly, the jurors were hung on Cherney's claim of having been falsely arrested. Incomprehensible, but a sidebar to the body of the text.

The first juror to speak out, a white woman, then revealed she was an airline ticket agent, but raised in the turmoil of foster homes in a black neighborhood where frequent police investigations were daily events. Her revelations of the dynamics in the jury room were fascinating. Not one of the jurors bought the official version that the bomb belonged to Bari or Cherney, but they had to be brought along miraculously by a white woman who had grown up black. She described how she had to educate incredulous jurors that the authorities could and did overstep legal bounds. She became the catalyst for leading them through the labyrinth of official mistakes and wrongdoing.

She, in her words, had Judi's "back." She had been deeply moved by the outpouring of love by the scores attending the trial every day, and she was going to protect someone she'd come to love. She patiently and persistently moved the jurors to the verdict, compromising downward from the $40 million she wanted to award the plaintiffs. It must have been an act of persuasion worthy of *Twelve Angry Men*. In the end her participation proved pivotal to the outcome, yet somehow accidental, chastening the egos of warriors like me who'd spent more than seven years in battle, to no particular purpose. Could America continue to rely that it would be saved by unlikely heroes?

The feds and locals finally and begrudgingly declined to appeal and paid, never apologizing or retreating from their assertions of having acted correctly. They also had to cough up legal fees, which were, I guessed, astronomical.

The case inspired Kate Coleman to write a critical analysis of Bari's life titled *The Secret Wars of Judi Bari*. The work was described as "gossip and often unflattering," relating Bari's "secret wars" with a former husband, the FBI, and other adversaries, and reveling in her celebrity. The book was published in 2005 by Encounter Books and financed by the conservative Bradley Foundation. They'd done other books critical of liberals. Judi's defenders cited hundreds of errors and falsehoods. It sparked lively encounters between the author and Bari's friends at book readings.

Dennis Cunningham's daughter, Bernadine Mellis, directed a documentary on Bari, "*The Forest for the Trees*".

I had, over the years, put in over seventy hours, not counting the deposition, which the defendants paid. But nothing happens that fast, especially cases such as this. On June 3, 2004, I got a letter from Dennis, concluding the case and enclosing a check for $14,150, and referring to a tough editorial in the *Wall Street Journal* on the verdict, accusing plaintiffs of gaming the system and of playing *Who Wants To Be a Millionaire*?

Cunningham went on to credit the influential juror, a typically generous act, and concluded with, "Thanks again, Comrade, for all your help and insight, the passion you showed to the jury, and, especially, the encouragement you always gave me. It has meant a whole lot to me, honest, and still does. It's been great working with you, and I hope we get another chance."

We would, and soon. The man represented full employment for me, not just in his cases, but in the many in which he recommended using me to other lawyers—the Central Park jogger (*Case21: The Central Park Jogger*), being the most prominent of all.

No case, however, has ever given me the satisfaction of *Bari v. Held*. The case had legs.

PART II:
CASES DECLINED, BUT
WORTH NOTING

CASE 54: MINOR VICTORIES

I've gradually come to see expert witnessing as a pretty effective way of altering police behavior on the street for the better. That reform occurs through the impetus of fear—the terror that lawsuits inspire—not only doesn't faze me, it actually confirms my view that this is the most effective route to reform.

This was substantiated around 2003, when a lawyer I didn't know called to say he had a case against two Minneapolis cops who'd abused his client. Did I want to know the cops' names? No, it made no difference to me. He sent the material and I was surprised to recognize one of the cops as having been involved in a bitter case in which he'd abused a pornographer (*Case 2: The Constitution in the Porn Parlor*). I felt the officer had lied on the stand, which pissed me off, so I examined this case with a measure of secret glee.

Two white males are finally ejected from a bar where they have been drinking. They spill into an alley. Two plainclothes cops, on patrol to quell "quality-of-life crimes," sense a violation, back their van, and catch one of the two guys urinating openly in the alley. Other patrons are exiting the bar.

A dispute evolves as the cops try to issue a citation. The guys challenge the cops to prove they are really police, even after badges are flashed. A struggle ensues in which the cops wrestle the pisser to the ground and apply a lateral vascular neck restraint to the point of his succumbing, but not before he has kicked and damaged the police van, called on the drunken oafs exiting the bar to come to his aid, and stirred up much angst until other cops respond to the call for help.

The non-pisser breaks free and flees. He returns to help his friend and interferes with the arrest and threatens the cops. The guy jumps into a cab, but the driver heeds the cop's warning to halt. The cop jumps into the cab and punches the guy into submission. With the help of other cops, the officer gets him out of the cab and cuffs and arrests him.

Both prisoners refuse medical attention and are taken to the Hennepin County jail. One is bailed out, but the pisser is still there the next day, and the arresting officers interview him and tape the exchange. In his taping he admits his acts and basically supports the details of the police version.

The documentation I received for review surprised me for containing a comprehensive account by the police by various members. Could they have been anticipating a lawsuit? I hoped the answer was yes, if it got them to document their actions.

The plaintiff's complaint was inaccurate: it failed to mention the chase, it was hysterical in its depiction of the police as being clad in camouflaged clothes, and it described a vicious assault that had no relation to the injuries reported following the event. I concluded the guys were two drunken assholes and one of them—the pisser—now saw a chance at a payday through a lawsuit.

I did derive satisfaction at the contrast between this case and the earlier one I had against the officer, who wound up chasing and arresting the nonsuing accomplice. It seemed to me that the earlier lawsuit had concentrated his mind wonderfully and altered his tactics, even down to documenting events thoroughly and securing evidence of his innocence (the taped interview). This seemed precisely the sort of reform I sought, and knowing how the earlier case had affected the present one took a lot of the bitterness I felt about the pornographer's case out of my head.

The case at hand brought out my law and order instincts. Notwithstanding my residual antipathy to a cop who'd behaved brutally and lied on the stand in a previous encounter, I thought the cops completely right in the current case. The prisoners were arrogant, mostly drunken bums, and it was poetic justice they got locked up. The pisser's effrontery in suing struck me as a leitmotif of the age: being wrong, yet whining and seeking some gain from it all.

I told the guy's lawyer I didn't like the case and wouldn't take it.

The criminal case was continued (postponed) pending a clean record and ultimately dismissed. I saw it as an admission of the essential elements of the case and another nail in the plaintiff's coffin.

Odd that the cops' attorneys would never think of hiring me as an expert for their side. Theirs was a case I would've taken.

CASE 55: THE RIGHT TO KILL

I have no compunctions about taking cases involving former employers.

When, in 2003, an attorney called, describing police abuse of her client, the issue sounded promising and I asked her to send materials. The contents were, to put it generously, at odds with the lawyer's interpretation of events, although I could not say she'd lied or misrepresented the issues grotesquely. She was just naïve, I thought, someone with little experience in these matters who'd been taken in by a shucking, jiving, streetwise character.

It involved a drug bust. Minneapolis cops had dealt with one of the two suspects, purchasing small amounts of marijuana, which would, they hoped, lead to a real seizure. A date was made to buy half a pound of grass, but the sellers insisted on doing it in St. Paul. The Minneapolis Police Department, knowing how closely information like this must be held, properly waited to notify the St. Paul police only a short time before the deal was to go down, still leaving them plenty of time to react.

At 6:30 p.m. on November 24, 2000, two black males, a twenty-nine-year-old driver and a thirty-nine-year-old passenger, pulled up to the rendezvous. Twelve MPD cops disguised in plainclothes were in the area, backed up by St. Paul police. The cops had badges around their necks and approached the pair in a parking lot. Both occupants had long and serious criminal records. The driver had been convicted, among other things, of beating a man to death in 1991. The passenger had convictions for drugs, robbery, forgery and burglary.

The driver gunned the car. Cops are strictly forbidden to fire at a moving car unless it is used to try to run them down. Deadly force can directed only at deadly force. The driver hit one officer and dragged another a short distance in trying to escape. Three MPD cops (including the dragged officer) fired twenty shots at the car, killing the driver and hitting the passenger three times, once in the shoulder and twice grazing his head. He recovered. The officers were not seriously injured.

Critical to my understanding this case were the statements of witnesses who buttressed the cops' stories.

No narcotics or weapons were found and the passenger was released without charges. Since he hadn't assaulted the cops with the car—a charge that would've been leveled at the driver—he was cleared. He claimed to have been an innocent participant in this deal. Implausible but acceptable, despite the hollow ring of his denials. The absence of proof was controlling.

A search warrant of the apartment turned up $100 in cash and a small amount of marijuana and other controlled (illegal) drugs. The death of the driver, whose apartment it was, precluded charges.

Since there were no drugs in the car, what could the two suspects have been up to? It smelled like a scam to screw the buyers (cops) out of the cash and take off. This may have accounted for the driver's alacrity in zooming out.

I though it a textbook example of how I'd want cops to perform in a case like this. They'd arranged for a buy, staked out the site, informed the local cops, wore their badges around their necks, and identified themselves. They fired only when deadly force was applied against them. Once again, I could have been a big help to the defendants in the civil suit (one MPD cop and the city), but I knew they would never think of calling me as an expert.

I had no problem deciding not to take the plaintiff's case and called the lawyer to tell her so. She asked why. I could have offered possible tangents to approach the case, and might still have been of some use to her, but she'd received $500 worth of service gratis and now wanted more. She'd not only failed to volunteer payment for my evaluation, she'd been a bit nasty and offhand with me. I certainly hadn't a high opinion of her evaluative skills. I thought I'd stop feeding this greedy soul and told her, "I just don't see an opportunity for reform," and left it at that.

I never did learn the outcome. My guess is that the case petered out as the lawyer's client pulled her chain and she finally cottoned to his hustle.

The vagaries of life could be seen in the absence of a suit on behalf of the deceased, while his partner pushed the envelope as hard as he could.

CASE 56: GRAY AREAS

One of the little understood features of the criminal justice system is discretion. Cops can arrest or not; prosecutors can charge or release. These are safety valves to adjust unpopular measures in an environment of shifting values.

The existence of a law on the books certainly grants the power to enforce it, but common practice usually winds up controlling the issue. Laws on sodomy remained on the books long after everyone had ceased enforcing them, for instance. Ditto for adultery. Across the nation small amounts of marijuana were effectively decriminalized through police lack of interest. The crack epidemic that peaked around 1985 shook the police, however, who stepped up enforcement even as their futility could be read in the availability and cheapness of all illegal drugs.

In Duluth, Minnesota, in 1994, the police found it impossible to ignore a shop openly selling drug paraphernalia, such as pipes for smoking marijuana. They sent in a cooperating informant who made a series of purchases. These devices might arguably be used innocently, so to preclude such a claim, the buyer was instructed to ask for a "pot pipe" and make it clear that it would be used to smoke marijuana. Such implements violated statutes.

The informant made several buys from different clerks to establish the pattern and preclude the defense of a renegade employee acting independently. A search warrant was secured and illegal implements seized. The establishment had a freaky title, sure to offend "respectable elements": *The Electric Fetus*.

The prosecutor declined to press charges and the persons cited were released from criminal liability. The seized implements were not returned. The shop owners, who had three stores in the state selling gifts, music, jewelry, tobacco, et cetera, sued for return of the items, to have the police department's actions ruled harassment, and to pursue damages against the city and for the employees, whose civil rights had been violated.

Larry Leventhal, a lawyer I greatly respected—he took good cases, didn't collect unless he won, and listened to the oppressed sympathetically and helpfully—called to hire me as an expert. The usual pile of motions and countermotions accompanied his letter. The plaintiff's briefs seized upon a series of mistakes and some overreaches by the police. My job was to place all of this within the context of my experience and decide whether the practices were sound or actionable.

This was, as was typical, two years after the event.

None of these cases is perfect. Mistakes occur. Human actions are flawed. It is always possible to point to errors and use these as wedges into courts and judgments, or settlements. It was clear to me that the cops had acted not just in good faith but had exhibited a decent regard for constitutional niceties. It was, on the whole, the sort of police behavior that needed to be encouraged and supported.

I was certain the cops would never solicit my aid in the cases. They virtually never did. I couldn't figure it out, but it was possible they simply saw me as the enemy.

I told Larry I wouldn't take the case, explaining that I agreed with the police actions. I was sure the cops would win the case, but I never learned the outcome.

CASE 57: MALL RATS

So what became of the corner hangout that was the Village Green of my youth? It morphed into a mall. These modern marts became the magnets for teens, and a headache to those thinking of security for these quasi-public-private spaces.

The Bloomington, Minnesota, police chief, Robert Lutz, was both an aide and a favorite of mine who confirmed my confidence when he thwarted a Mall of America initiative to reduce or even eliminate bus service that many black teens used to get to their favorite hangout. So when three black females, two fourteen-year-olds and one-fifteen-year-old, charged abuse by mall security, where many actions (not this one) are taped by video camera, I knew I'd get sharply divergent versions. Truth was usually the first casualty in these controversies, as it is in war.

The plaintiffs' complaints read like the essence of reasonableness, except where it becomes essential to describe conduct, and then such euphemisms and evasions as "protested this order" (to move on) or "failing to obey" a guard's order to leave.

The events occurred in May 1995, when the three girls were detained, interrogated, and given a thirty-day trespass notice that forbade their return to the mall for that period. This, under a Bloomington ordinance adopted to meet the problem of congregating, noisy, somewhat threatening youngsters who, at least in the eyes of shop owners and some elderly customers, needed to be controlled.

Less than a month later, one of the three girls had another—disputed as to circumstances—encounter with security. She alleged an assault by the security officer, was handcuffed, interrogated, and detained, and this time given a notice forbidding her appearance at the mall for one year.

Six months earlier another black female was detained and given a trespass notice.

The three cases were virtually identical. One of the young women was four months pregnant and later gave birth to a daughter.

The group of three women filed a racial discrimination complaint with the Department of Human Rights and sued the Mall of America for injuries, false imprisonment, and related issues. The complaint paints the inability to go to the mall as a serious constitutional deprivation. Modern times.

Mall security forces were issuing about one thousand trespass notices a year since the practice began in 1992. This, I thought, attested to the utility and value of a process that replaced the physical contact and "escorting out" function that inevitably led to serious abuses. Such informal expulsions had placed security personnel in untenable situations and shaky legal ground.

The accounts of the security personnel were not recognizable in the plaintiffs' descriptions of demurely going about their business and being set upon by guards without provocation. The guards' accounts, filed in reports to their bosses, described the girls as blocking access to an escalator, profanely refusing repeated requests to move, threatening officers, and being physically abusive.

I was aware of the continuing problems caused by kids using the mall as their corner hangout and of repeated clashes with security. I had also had cases that thrust me into the operations of mall guards, and I came away with the view that they were carefully monitored and that management was eager to avoid confrontations and lawsuits.

Many of the guards were minorities, including some of those involved in this case, and no one alleged racial slurs or other unacceptable comments by security. No witnesses came forward to attest to the young ladies' innocence, and the mere fact that they were women indicated to me that security would likely have been careful to avoid charges of brutality. There were no injuries to buttress the girls' contentions of having been assaulted by the guards.

The complaint also attacked the trespass ordinance as unconstitutionally vague, calling for action in cases of "failure to comply with requests of management," "loud and abusive language," "failure to move along," "inappropriate attire" (a tough one, I'd admit), and "obscenity." Nevertheless, one of the young women was convicted, by a jury, under this statute.

The case was a familiar societal dilemma—controlling teenage behavior in places mostly regarded as public gathering spots, but which have a private and commercial component. My sympathies were with management. I saw no evidence to justify charges of racism. The guards documented their actions. No serious injuries occurred. A jury supported management on the criminal charges and it just seemed illogical that the guards would have acted so energetically, detaining and summonsing the girls, in the absence of demonstrable provocation. After all, the place was full of teens and these came, stayed, and went without incident.

I'd support the guards, so I declined the case. It petered out and I assume it was dismissed in federal court, since I was never contacted after the initial evaluation. Then came a news report that irritated me. The mall had settled with the three black girls who said they'd been discriminated against and mistreated by security guards.

Another case of pusillanimous surrender, most likely by an insurance company that didn't want the trouble and expense. No doubt it would've been a minimal amount, but the message could not have been more corrosive: right or wrong, it pays to sue.

"Frivolous lawsuits" received new adherents. Justice had not been served.

CASE 58: AVOIDABLE PROBLEMS

While there have been indisputable similarities in the cases I've taken, the differences in them certainly have not been subtle. No formulaic approaches work for me. I need everything that's specific to each case: a sense of the lawyer and his/her motives, a handle on whether the cops were trying to do something right, the response of superiors and policymakers, the motives of the plaintiff, and so on. I finally decided that what I was bringing was tons of experience—in my case, meaning mistakes I'd learned from—and this gets distilled, after over three-quarters of a century, into something we label, with hubris, wisdom.

The hare-and-hound chases between security and teens at the Mall of America seemed a ready source of business. Somehow no one had ever cautioned black teens to be obsequious with authority. Just the opposite, many seemed to see these encounters as intrusions into their personhood, challenges to be faced down. A ruinous decision played out, again and again, into urban tragedy.

A prominent black attorney—and, to me, race seems to be always relevant in these cases—called to inquire about my availability. The case again involved Chief Robert Lutz of Bloomington, my former aide and protégé. I assured the lawyer this wouldn't be an impediment. I'd crossed swords with him, and a lot of other friends and associates, before without a problem. Our paths, in fact, would even cross later as opposing experts (*Case 35: A Victim Perennial*).

These cases—and this was one—often taught me practices I didn't even know existed. Theater-hopping, for instance, a cultural artifact brought into being by multiplex cinemas. I'd grown up in the era when movie houses were often opulent and resplendent palaces, seating thousands, standing serenely alone, and offering double features. And I went in regardless of starting times and left when "this is where I came in." Now teenaged mall rats enter buildings housing eight, sixteen, or more small theaters, buy a ticket, and hop from movie to movie endlessly.

The dominant culture adjusted and invented "theft of services" to add to disorderly conduct statutes that regulated minor incidents that threatened commerce or serenity. Officers now check and, if you don't have a ticket for the movie you are watching, you are asked to leave.

The date is October 11, 1997, and it's almost 11:30 p.m. at the Mall of America. Two black women enter a movie titled *Gang Related*, and a security guard advises them there are only forty-five minutes of the movie left and they can't have a ticket for it. Both are twenty-three.

Writers should consult police complaints for dialogue.

One of the women is alleged to have said, "Fuck you, punk-ass motherfucker toy cop."

Even if she didn't say it, the sheer inventiveness dazzles the imagination.

The audience stirs, turns.

As it happens this isn't a "toy cop" but a Bloomington police officer assigned to prevent disorders and thefts of services in response to management's complaints and pressures.

Now the women turn and walk away and try to enter the ladies' room. The officer grabs the colorful speaker's arm. Two black men approach. The cop lets go and calls for help. A cop responds. They wait. The women emerge and are not allowed to enter the theater. They refuse and march into the movie. A male, brother of one of the women, twenty-six, said they all had tickets. They are offered a refund. Both cops are white.

The strategies are impressive for the parries and thrusts honed over dozens of frustrating encounters.

The two women become "confrontational" and "disruptive." Patrons are "hearing their behavior." Not exactly a riot in progress.

Less imaginative insults are hurled at the cops by a third female, also twenty-three and black. She is told she is under arrest for disorderly conduct. The Rubicon has been crossed. She gets loud, combative, and moves to depart. The cop handcuffs her. Yelling profanities now, she attracts a crowd. The brother says the cops are not taking the cuffed prisoner. More help is summoned as events escalate. The brother is now arrested. He moves to go and is blocked by the second cop. The attempt to handcuff him is resisted. Another of the three women interferes. The brother starts to run off. He is chased.

Meanwhile, the original officer is struggling with the cuffed female, who is kicking and flailing her arms.

When the chasing cop gets to the brother, he uses his baton on the man's arm and orders him down to the ground. The fleeing man strikes the cop on the head with his fist. The officer gets him down. One of the women appears and begins kicking the cop in the groin and thigh. Help arrives. The man is cuffed. The crowd is kept back. As she is led away she asks the cop how he liked his "kick in the nuts." The cops omit few damaging comments in their complaints.

Surprisingly, the cops did include the brother's comment that his hitting the officer was an accident. I was not accustomed to exculpatory inclusions. He was charged not with felony assault, but misdemeanors. An act of surprising generosity by the police.

The plaintiffs' complaint alleges that the male, twenty-six, had gone to the movie with his mother, his sister, his girlfriend, and her sister, fourteen. They bought tickets to Soul Food.

The guilt described in the cops' complaint is matched by the innocence in the plaintiffs'.

The guy went to the bathroom. The two women went to check if a friend was in the other movie. They were ejected. The cop spoke in a "rough tone." The women "took offense," "words were exchanged" (an uneven repartee).

The fact outlines are consistent, even to the ladies' room refuge, encounter, and confrontation. The officers were rude. The women objected. One was arrested for disorderly conduct. The brother emerged from the men's room and "observed the scene." (You gotta love the prose.) The women complained and the female was handcuffed.

The plaintiffs reported that "a discussion ensued." They were "understandably upset" but not "violent, disruptive, or out of control." A slow-motion chase is depicted, with the officer trying to grab the brother's arm and he moving away.

The officer is charged with spraying Mace over the "peaceful" brother. No provocation or justification. The brother, sprayed again, attempted to get away and was struck in the leg with the baton. The officer then struck him six or seven times more, causing pain and injury. The second woman was arrested and the police now had three prisoners, the brother and two women.

The plaintiffs said the crowd was upset with the officers but calmed when given their badge numbers. The behavior of security was described as a familiar pattern of racist police action aimed at blacks. White citizens "would not have been confronted or harassed." Blacks were "more likely to be accused of 'ticket hopping' and less likely to be treated civilly."

Most of the violence in this encounter was captured on video by a security camera. The case, filed less than two months after the incident, was likened to Rodney King redux (*Case 8: Rodney King*). The brother is six foot four and weighs 330 pounds.

I never did learn the outcome of the criminal charges, which would have been important but not, in this case, controlling, for me.

I reviewed the materials and the tape, which showed only one baton strike in an attempt to subdue. I was impressed by the officers' fairness in not charging the male with assault, an almost automatic inclusion in these cases. And the plaintiffs' complaint essentially confirmed the police reports and relied on racism as the rationale for the cops' actions.

I concluded that the cops were there precisely to address the breaches of law admitted by the plaintiffs. Their claims rang hollow. I declined the case, but still I wanted to be helpful and participated in a conference call with the plaintiffs' lawyers, describing my impressions. I did not charge any fees and never learned the outcome of the suit.

While I sided with the cops, I was not surprised their chief, my former aide, never sought my input.

CASE 59: INNOCENTLY WREAKING HAVOC

I make it a practice to take everyone's psychic and emotional temperature as I listen to their voices. To me the phone is a measuring instrument of delicious delicacy. Hesitations, eagerness, gloominess, victory or defeat, and a range of other possibilities dance over the wire. Arrogance and condescension have caused defeats with me that the caller never suspected or expected. Ingenuous reactions excite my sympathy. Perhaps mistakenly I rely on these judgments.

A young lawyer gushing with admiration for my wonderfulness called. A grief-stricken mother had impressed him in her cause. I always, whatever my impression, invited lawyers to send material and he promptly dispatched the usual hernia-inducing poundage. The case, though, was very simple.

A psychotic twenty-seven-year-old white man experienced another in a series of scary episodes dotting his life. On his medicine, he functioned but, in common with other similarly afflicted, he hated it and stopped taking it. A bachelor with two siblings, he lived at home with his mother in Duluth, Minnesota.

On January 7, 2002, she called the police. It was around 4:00 p.m. and three cops responded. They had a caution notice for the location because of previous problems with the son over a seven-year period. A cop went to the basement where the young man was slumped, seated and had a shotgun in his hands. As he moved around, the cop fled, alerted his partners, and all called for help. About twenty cops soon responded. These were the special teams organized for such stand-offs. They phoned but the man didn't answer. They tried a public address system but no response.

After about ninety minutes the young man emerged, in a surrender posture but with the shotgun in his hand. He yelled at the cops to shoot him. Suicide by cop, it's called. He'd tried to burn down the house with gasoline in a previous suicide attempt and, in another, threatened his parents that if they didn't kill him, he'd kill them and then himself. The cops retreated, maintained a perimeter, and maneuvered to contain him. He got into his car and drove off. The chase ensued, never exceeding 50 mph, with the cops radioing for intercepts.

State Patrol arranged strips that would puncture his tires and he went over them, lost control, and went off the road and the car overturned. A fire began in the engine and the cops shot out the windows with less lethal bullets to permit the fire department to try and extinguish the blaze, but having to proceed cautiously because of the weapon. The young man was inside, dead, with a shotgun wound through his mouth. The autopsy revealed he'd died before the fire could injure him. A clear-cut suicide, and no one disputed this version.

The mother hired a private investigator whose report was full of should'ves and could'ves, criticizing the police. Sophistry. The mother faulted doctors for taking her son off medication and for not confining him to institutional care. She faulted the cops for not preventing the suicide.

The young man's history was marked with hallucinations and delusions that prompted dangerous actions. His mother had previously referred to him as a "powder keg" and dangerous. He'd slashed a man's face with a knife and stabbed him in the arm in 1997; had a two-and-a-half-hour stand-off with the police in 1996, when he tried to burn down the house with a gasoline can; he assaulted a female neighbor in 1999, causing her to get an order of protection against him; and the police had to be called, later in 1999, when he threatened to kill his parents if they didn't kill him. Once, while in custody, he was assaulted by an inmate and had his jaw fractured in three places. This event traumatized him mentally as well as physically and he developed a paranoiacal fear of being assaulted. Thus, he struck preemptively.

In this 2002 incident, as well as in previous ones, he'd been drinking heavily and his mother had fought to have him committed. He once was held for six weeks, placed on medication, and released.

The young man never married and had no children. He was not able to work.

The lawyer, clearly moved by the mother's attempts to bring something of use to her son's life and death, was inspired by her devotion to help her. He hoped I'd at least speak to the mother before making up my mind.

Suicides leave two effects in their wake: survivors and guilt. I'd seen the results, particularly in mothers. One went literally crazy with grief over a son stabbed and killed in a child's game. He'd died in our arms after staggering into the 10th Precinct Station House in 1955.

I'd presided over a number of similar incidents in the Bronx. A mother is terrified. Her son is going wild, swinging a big kitchen knife. She calls the cops. They wind up in a small bedroom, blood everywhere, the berserk male in a corner. He lunges. They shoot. A funeral. Another mother shattered. She sues the doctors and the cops. I supported the police action and had to face the distraught parents in a pre-staged TV ambush.

In this case I saw no fault by the police. They'd behaved most sensitively. I didn't even see any need for training or altering procedures. What I did see was the "powder keg" the mother described, whose innocent trajectory would produce carnage. In the cruel calculus of life this man had been right. His death would be the solution.

Liking the lawyer and admiring his motives I called him the very day I received the materials, explained everything I knew, thought, and felt about the case. I declined the case and declined to send any bill. There was no point in speaking to the mother and that issue never arose.

I never learned if the lawyer continued to work the case, but it didn't seem like a promising enterprise.

WHY HIRE AN EXPERT WITNESS?

GUNSLINGERS

Gunslingers. That's how a lot of folks view expert witnesses. Guns for hire by the highest bidder.

The guys I know who serve as police expert witnesses (and they are all guys, though I'm certain this will change) will, in fact, argue any position for money and require payment up front. And they're paid well, up to $250 per hour, plus expenses and a flat fee just for reviewing the case. Most of them are like me—former police executives with academic credentials, with the occasional criminologist thrown in. They are intelligent, experienced, and knowledgeable, ready to put their skills and powers of persuasion to the use of their clients in lawsuits involving questionable police behavior. What they lack, however, is integrity and conviction. Each one is, in fact, a gunslinger, although more sophist than desperado.

I've never accepted that view. When I took a case, my intention was to help fix what's broken in the cult-like world of police. I told the truth, even when it was contrary to my clients' interests. I accepted payment, but only when my work was done, rarely if we lost. The principle's the thing, and for me the overriding principle is holding accountable those cops who have compromised the constitutional rights of others.

While the Constitution does not lack for champions, it has few defenders in arenas where unpopular causes breathe life and meaning into its words. Great constitutional questions are usually embodied in the defense of derelicts, molesters, psychos, murderers, and other pariahs that society finds easy to loathe. Accepting that their rights represent the advance guard of our rights is what is so hard for most of us to grasp.

Like the expert witnesses they hire, litigation lawyers are intelligent, experienced, and knowledgeable. They're good at evaluating a case, researching the law, preparing a complaint, analyzing and responding to motions, screening evidence, taking depositions, examining witnesses, and arguing the case. So why would they hire an expert witness in cases involving police misconduct against their clients?

Understanding police behavior is often more difficult than it appears. Even those lawyers who devote their lives to litigating against cops need help developing a cogent theory or evaluating the significance of evidence, or figuring out what matters and what doesn't. They need an insider to describe for them, and in some cases for judge and jury, the mysterious internal culture of the police. They need an insider to expose the hidden tip of the law-enforcement iceberg, to help them understand and explain what lies beneath the surface behavior of cops. What values, motivations, and tacit understandings drive police conduct? Why do cops react as they do? How are they likely to testify?

Police departments across the United States all have manuals professing how their officers should respond to various problems they can anticipate. The scripts are eloquent testimonials to each agency's commitment to truth, beauty, and the American way, and just as likely to be devotedly pursued. But police culture is unexpectedly complex and at odds with its public persona.

Discretion adds to that complexity. Discretion permeates the police world, indeed the entire criminal justice system. Cops can arrest, cite, or merely warn; DAs can prosecute or drop charges; judges can be lenient or strict. It takes an expert to determine whether an exercise in discretion by a cop is prudent, rooted in practice and precedent, or arbitrary, willful, or corrupt.

The fact is that too many cops practice bad law enforcement—racial profiling, excessive force, failure to protect the rights of those they serve. And too many of them cover it up and deny it all, choosing to falsify reports or testilie in court to protect sibling officers rather than break ranks and tell the truth. The "blue code of silence" exists only to protect cops from being discovered as "wrong." It is a harsh reality, but you'd never know it from the legal testimony of police officials of all ranks, persuasions, and jurisdictions. Since virtually everywhere in the police world chiefs are up-from-the-ranks beat cops, they too have been acculturated to corruption within the force and to keeping that corruption under wraps.

Silence and secretiveness isolate cops from the larger society, driving them further into a world of work and play in which they associate mostly with their own kind. Policing isn't just a job; it's a calling in which its members quickly discover only other cops understand the complexities of human existence, especially when viewed from the underbelly of the angry, drunk, or psychotic beast that has to be controlled. In this hermetically sealed environment, unbelievable bondings attend such partnerships. It's all that shared danger and late-night confessing in the confines of a patrol car. Policing becomes a way of life more than a job, with the harshest exclusions and punishments reserved for squealers. Those who adhere to the code of silence look at those who don't as rats and traitors.

The rare reformer has appeared, like Frank Serpico, who joined the New York Police Department six years after I did, and later blew the whistle on plainclothes corruption in the force. Frequently those reformers are chiefs, but they've concentrated mostly on technological and procedural innovations, productivity and performance standards, physical plant and equipment modernizations, and other administrative upgrades. The underlying culture of secrecy, mutual protection, and hostility to finks usually goes untouched.

During my stints as Bronx commander of the NYPD and police chief of Minneapolis, I became one of those reformers. I hoped to better the institution I had worked in since 1953. I wanted to create systems in which the pressures were to conform to the rule of law, not to be coerced into behaviors that I thought were oppressive, often illegal, at odds with the expressed ideals, or simply wrong. It's why, in 1990, I wrote *The Police Mystique*. The book was the equivalent of a mafia capo revealing the inner workings of his organization. A grandiose assertion, to be sure, but one I believe to be true.

My efforts at real reform while I was on the force didn't take. Civilian review boards also missed the mark. There wasn't one that worked anywhere in America, and I'd resisted the imposition of such a board in Minneapolis for nine years. The city adopted one after I left and wasted millions on its bureaucracy, while judgments and settlements in the swelling totals of lawsuits dented the Minneapolis budget.

Eventually I realized that the only way to reform police agencies—other than through a tough chief, like the NYPD's Pat Murphy—was through the courts and attention-getting lawsuits, media disclosures, and occasional investigations of the FBI, when that agency can be coerced into action.

So since 1989, when I retired after thirty-six years on the New York and Minneapolis police forces, I took another tack. By then I'd already done a bit of expert witness work in connection with getting women, blacks, Hispanics, and gays hired on police forces throughout the country, and I'd often testified in court in connection with police issues, practices, and policies. Now I would testify against cops as my way of reforming the institution I loved.

FIXING WHAT'S BROKEN

America was founded on the principles of liberty and justice. All of us, without exception, want to be treated fairly. But what is justice? How does our justice system, civil and criminal, work?

My answer is that it works, but not the way you think. It works fitfully, unexpectedly, complexly. The system is a maze, and you'd better know how to navigate your way through it or hire a skillful pilot if you want to avoid the shoals.

Yet I continue to believe in the justice system, and as an expert witness, I've found ways of contributing to the system's more effective workings. In other words, after analyzing a case I've provided arguments that support the proposition that holding officials to account improves the quality of justice. Demonstrating the involvement of higher-ups, in the actions of those on the street, became a key component of my approach. It gets back to the Watergate question of what did the chief know and when did he/she know it, with the added fillip, "And what did he/she do about it?"

THE ROLE OF EXPERT WITNESS

My job as an expert witness was to guide the plaintiff's lawyer through a thicket of practices, policies, and procedures that misrepresent police misconduct as constitutional.

An adversarial system often places the truth between contending forces. The cops tell their version, which is biased to protect the police, institutionally and at all rank levels, and they engage the police union in the effort. The plaintiffs tell their version, usually represented by liberal attorneys who have an unblinking suspicion of, and hostility to, a lot of police actions. My task as an expert witness: find the truth without regard to the wishes of either. One way is to reject cases; another is to accept them but to concede the points of the opposition with which I agree, regardless of my employer's wishes. It is a balancing act.

Meanwhile, the defendant's lawyer is gathering evidence in support of the misbehaving officer and petitioning the court to dismiss the suit, usually on the basis that cops have a tough job and that their enforcement activities shouldn't be inhibited for fear of "litigaphobia."

Jury selection, deciding on the value of various documents, and preparing for depositions, trial and evidence collection requires experience and knowledge. And new wrinkles – the endlessly ubiquitous videotapes, for example– offer new opportunities and challenges. Battling the inevitable motions to dismiss, evaluating the complicity of higher ups, and deciding between a steward's and an insurer's responsibilities require an insider's grasp.

Tackle the criminal phase first or the civil? What are the stakes involved in a seeming bargain of an offer of leniency for a pro forma admission of some guilt? Take a settlement (and how much for) or go to trial? The relevance of racial profiling and other forms of prejudice need to be factored.

When I was hired as an expert witness, the cases usually followed a distinct pattern: A lawyer calls with a brief description of the case. Maybe he's heard of me from another attorney or he's seen a reference to me posted on the Internet by someone who's worked with me. Maybe he's read one of my books. Regardless, it's all word of mouth. I never advertised or solicited cases.

If the case sounded like the kind I usually take—one involving blatant police misconduct—I'd ask the lawyer to send me background material. If it didn't, I'd decline. I never accepted an assignment unless I could embrace advocacy without reservation. I always give the cops the benefit of every doubt.

Case in point: A lawyer called me in 2004, describing the Chicago Police Department's practice of attacking "quality of life" issues—pissing on the sidewalk, public drinking or drunkenness, graffiti, aggressive begging, loitering, camping out, and other public nuisances. The cops gave out about fifty thousand citations annually but physically arrested and took in about a fourth of these. The summons were issued "in lieu of arrest," so the taking in for verification (warrants, identification, sobering up, et cetera) was unquestionably legal.

What the lawyer objected to was the length of detention, varying from four to twenty-three-and-a-half hours. Why twenty-three-and-a-half hours? Because the cops had a strict rule forbidding holdings of a day or more. Any evidence of racial profiling or other discrimination? No. Were the detentions distributed over a normal bell-shaped curve or bunched up at the longer periods of twenty hours held or more? They were evenly distributed.

The cops were obviously chary of being sued for overly long detentions. Notwithstanding dumb and excessive delays in releasing those held, I gave them the benefit of the doubt. I declined the case.

When I did accept an assignment, the background material arrived by FedEx, often in a package of formidable dimensions. I read (or viewed on video) all of it, took notes, and quickly got back to the lawyer with my take on the case, including a summary that lists critical points, items of evidence that matter, additional facts he or she should pursue, and names of witnesses to question and specific questions to ask them. I also suggested questions to ask the cops when they were deposed by the lawyer hiring me.

Then, after a lengthy phone discussion or personal conference (usually in my living room), I would write a formal report (in longhand, to the dismay of the lawyers with whom I've worked.) The report was accompanied by my resume and a list of lawsuits on which I'd worked, from those brought by everyday citizens against cops to those involving Rodney King (*Case 8: Rodney King*), the Central Park jogger (*Case21: The Central Park Jogger*), and Attica Prison (*Case 31: Attica Prison*). If the report met the lawyers' needs, they'd have it typed and substantially edited before I signed the final version.

After advising the lawyer as to what happened and, more important, why it happened, I often had to convince the jury that what they have heard solemnly described as textbook-perfect practices by the police involved are wrong, malicious, corrupt, or illegal. Such refutations can come only from a knowledgeable and credible creature of the establishment.

First, however, once my involvement is revealed to the opposition and my report is parsed, the defendant's attorney usually wants to see how I'll testify in court. They demand to take my deposition, which is nothing more than an extended cross-examination under oath in a law office, with a stenographer writing down every word and preparing a transcript. The deposition is followed by the defendants moving to strike my appearance on the basis that I don't know what I'm talking about and that the notion that I'm an "expert" is laughable. This is the second major hurdle a litigation lawyer has to overcome. It's less commonly successful than the first major hurdle, which is the dismissal of the complaint motion.

Lawyers were sometimes reluctant to show me the defendant's affidavit to exclude my appearance. They were concerned I might lose my cool and effectiveness after being called a shill (and worse) in these solemn documents. Truth is, I found the assaults on my competence, intelligence, experience, or status so strident as to be funny. I was also flattered that my testimony was viewed as so potentially damaging that it merits such outlandish legal assaults.

Clearing both obstacles leaves the gloomy prospect of a trial, a contest no one cheerily anticipates. Impending courtroom drama makes for good TV, but its prospect usually accelerates movement toward settlement of a case. At this point my usefulness entailed suggesting what might constitute a reasonable settlement. This even included my attempts (with the lawyer's encouragement) to persuade the plaintiff to accept a reasonable offer to settle, especially when the aggrieved was driven by emotion or dreams of sugarplums and fairies.

IF THE CASE GOES TO TRIAL

When a case does go to trial, jury selection is the key to a successful outcome. There are many good reasons to extol the process—it's noble and democratic to be judged by your peers—but, God, are juries ever fallible. Clever lawyers, just like in the movies, play jurors like fiddles. If I were guilty, I'd go with a jury trial. If I were innocent, I'd take my chances with a judge and no jury. Curiously, most cops would respond the same way, which is why the path they choose when facing justice is a great litmus test to insiders watching the process.

As a rule, poor jurors have more experience with the police than middle-class jurors. Black jurors are likely to be more skeptical of the police version of a story, given their or their friends' or relatives' often unhappy encounters with cops. White middle-class jurors, on the other hand, love cops. They are grateful for the blue line protecting them from pillage, rape, and slaughter, and will usually accept the testimony of impressibly uniformed officers on the stand. Such weighers of fact need the detoxifying testimony of someone who knows better. They need to hear an expert witness suggest a credible alternative version. The police practice of testilying is terra incognita to such jurors.

THE EVER-POPULAR GOOD FAITH DEFENSE

Cops take umbrage over legal questionings of actions taken in good faith. This, on the surface, appears reasonable enough, yet it is a logical, legal Trojan horse slipped into the system calculated to win over not only a gullible, unknowing public, but even the news media. The painful reality is that the law recognizes that even actions taken in good faith can produce such horrendous results as to demand an accounting.

Let's say some plainclothes cops are on the hunt for a felon. One night they spot a suspicious-looking black male. They shout questions and instructions. A foreigner, he is confused and reaches for his wallet. One of the cops stumbles. His gun goes off. In the adrenaline rush the three other cops think he's been shot. They fire about forty times (a counterintuitive action that occurs frequently and is rarely understood by outsiders). The black male is hit multiple times and dies.

The cops are tried for murder, a palpable yet excruciatingly subtle attempt by a knowing prosecutor to satisfy black constituents calling for blood without alienating the police union, which has come all out to the cops' defense. The union understands the ploy: murder requires a specific intent to kill, which is altogether lacking in this case.

The cops are acquitted. The protesters are gulled into believing that the prosecutor has done his noble best and lost. The cops are off the hook. The mother is left with her grief. And so it ends, except for one little thing: the cops and prosecutor had closed ranks within the criminal justice system and scammed those outraged by this killing. The mother's only recourse now is a lawsuit. The protesters' only serious option is to scare the FBI into undertaking a federal investigation.

So what should have happened? The law wisely considers the consequences of action taken in good faith that produces tragic and unallowable results. In this case the officers were not faced with a real (as opposed to imagined) threat of deadly force and responded illegally. The crime is the unintentional killing of one human by another in which any legal justification for such killing is absent. By pursuing murder charges against the cops, the district attorney showed the world how tough he was, even as he guaranteed the exoneration of the officers.

So much for good faith actions.

The Expert's Most Important Contribution

Countering the official version of the police testimony in the courtroom is the most important contribution I could make to a case. Addressing the jurors directly, engaging them personally with eye contact, is critically important. Conceding points during cross-examination added to my credibility. If the cops being sued have done some things right, I would say so. If I didn't know something, I would admit it. If I'd changed my mind, I confessed that too. I have freely granted a good job by the opposition and concentrated on what I thought were the flaws. There seems no point in doing just what my employers want—to give perfect answers. If I make them unhappy, so be it.

The point is to respond truthfully. Truth is the only weapon that works on the stand.

EPILOGUE

MY MOST IMPORTANT WORK

When Boston activist and author Howard Zinn told me that expert witnessing was the most important work he'd ever done, it resonated powerfully. He was right. My cases not only helped secure justice for the downtrodden, they served as powerful vehicles for reforming the agency. But some former associates, and even one friend, have suggested I am a traitor for testifying against cops—and for money. This is a legitimate cavil and deserves an answer.

Like writing, expert witnessing as I did it was not the way to wealth. The largest and most productive amount of effort—thinking about a case—never appears on a bill for fees. This is where I've spent the largest chunks of time and the area that has produced the best and most useful perspectives on the cases.

The money came fitfully, if at all. At first I did a fair amount of pro bono work, but I discovered to my dismay lawyers yawning and losing interest. It has long been clear that our society places a dollar value on worth. Volunteers seem to get a lot of scorn. When I started charging, lawyers listened, took notes, followed advice, and ended meetings promptly.

I sent bills only at the end, and only if we won. Sometimes I've been paid, sometimes I haven't, and sometimes I didn't send a bill. My affordability would have been an insuperable obstacle for the fucked-over poor blacks who were my principal clients. And I have worked mostly for dedicated lawyers who mirrored my approach. If these folks could suck it up and sue, I could wait to be paid.

My work as an expert witness hasn't cost cops money. Despite a pervasive litigaphobia in the ranks, I've never heard or known of a single cop, of any rank, ever laying out a penny for damages, however egregious the wrongdoing proved. The government—that is, the taxpayer—coughs it up. In fact, I had a case in Minneapolis in which one of my "thumpers" physically mistreated revelers. They sued and won, even exacting punitive damages against him. I disciplined him and then went before the City Council to argue—pretty vehemently—that he, not the taxpayers, should pay the $35,000 judgment. The council ignored their police chief's entreaties and paid the judgment. It created no stir whatsoever.

My work as an expert witness has, however, cost several cops, in some measure, their reputation and credibility.

I do owe an apology to the enormous body of cops who perform faithfully, day in and day out, across America. I've roughly calculated that about 98 percent of them do the job, from mediocrely to heroically and brilliantly. They're trying.

But then there are the 2-percenters. I could actually prepare a list of these misfits in every agency I have worked. The thumpers, grafters, malingerers, psychos, alcoholics, women-beaters, and bullies are the objects of my reform efforts. In the New York Police Department they were distinguished from the larger body of "grass eaters" with the sobriquet "meat eaters." The painful and unobvious truth is that many heroes and leaders come from this group. The same cop who beats a hapless prisoner to death is also the first through the door, facing bullets, or the organizer of blood donations for a fallen comrade, or the leader of the pack hunting his assailant. Alpha males, mostly. The Oscar-winning movie *Crash* captures the genre's duality perfectly.

The police union, sadly, becomes defender and apologist for this tiny fraction. And the chief spends a bitterly resented, disproportionate amount of time and energy attending to the problems created by this minuscule body. Yet he/she is wrong to resent it, because in controlling this band lies the secret to controlling the agency. This direction can be achieved only through terror. If these tough cases aren't afraid of you, they'll be running your agency. The vast majority of cops may hate the methods chiefs employ to gain ascendancy, but they'll make even hated reforms work. I hope that critical fact emerges from these pages, and I hope the apology is accepted.

As it happens, reform—controlling the 2-percenters and making the agency more efficient—means war with the blue community within. That is why the Pat Murphy's of the police world are so rare. He was certainly the only one I saw or heard of in my thirty-six years of police work, and he was washed aboard on the wave of a colossal scandal.

There probably isn't a single reform chief anywhere in the nation, allowing for a bell-shaped curve of caretakers, from those mildly inclined to make needed changes to those in bed with the union and its charges. Civilian review boards certainly don't reform any agency anywhere. They are resisted, co-opted, or evaded. The FBI can be stirred to effective action—in the form of investigating police wrongdoing—but it usually takes a massive black riot to get their attention. The news media are our sturdiest pillar for reform, yet they can be painfully fallible. Of certain journalists the NYPD said, "He's pissing in your pocket and telling you it's raining." Police inspectors general have had some notable successes within the federal government, but they have not yet been tried at the local level. The NYPD's sole venture into this area ended unfortunately. Politicians and prosecutors are mostly nonplayers in the reform game.

These are broad accusatory strokes, but I hope and believe the preceding pages illustrate the points, chapter and verse. If no glint of recognition emerges in the reader's mind, I've failed.

The issues of justice can be hopelessly clouded or confused, leading us to question whether the system will work for us when we need it. O. J. Simpson muddied the waters with his unexpected acquittal on two murder charges and compounded the complexity by being convicted of civil responsibility. The cops in the Rodney King case (*Case 8: Rodney King*) were first found not guilty of assaulting him, in state court, then, under the pressures of rioting blacks and a furious community, the FBI secured their convictions in a federal court.

The system is a fallible institution, and more to the point, it is a human institution. But it mainly works. Fitfully, to be sure, even for screwed-over black folks. These perceived menaces from the underclass embody the rights we must protect if ours are to be preserved.

I hope that, in these pages, I've shown how complicated the question of our rights can be. It is a lesson that took me many years and lots of mistakes and hard experiences to grasp.

Lawsuits constitute truly effective vehicles for reform now. When and if the public wakes up to the costs it is subsidizing through its ignorance or lack of interest, lawsuits hold the promise of marvelous progress through savings and avoided sufferings in the future. Damage suits concentrate the minds of apparatchiks wonderfully. As we can see here in several cases, Chicago has paid dearly for its indifference. And Illinois has mercifully stopped executing the innocent because of such litigation. Is this progress or what?

In the criminal justice field most cities are self-insurers, sparing themselves the fiscal agony of being at an insurance company's mercy. How much more pain they could avoid by simply insisting that their employees behaved better doesn't seem to interest the taxpayer footing the bill, at least not yet. This—the enormous cost because of police chiefs' unwillingness to control officer behavior on the street—is the great stealth scandal of American policing.

Occasional headlines like "A Legacy of Giuliani Years: Damage Suits Against the City" (*New York Times*, December 24, 2004) are simply swallowed whole. There are seemingly no political consequences to an administration's indifference to the behavior of its minions. After all, it's just a nickel here and a dime there, right?

And yet "Chicago Rethinks Its Use of Stun Guns" (*New York Times*, February 12, 2005) was inspired by the death of one man struck by a Taser gun and the injuring of a fourteen-year-old boy. The telling comment came from a high-ranking politician: "Once we are put on notice like this, the liability that then is created is substantial." And the Los Angeles Police Department, following rampant and uncontrolled use of less lethal weapons—in violation of its own policy, the law, and even the manufacturer's requirements (as we have seen, a ubiquitous hypocrisy)—decided to withdraw some of the weapons and rethink their employment in the wake of yet another lost lawsuit.

In a Sherlock Holmes mystery the key clue is of a dog that didn't bark, the deduction being that he must have known the intruder. What I think and hope we've seen in these cases is that the system is loaded with watchdogs that don't bite. My involvement has been aimed at putting a bite into the system.

ABOUT THE AUTHOR

Tony Bouza was born on Oct. 4, 1928 in a small village in the northwest corner of Spain, the younger of two children born to a Spanish stoker on American ships and his wife, also a local. In December 1937, at the age of nine, his father brought his mother and sister to America – a very traditional maneuver but one that entailed real poverty, given his humble job. They moved into a Brooklyn tenement under the shadow of the bridge and his mother took in lace trimmings for work at home. A tough struggle ensued for the Bouza family, including rheumatic fever for Bouza's sixteen year old sister requiring her removal from school never to return and the usual humiliations of the underclass.

Bouza's father died in 1944 at the age of 54 and his widow supported the penniless three by responding to signs for "Operators Wanted" and operating a sewing machine. There was no social security for them. His sister married a cop, inspiring Bouza's mother to suggest the force to Tony, who after two years in the Army, joined the NYPD (New York Police Department) on Jan. 1, 1953.

My life was permanently transformed by joining the police force. After graduating from high school in 1947 I was a corner hangout, a hopeless member of a great army of Brooklynites headed for oblivion in sports-besotted ignorance.

When people asked years later why I'd chosen to be a cop, I said I never felt I had a choice of careers and I was damn glad and unbelievably lucky to have found this one. I sought a salary (in 1953 about $250 a month) and a pension of half-pay after twenty years. Tenure came with probation at the end of nine months. After that, it would be really hard to be fired. Civil Service conveyed the sense of a magical mantle of protection.

A climb followed through every rank and position, culminating in four years as commander of the Bronx NYPD forces, starting in late 1976. Next came three years as the number two in the New York subway police, followed by nine years as Chief of the Minneapolis Police Department.

In 1989, Bouza began to function as an expert witness, testifying on police practices, procedures and programs in cases involving brutality, false arrest, and other acts of police wrong doing. This went on through 2012 and encompassed about eighty cases.

In between, there was a bachelor's and a master's degree, countless courses, eight published books on policing and related activities, as well as marriage and family.

BOOKS BY TONY BOUZA

Police Unbound:
Corruption, Abuse, and Heroism by the Boys in Blue (2001)

The Decline and Fall of the American Empire:
Corruption, Decadence, and the American Dream (1996)

How to Stop Crime (1993)

A Carpet of Blue:
An Ex-Cop Takes a Tough Look at America's Drug Problem (1992)

Bronx Beat:
Reflections of a Police Commander (1990)

Gambling in Minnesota (1990)

The Police Mystique:
An Insider's Look at Cops, Crime, and the Criminal Justice System (1990)

Police Administration (1978)

Police Intelligence:
The Operations of an Investigative Unit (1976)

Made in the USA
Lexington, KY
02 May 2013